Political Journeys in Health

Political Journeys in Health

Essays by and for Amit Sengupta

Edited by
Prabir Purkayastha
Indranil
Richa Chintan

LeftWord

First published as an ebook in July 2020
Offset edition first published in February 2021.
Digital print edition, February 2021.

LeftWord Books
2254/2A Shadi Khampur
New Ranjit Nagar
New Delhi 110008
INDIA

www.leftword.com

LeftWord Books and Vaam Prakashan are the publishing divisions of
Naya Rasta Publishers Pvt. Ltd.

Publications details for essays by Amit Sengupta reproduced in this volume have been provided in the Acknowledgements.

ISBN 978-81-947287-8-8 (paperback)
978-81-945925-3-2 (ebook)

'Unethical behaviour of healthcare providers is directly linked with the fact that if care is linked to profit, more ill health means more profit! . . . Governments, not markets, can ensure that health systems address the needs of the poorest and the most marginalized. It is also true that there need to be conscious elements within public systems that promote equity. . . [Public health services] should be seen as attempts to provide the best services possible to all, while addressing the special needs of those most vulnerable . . . For such a system to work optimally, it needs to regularly connect with peoples' needs and priorities. This is best achieved when popular participation ensures that the public is not just a recipient of public healthcare but is also involved in its planning and execution . . .'

AMIT SENGUPTA

Contents

Foreword

PRABHAT PATNAIK

History has a habit of playing tricks with Left activists. Each generation of Left activists dreams of bringing about a basic social transformation; or, short of that, at least pushing society much further Left from where it found it. History, however, does not grant this privilege to all. For some, preventing a slide-back to the right, struggling against the re-assertion of ruling-class hegemony, becomes the primary task, the quintessence of their historic role, which is less exciting though no less important. The generation to which Amit Sengupta belonged was one such; to it belonged the task of fighting against such a re-assertion of metropolitan hegemony.

Science activists of an earlier generation who had been associated with the anti-colonial struggle, like Sahib Singh Sokhey, Nitya Anand, and K. Ganapathi, played a stellar role in promoting self-reliance in the country in drugs and pharmaceuticals. They helped build up the production base and struggled against the patent regime inherited from colonial times. The culmination of their efforts was the Indian Patents Act enacted in 1970, an Act many consider a model piece of legislation for all countries.

But matters had taken a turn by the time Amit and his colleagues came on the scene. The postwar conjuncture had formally ended with the collapse of the Bretton Woods system. The globalization of finance that followed, ushered in neoliberal policies in one country after another, aided by the fact that the old *dirigiste* regimes had reached a dead end by then. All this, soon followed by the collapse of the Soviet Union, created the context in which metropolitan capital launched a fresh offensive to reassert its hegemony. A key weapon it used was the imposition of a new patent regime for the world.

In almost a parody of the wildest conspiracy theory, a group of American and European multinationals got together to prepare a new patent regime for the world. This was first sold to the US government, and then, through it and its allies, got enshrined in the form of the TRIPs agreement at the WTO; and member-states were enjoined to make their domestic patent laws 'TRIPs-compatible'. For India this meant amending the Indian Patents Act, among other things, to extend the life of patents and to recognize product patents that the Act had de-recognized, which would have virtually rolled back all domestic advances made in this sphere.

This is when Amit and his colleagues began a massive resistance against this move. I had known Amit for long but had never been directly involved with his work. This was the first occasion when I did get involved, in a limited sort of way, as a member of the People's Tribunal that was set up at B.K. Keayla's initiative, by Amit and his colleagues. They mobilized Members of Parliament (MPs) from all parties and made the resistance into a people's movement.

The time of course was favourable for such resistance: the Left parties together not only had the largest number of MPs they have ever had in post-Independence India, 63 altogether; but the government under UPA-I was also crucially dependent upon Left support. With the inputs provided by Amit and his colleagues, the Act was amended through Left intervention in a manner much less damaging to the country's interest: product patents were *greatly limited in scope* and the provision for a strong compulsory licensing regime in public interest, which the Doha Declaration of WTO had permitted, was retained.

This provision of limiting product patents has enabled India to meet today 80 per cent of the AIDS medicine needed by the world at affordable prices. This is much to the chagrin of the Big Pharma, which have no compunctions about charging such exorbitant prices for their AIDS drugs that the annual AIDS treatment expenditure of patients in certain countries can exceed even their GDPs.

This provision of compulsory licensing is likely to come in handy in the context of the Coronavirus pandemic. At the recent World Health Assembly, the US opposed the resolution of putting drugs or vaccines for Covid-19 in a voluntary common pool, for manufacture at concessional rates by any country. This means that if a drug or a vaccine is developed by a US firm, or with US funding, it is likely to be patented, and hence available only at an exorbitant price, well beyond the reach of most people. But in such an event, India would be able to manufacture the drug under a compulsory licence, both for its own use and also for use by other countries. For making this possible, we have to thank the strong resistance put up by Amit and his colleagues earlier against the wholesale dilution of the 1970 Act.

The world at present, however, is on the cusp of yet another turn. Even before the Covid-19 pandemic, the regime of neoliberal globalization had palpably reached its limits. The world economy had slowed down causing high unemployment everywhere; and there was little scope for any fiscal stimulus because the hegemony of globalized finance made it near impossible. The only two ways in which larger government expenditure must be financed, if it is to have any expansionary impact, are through larger taxation of capitalists or through a larger fiscal deficit; and finance was opposed to both.

It had become clear even before the pandemic that a moment, analogous to the Keynes–Roosevelt moment of the 1930s, had arrived in the life of the capitalist system, when it had to adopt an altogether new course, against the wishes of globalized finance and different from what neoliberal globalization had entailed, for its very survival.

The pandemic has emphatically underscored this fact. Its destructiveness was vastly enhanced by the running down of public healthcare which characterized neoliberalism. In Britain, the reduction in the number of beds in public hospitals is now recognized to have had damaging consequences. In Spain the government has even temporarily 'nationalized' private hospitals for treating Covid-19 patients; similar emergency measures to expand public healthcare have been undertaken elsewhere as well. These entail a reversal of the trend under neoliberalism. Likewise, in many countries, governments have adopted relief measures for the people during lockdowns that have involved hugely expanded fiscal deficits, and gone against the financial orthodoxy demanded by globalized finance. India alas has neither provided much relief to the people, nor temporarily 'nationalized' private hospitals to prevent their charging exorbitant rates to Covid-19 patients; but India is more an exception in this regard. The pervasive tendency has been a reversal of neoliberalism.

Finance will certainly resist a continuation of these measures once the fury of the pandemic has abated. But removing these measures and re-imposing 'austerity' will be strongly resisted by the working people in all these countries.

A period of intensified class struggle is thus on the horizon. And even in India, which has kowtowed to the dictates of globalized finance and provided little relief to the distressed people during the lockdown, a continuation of this insensitivity will call forth strong class struggles once political activity becomes possible.

The main immediate focus of such struggles will be for welfare state measures, including above all for free and universal healthcare as a right, which would require greater government provisioning of this and other essential services. The post-Independence *dirigisme*, in other words, which had been superseded by neoliberal globalization, will once again have to be revived, even with the consent of sections of the ruling classes, in a new context and under new conditions.

The dreams of Amit's generation of Left activists will return once more to the agenda. Amit's own writings, some of which are collected in this volume, will acquire urgent relevance. Amit will not be here to see that; but his dreams will be here—centre stage.

Introduction

PRABIR PURKAYASTHA

The Covid-19 pandemic throws into sharp relief all the underlying problems of our society. Like other pandemics, Covid-19 holds up a mirror: it forces us to see, clearly, the chronic conditions we live in, the gross inequalities, the collapse of public health systems, and the greed of big capital. There is more than one virus attacking our lives here. The politics of the pandemic is located on a terrain where a much larger battle—a battle over our future—must be fought. What will our world be like when we emerge from this pandemic? Will existing inequalities sharpen? Will even more of our failing public health system be privatized? Will Big Pharma grow stronger? Or will the inhumanity of the rulers during this pandemic discredit the system to such an extent that change is imminent?

We have recently been hearing people repeat the words of the arch-imperialist Winston Churchill: 'Never let a good crisis go to waste.' Presumably, it is this philosophy that led Churchill to suggest, at the time of the British-made Bengal famine, that since Indians breed too much, a famine was a good way to curb their numbers. The same philosophy seems to be in practice in India during the present pandemic. The Modi government has been using the pandemic to launch a brutal attack on labour—by its assault on labour laws; by privatizing the public sector; by removing restrictions on privatization of land; and by allowing in foreign capital, even in the area of defence. All this has been described as developing 'self-reliance' in times of Covid-19. Even the bailout to big capital comes in the name of an economic stimulus to fight Covid-19. (That other strongman, Donald Trump, has gone even further. Instead of fighting a pandemic with international cooperation, Trump's US seems to believe that the pandemic is a 'good crisis' for its trade war, its economic de-coupling[1] from China, and even its vaccine war.[2])

In fact, the pandemic needs to be fought on three fronts: science, health and politics. Understanding science is the only way to understand the microbe—SARS-CoV-2—and what it does to our bodies. Trump's bleach and sunlight, or his Indian counterparts' *Ganga jal* and *gau mutra*, are only good for a sad laugh or two. Fighting a pandemic requires a well-functioning public health system. The crisis created by the Covid-19 pandemic in the 'advanced countries'—supposedly the best prepared—has shown us the peril of hollowing out public health systems to make way for 'efficient' privatized healthcare.

This time in our collective lives, a global pandemic, is the right time to recall Amit Sengupta. He should have been here to help us understand what we are going through, why we are where we are, and the way forward. But he is not here. Instead, we recall his life, his ideas, his convictions. We see that the pandemic brings out the three elements that defined Amit's work: as a science activist, a health activist, and a political activist. He made no pretence that he viewed science and health activism through the prism of his politics. He chose this battlefield since he was trained as a doctor. He did not believe that the doctor's job was just to heal sick

[1] Yan Liang, 'The US, China, and the Perils of Post-COVID Decoupling', *The Diplomat*, May 8, 2020 (https://thediplomat.com/2020/05/the-us-china-and-the-perils-of-post-covid-decoupling/).

[2] The US project Warp Speed for a vaccine aims specifically at protecting the US, and keeping China out. It is Trump's response to the US failure in handling the pandemic, a form of throwing money at the problem. See Jon Cohen, 'U.S. "Warp Speed" Vaccine Effort Comes Out of the Shadows', *Science*, vol. 368, no. 6492 (May 15, 2020), pp. 692–93 (https://science.sciencemag.org/content/368/6492/692).

individuals; the bigger task—perhaps the real task—was to build a society with a system to prevent its people from getting sick. And if people do get sick, such a system, in such a society, will care for them whether or not they can pay for treatment. In other words: health is a fundamental right of a citizen. Capital's objective—both Big Pharma and private healthcare—is to profit from people falling ill. This is the fundamental contradiction between capital and people. Amit knew this.

But this book does more than recalling Amit Sengupta. It traces how his work and his personal and political development as an activist were integral to the history of the health movement. The sections here trace this development, from 'medicines for all' to 'health for all'.

Amit became a part of the Delhi Science Forum (DSF), one of the organizations to found the people's science movement—which emerged from two *vigyan jathas*[3] as the All India Peoples Science Network. Soon after joining the DSF, he was confronted with the Bhopal Gas Tragedy, where the DSF played an important part in analysing the disaster created by Union Carbide. Amit worked with a set of doctors to survey the Bhopal gas victims and identify the scale of the disaster through the extent of injuries and their long-term effects.

The DSF was part of the All India Drug Action Network (AIDAN), and Amit also became active with AIDAN, beginning his lifelong engagement with people's access to medicines. The People's Health Movement, of which he was one of the co-founders, was a natural progression—from the issue of drugs to the larger question of people's health.

This engagement began with looking at rational combinations of drugs that should be used for treatment; and the two issues of

[3] No exact English translation exists, but loosely a *jatha* is a travelling group with a common purpose. The two *jathas* are: the Bharat Jan Vigyan Jatha (BJVJ) which took place in 1987, and the Bharat Gyan Vigyan Jatha (BGVJ) in 1990.

intellectual property rights—brand names versus generic names, and patents. It led to Amit's engagement with GATT negotiations: with its metamorphosis as the WTO; the emergence of the Trade-Related Intellectual Property Rights (TRIPS) Agreement in the WTO; and the radical change it made to India's patents law. With biologics as the new era in medicines, Amit became part of an international coalition addressing the new barriers that the US and European Union regulators were creating to extend the monopoly rights of Big Pharma.

Kajal Bhardwaj refers[4] to a generation gap among the activists who worked on patents and intellectual property rights issues. Their generation, who came of age as a part of the AIDS movement, was unaware of an earlier fight—one fought in the 1980s and 1990s by an earlier generation—against changing the structure of trade and intellectual property during the Uruguay Round of the GATT negotiations and the formation of the WTO. It was only during the 2004 Amendment to the Indian Patents Act, and after, that the two sets of activists combined and worked together.

What Kajal may also not know is that many of us in the older lot, Amit included, who became involved with intellectual property rights issues in the 1980s, were equally unaware of an earlier generation's fight. This was the fight for a self-reliant drug industry, freed from the clutches of global multinationals. We came to know about this earlier generation of activists during our seminar on 'Drug Industry and the Indian People' in 1986. We learnt then of how they had begun the movement for self-reliance in the drug industry—a movement that had its roots in India's struggle for independence and grew to encompass the struggle against the continuation of the colonial-era Indian patents regime.

This earlier generation included the key figure, Sahib Singh Sokhey—whom J.S. Majumdar refers to in his short piece on the

[4] See K. Bhardwaj, 'Medicines for All: A Reality Check, a Glimpse of Hope', in Section 1 in this volume.

1986 seminar, in Section 4. Sokhey, even though he was a Colonel at the time in the British Indian Army, headed the health section of the Planning Committee[5] set up in 1938 by the Indian National Congress, with Jawaharlal Nehru as the chairman. Sokhey[6] was the first Indian director of the Haffkine Institute and built it as a premier research institution that could also produce vaccines and medicines at an industrial scale. Despite opposition,[7] Sokhey laid the foundation of two public-sector units that began India's journey towards self-reliance—Indian Drugs & Pharmaceuticals Ltd (IDPL) and Hindustan Antibiotics Ltd (HAL).[8]

Sokhey was clear that the Indian Patents Act needed to change if India had to develop its indigenous pharmaceutical industry. (Unfortunately, this part of the Sokhey Committee report had to wait more than two decades to be enacted as the Patents Act 1970.) Sokhey knew that the challenge of the emerging pharmaceutical industry was three-fold: a) India needed scientific knowledge to produce existing drugs as well as a new generation of drugs; b)

[5] Sokhey Committee Report, 1948 (http://www.communityhealth.in/~commun26/wiki/index.php?title=File:Sokhey_Committee_report_1948.PDF.pdf).

[6] K. Ganapathi, 'Sahib Singh Sokhey, as I knew him', in *Biographical Memoirs of Fellows of the Indian National Science Academy*, vol. 4, 1976, pp. 134–53.

[7] Despite Nehru's backing, the Western MNC lobby, aligned with sections of the Indian government, bitterly opposed the setting up of public-sector drug companies. Sokhey had to bring in what he and his associate, K. Ganapathi, had already designed, with support from the UNICEF/WHO. Again, it was Sokhey who was instrumental in bringing Soviet technology to IDPL. For more details on this bitter battle, see Nasir Tyabji, 'Gaining Technical Know-How in an Unequal World: Penicillin manufacture in Nehru's India', *Technology and Culture*, vol. 45, no. 2 (April 2004), pp. 331–49 (https://mpra.ub.uni-muenchen.de/84236/).

[8] Harkishan Singh writes that Sokhey understood that self-reliance in medicines meant building a self-reliant chemical industry. Harkishan Singh, 'Sahib Singh Sokhey (1887–1971): An Eminent Medico-Pharmaceutical Professional', *Indian Journal of History of Science*, vol. 51, no. 2 (2016), pp. 238–47 (https://www.insa.nic.in/writereaddata/UpLoadedFiles/IJHS/Vol51_2016_2_1_Art06.pdf).

India needed the ability to produce such drugs at an industrial scale and not just in the laboratory; and c) the drugs produced had to be cheap enough to make them accessible to the Indian people.

People today may have forgotten that the life expectancy of Indians was 32 years at the time of Independence—lives were cut short by infectious diseases, epidemics, and malnutrition. The Patents Act was only one issue for pioneers such as Sokhey. The other issue was setting up public-sector units to produce drugs, and developing research institutions that would help make India self-reliant.

The laboratories of the Council of Science and Industrial Research (CSIR) created the scientific and technological knowledge infrastructure required for an indigenous Indian pharmaceutical industry. Without the CSIR infrastructure, the Patents Act changes introduced in 1970—changes that did away with product patents—would not have removed the stranglehold of the global MNCs. The National Chemical Laboratories (NCL), Pune, and the Central Drug Research Institute (CDRI), Lucknow—both part of the CSIR, and set up precisely to develop this capacity—became the two key institutions that made this transition possible.

There are also figures of interest—other than Sokhey—during this transition period of the pharmaceutical industry. One is Khwaja Abdul Hamied, the founder of Cipla,[9] a follower of Gandhi and an ardent nationalist. Along with Sokhey, Hamied was a member of the committee for the expansion of CSIR[10] and continued to be associated with CSIR. His son, Yusuf Hamied, followed his father's philosophy of cheap medicines for the people: Cipla, sometimes described as the Robin Hood of drugs,[11] provided AIDS drugs that

[9] Cipla was founded in Mumbai by Khwaja Abdul Hamied as The Chemical, Industrial & Pharmaceutical Laboratories, in 1935. The name of the company was changed to Cipla Limited on July 20, 1984.

[10] Harkishen Singh, 'Sahib Singh Sokhey'.

[11] Lisa Goldapple, 'India's Robin Hood of drugs', Project Breakthrough, September 19, 2016 (http://breakthrough.unglobalcompact.org/briefs/cipla-in-

people in developing countries could afford. Another figure of note is Dr Nitya Anand; as the director of CDRI, he pioneered research into the new processes required to make pharmaceutical products for the market. He would later chair (along with S.P. Shukla), the National Working Group on Patents Law which B.K. Keayla had helped set up.

We knew well the story of 'later pioneers' such as Nitya Anand, Abdul Hamied, or Ranbaxy's founder Bhai Mohan Singh.[12] What we ourselves did not know was the legacy of the earlier generation of activists—progressives and anti-imperialists, a part of the independence struggle, whose struggle we had inherited.

Soon after Independence, a committee, chaired by Justice Bakshi Tek Chand, formerly of the Lahore High Court, was set up to examine changes to the patents law. The Committee observed that the colonial-era law had led to high cost of medicines, but it failed to come up with an alternate framework. India had used the public-sector route to develop the indigenous manufacture of antibiotics in the 1950s; but the bulk of medicines in the Indian market was still in the hands of multinationals.

In 1957, a committee chaired by a retired judge of the Supreme Court, Justice Rajagopala Ayyangar, was again set up to suggest the way forward on patents. In his report, Ayyangar acknowledged the role of Sokhey's close associate, K. Ganapathi, in understanding the implications of patents for the pharmaceutical industry. While Ayyangar did not go as far as Sokhey wanted[13]—abolishing patents altogether—he did suggest changes to remove product patents in the food, drugs and chemical sectors. Instead, he suggested the

dias-robin-hood-of-drugs-yusuf-hamied/).

12 After Bhai Mohan Singh handed over Ranbaxy to his son, Parminder Singh, Ranbaxy switched sides. Parminder Singh decided that partnership with multinationals on patented drugs and manufacturing generics made for a better business strategy for Ranbaxy.

13 Sokhey was close to the Communist Party of India, and headed the All India Peace and Solidarity Organisation affiliated to the World Peace Council.

granting of only process patents in these sectors, and that too for a shorter period. A draft bill based on the Ayyangar Committee Report was first introduced in Parliament in 1965. It was then referred to a joint parliamentary committee which submitted its report in 1966,[14] and was finally passed by Parliament in 1970.[15]

In this post-Independence period, the MNCs continued with minimal manufacturing capacity in the country, and used their control over new drugs[16] to maintain super profits,[17] the bulk of which flowed back to the parent companies.[18] The prices of medicines were high, and out of reach to most Indians. The British India Patents Act of 1911 should have been changed soon after Independence. But it actually took more than two decades—an indication of the strength of the multinationals as well as the neo-colonial lobby[19] in India.

It was obvious that patents held by MNCs meant expensive medicines, and less access to medicines for most Indians. Then why—and how—did this delay in changing the patents law take place?

In countries such as India, the battle over pharmaceuticals

[14] *The Patents Bill, 1965*, Report of the Joint Parliamentary Committee, November, 1966 (https://www.eparlib.nic.in/bitstream/123456789/755572/1/jcb_03_1966_patents_bill.pdf).

[15] Though the Act was passed in 1970, it became operative with the Patents Rule being notified in April 1972.

[16] P.G. Sampath, 'Economic Aspects of Access to Medicines after 2005: Product Patent Protection and Emerging Firm Strategies in the Indian Pharmaceutical Industry', paper submitted to the United Nations University-Institute for New Technologies, 2005, Chapter 2 (https://www.who.int/intellectualproperty/studies/PadmashreeSampathFinal.pdf).

[17] The Report of the Joint Parliamentary Committee on the Patents Bill (1966) gives various examples of MNCs exploiting their patent monopolies to charge exorbitant prices.

[18] The Hathi Committee Report, Sudip Chaudhuri and P.G. Sampath have all written about the control of the MNCs over the Indian pharmaceutical market.

[19] Tyabji, 'Gaining Technical Know-How in an Unequal World'.

was as much a battle for self-reliance as for affordable medicine. But the West viewed this attempt to build a self-reliant industry, free of multi-national control, as an alignment with Communism. This is also how the West perceived non-alignment. Indeed, with control over knowledge becoming something of a strategic battle with the 'reds', the pharma companies considered themselves Cold War warriors. In his testimony[20] to the Kefauver Committee's Congressional hearings on the drug industry, the president of Merck & Co, J.T. Connor, spoke of how Merck, a Big Pharma player, had allegedly won '... an initial skirmish with the Soviet Union in India last year, as Merck and the Soviet government fought for the right to establish a manufacturing plant in India'. This is a reference to Sokhey's attempts to bring antibiotic technology to India. Connor went on to claim that '... our industry has grown into a significant national asset, these daily contributions to the war against disease are well known ... but [their] potential contributions to the world struggle against communism are only beginning to become apparent'.

Merck's CEO positioned Big Pharma's battle to maintain a strong patents regime as a global battle against the Soviet Union. Big Pharma was fully aware that any country with a reasonable industrial base would be able to manufacture drug and pharmaceutical products. Hence patents for new drugs were crucial for Big Pharma's global monopoly. And India was not just another market. The country was developing its science institutions; it had built capacity in the cutting-edge technology of the day, antibiotics; and it had a huge internal market. The stakes in India went far beyond India: this is why the battle took more than two decades before India could change its patent laws. And India's success was, precisely, a case of fears-come-true for global

[20] Dominique A. Tobbell, 'Who's Winning the Human Race?: Cold War as Pharmaceutical Political Strategy', *Journal of the History of Medicine and Allied Sciences*, vol. 64, no. 4 (October 2009), pp. 429–73 (https://academic.oup.com/jhmas/article/64/4/429/667871).

capital: its global market was truly being endangered.

The Kefauver Committee's Report, submitted in 1961, pointed out how the US drug companies charged as much as 7,000% of their costs. And who was charged this highest price[21] in the world? The poorest people, namely people in India. This made big news in India, and gave a further fillip to the demand to change India's patents laws.

The Kefauver Report[22] suggested limiting product patent monopoly to three years, pointing out (as the Ayyangar Committee had also done), that advanced European countries such as Germany, Switzerland, Italy, France did not give product patents, only process patents.[23] The Report also suggested that patents should be given only when the new drug had a different molecular structure, and significantly greater therapeutic effect.[24] This was in a similar spirit to India's amended Patents Act of 2005.

The new Patents Act was supplemented by the Drug Price Control Orders and the Hathi Committee Report[25] in helping indigenous drug manufacture. The results[26] were visible: the

[21] 'Study of Administrated Prices in the Drug Industry', Subcommittee on Anti-trust and Monopoly, Committee on the Judiciary, US Senate, 87th Cong., 1st Session., S. Rep. 448 (June 27, 1961), showing India with the highest prices of the seventeen countries surveyed, which included the United States.

[22] Kefauver's Report would have died a natural death since it was bitterly opposed by the pharmaceutical industry and large sections of the US political establishment. But the thalidomide tragedy resuscitated it—as the Kefauver–Harris Amendments to the Federal Food, Drug, and Cosmetic Act that demanded proof of efficacy of a new drug before granting it a patent.

[23] See Michele Boldrin and David K. Levine, *Against Intellectual Monopoly*, January 2008, available online (http://www.dklevine.com/papers/imbookfinalall.pdf).

[24] Ibid.

[25] Report of the Committee on Drugs and Pharmaceutical Industry (Hathi Committee Report), 1975 (http://www.communityhealth.in/~commun26/wiki/images/b/b5/Hathi_Committee_report_1975.PDF.pdf).

[26] Sudip Chaudhuri, 'The Pharmaceutical Industry in India after TRIPS', in *The New Political Economy of Pharmaceuticals. International Political Economy Series*, ed. H. Löfgren and O.D. Williams, London: Palgrave Macmillan,

pharmaceutical market of the multinational drug companies in India came down from about 85% before 1970 to less than 40% by 1999.[27] India not only manufactured a significant part of its drug needs, especially of lifesaving drugs, it also went on to produce the active pharmaceutical ingredient (API)—which required a deeper industrial base—for most drugs. This transition in indigenous manufacturing was made possible by the scientific knowledge India had; by people who had the necessary industrial experience; and also by the CSIR laboratories that helped India develop alternate processes.

By the 1990s, India had emerged as an important global player in generic drugs, as well as APIs. The Indian pharmaceutical industry is currently the largest global supplier of generic drugs—with an estimated share of 20% of the world's generic market.[28] This was exactly what Big Pharma had feared: that weakening the inherited colonial-era patents laws of most newly-independent countries would also weaken the control of Big Pharma over the global market. This fear was not limited to losing the market of the ex-colonies; it extended to the threat posed to their home markets.

The changes in the Patents Act were necessary for the Indian pharmaceutical industry to emerge, first in India, and later at a global level. What is often forgotten in the story of the Indian drug industry is the contribution of the public-sector undertakings, IDPL and HAL. Just as these two units had benefited from the Haffkine Institute's experience in making vaccines, serum, and later drugs, the Indian private sector also 'borrowed' people[29] and knowledge from the public sector. The public sector may be

2013.

27 Sampath, 'Economic Aspects of Access to Medicines'.

28 Uday S. Racherla, 'Historical Evolution of India's Patent Regime and Its Impact on Innovation in the Indian Pharmaceutical Industry', in *Innovation, Economic Development, and Intellectual Property in India and China*, ed. Kung-Chung Liu, Uday S. Racherla, September 2019.

29 An example is the founder of Dr Reddy's Lab. He got his PhD from NCL, then worked for IDPL before starting out on his own.

sick today, but we have to remember that our successes in the pharmaceutical sector owe much to its contributions.

Going beyond India to a global view, we see a parallel: countries such as Brazil, Argentina, Mexico changed their patents laws in the 1970s to weaken the control of monopolies. Developing countries in fora[30] such as the Berne or Paris Convention began to ask a critical question: Did patents and copyright work to diffuse knowledge or appropriate it? The question naturally led to resisting the MNCs' control of knowledge, and the support such control got from the West in various international fora.

There was a fight-back of course. A group of pharma and chemical MNCs launched the fight against the developing countries, with support from the US, the EU, the UK and Japan. Having failed to use the WIPO (World Intellectual Property Organization) to strengthen patent protection, these countries decided to shift the forum to GATT, where they felt they had more clout.

In his essay in this volume, S.P. Shukla describes the fight-back of global capital in GATT, and the collapse of the resistance of countries such as India and Brazil. Shukla also recounts how the Communist Party of India (Marxist), or CPI (M), asked him to join its Members of Parliament during the negotiations with the Manmohan Singh government on the Draft Patents Bill. Out of these negotiations—that made use of the TRIPS flexibilities[31]—emerged India's Patents Act in 2005. The essays in this volume,

[30] The Berne Convention aimed at copyright protection of original works, while the Paris Convention focused on protecting industrial property—patents, trademark and industrial designs. The concept or the usage of intellectual property for both is a later 'invention', and became popular only with the Uruguay Round of GATT negotiations.

[31] A number of threats were made about taking India to the WTO's Dispute Settlement Tribunal, but a reading of the TRIPS Agreement makes it clear that India used the TRIPS flexibilities to create a TRIPS-compliant law. That is why the US threatened India under its domestic laws, but never sought to use the WTO's dispute settlement process against India.

particularly those by Amit, indicate that the scope of the Left's intervention was not limited to Section 3(d)[32] of the Patents Act; it also extended to the Act's provisions on compulsory licensing, pre- and post-grant opposition, and its treatment of mailbox patents. As we confront the Covid-19 pandemic, provisions on compulsory licensing for vaccines and medicines are even more relevant today.

For many of the health activists in the 1980s, the key struggle was a rational drug therapy, creating an essential drug list, and regulating the prices of these essential drugs. The underlying belief, shared by many in the world, was that infectious disease had now been conquered; and that we now had enough medicines in our kitty to control such diseases. The argument was that the latest patent-protected drugs could easily be substituted by older drugs in the essential list, and were, therefore, not necessary for poor countries. The WHO had prepared an essential drug list, and a number of health groups were fighting to reduce the number of drugs and drug combinations.

Those of us from the science and self-reliance movements agreed on the need to fight irrational drug combinations; but we also believed that poor countries do need the latest in medicines. The medicine required has to be decided by the disease a patient has, not by the person's ability to pay, and not by a country's wealth or poverty. And for India, the argument of restricting drugs to a small number of essential drugs made even less sense—the country already had a developing pharmaceutical industry with its capacity to manufacture a whole range of drugs.

It was the AIDS epidemic that brought the two sets—the health and the science activists—together. AIDS showed that the battle against infectious diseases was a continuous one; to think

[32] The 3(d) provision of what is not patentable is more well known as it was on this issue that the Glivec patent of Novartis was rejected. Amit Sengupta's essay in Section 1 brings out the importance of other amendments that the Left was able to insert in the Patent Act, 2005.

that the battle against such diseases was over was a foolish illusion.[33] Disease is always going to strike, or strike back, and new drugs are continuously required. This is what we have seen, once again, with the onslaught of SARS-CoV-2.

The AIDS epidemic also illustrated the utter heartlessness of Big Pharma, which was willing to sacrifice untold human lives in its hunger for profit. Big Pharma's price for AIDS drugs was $10,000–15,000 for a year's course—against India's price of $350 for a year's medicine. Big Pharma's price was something that 99% of the twenty-five million AIDS patients at the time (the number today stands at about thirty-eight million) could not afford. Even many countries could not have afforded this price which, when calculated for their affected populations, would have exceeded the country's GDP! The 'concessional' price offered was $4,000, twelve times more than the $350 at which Cipla was willing to sell the drug. Big Pharma did not stop there, and forty-one lawsuits[34] charging violation of patent laws were filed against South Africa for its attempts to import generic AIDS drugs from India.

India might have signed the WTO/TRIPS Agreement, but it still had a ten-year moratorium to manufacture drugs for its home market. Indian activists came together with global health activists to consider how to provide India's cheap generic drugs to countries in Africa that did not have an indigenous drug industry. They took on several questions: could India, under the TRIPS Agreement, still export its drugs to Africa? Or other parts of the world? Or do the WTO trade rules bar such exports?

The battle was finally won in the Doha Round of the WTO negotiations in 2001. The Round reached the agreement that under conditions of an epidemic or a health emergency—and AIDS was

[33] Amit's blood pressure would go up every time this issue of forgotten infectious diseases came up!

[34] Jennifer Hillmen, 'Drugs and Vaccines Are Coming—But to Whom', *Foreign Affairs*, May 19, 2020 (https://www.foreignaffairs.com/articles/world/2020-05-19/drugs-and-vaccines-are-coming-whom).

held to be both—any country could issue a compulsory licence. This held even for a company outside its borders, in this case an Indian company, to work its licence. This is how the Indian generic industry became the supplier of 80% of AIDS drugs in the world.

If the AIDS epidemic had exposed the weakness in the TRIPS Agreement when it came to dealing with public health emergencies, Covid-19 has brought out the underlying crisis of the health systems of the advanced countries as well. Why have countries with the most advanced health infrastructure, those with the strongest economies, failed to control the epidemic? The question becomes more pointed if we consider that a China, a South Korea or a Vietnam has managed better in controlling the epidemic.

In his book *Forgotten People, Forgotten Diseases,*[35] the molecular biologist Peter Hotez wrote about the two billion who face the threat of infectious diseases, people for whom Big Pharma is not interested in developing new drugs. The last malaria drugs the US developed were for its soldiers in the war against Vietnam. The most frequently used TB drugs are now more than fifty years old. The question is: who has forgotten these diseases? If we add tuberculosis, malaria, dengue and yellow fever to Hotez's list of forgotten diseases, certainly, the five billion people threatened by these infectious diseases have not forgotten them.

Since the Third Plague pandemic (1890–1950) killed relatively few people in rich countries,[36] the belief that only people in poor countries suffered from infectious diseases grew stronger. All the advanced countries had to do then was to keep such people—and their diseases—outside their borders. Like AIDS, the Covid-19

[35] Peter Hotez, *Forgotten People, Forgotten Diseases: The Neglected Tropical Diseases and Their Impact on Global Health and Development*, 2nd ed., ASM Press, May 21, 2013 (https://www.ncbi.nlm.nih.gov/pmc/articles/PMC2681134/).

[36] Figures indicate that about 1,700 died in Europe against an estimated 15 million in Asia, with about 10 million in India alone.

pandemic has once again proved that diseases will strike back: we are always only one mutation away from an emerging infectious disease.

This failure of the rich countries appears even more stark when we consider their predictions when the pandemic began in China. Johns Hopkins and the Nuclear Threat Initiative came together to produce an index of which countries were best prepared[37] to face the epidemic. At the top was the US, followed by the UK and other European countries. China, South Korea and Vietnam were all well below these countries. Needless to say, the index turned out to be pure fantasy.

For the people in the US, the threat of a new infectious disease is not even a part of their collective memory. In the less affluent countries, people still remember infectious diseases—plague, cholera, small pox, polio—and the public health measures that are needed during epidemics. Is that why the East and Southeast Asian countries, who have recently faced SARS and the dangerous H5N1 avian flu, fared better?

After the collapse of the socialist bloc, a triumphalist belief grew in the West—that the world could now be remoulded to suit the interests of global capital. Such a philosophy had many targets; one was the public health system, what was seen as 'socialist medicine'. Privatizing healthcare—including privatizing publicly funded drug research—was the new paradigm pushed by the World Bank and the other global think tanks that had mushroomed all over the world, and covered in Section 3. This was the neoliberal phase of capital, which did not spare healthcare, municipal services, and other public monopolies such as electricity, telecom, and railways.

The response of the health activists was to build on the global AIDS campaign and start an international health movement. The movement made the political choice to locate itself in the global

[37] Global Health Security Index, Nuclear Threat Initiative and Johns Hopkins School of Public Health, October 2019 (https://www.ghsindex.org/wp-content/uploads/2020/04/2019-Global-Health-Security-Index.pdf).

South, and not be led by global North NGOs, however well-meaning they may be. Zafrullah Chowdhury,[38] Amit Sengupta, and others realized that we cannot replicate the imperialist global order within the movement of resistance. This is why the People's Health Assembly was founded in Dhaka in 2000. This led to the formation of the global People's Health Movement (PHM) and the Jana Swasthya Abhiyan (JSA) in India. The PHM has built a network of health activists who have kept the issue of public health firmly on the agenda. They have been critical about the WHO's vulnerability to US pressure, or pressure from big private funders, to drift towards more privatized healthcare—a development that would mean retreating from health as a public good. The WHO Watch was a consequence of this larger engagement of health activists with the global agenda, which included issues from market-driven solutions of privatized healthcare to the battle over patents.

The engagement with the WHO made Amit focus, once again, on intellectual property in the newly emerging area of biologics. Biologics comprise the cutting edge of new medicines—for diseases from cancer to inflammatory diseases such as rheumatoid arthritis. Biologics have been making an entry even in antivirals. Biologics were priced very high, making it impossible for anyone in developing countries, except the super rich, to access such drugs.

An example is Nexavar, a cancer drug which Bayer was selling for $65,000 a year's course. India issued a compulsory licence for Nexavar to Natco to produce it in India. Marijn Dekkers, the CEO of Bayer, was quoted widely[39] calling this 'theft', and he 'candidly' explained the basis of Bayer's price: 'We did not develop this medicine for Indians ... We developed it for western patients who can afford it.'

[38] Zafrullah Chowdhury is the founder of Gonoshasthaya Kendra, and a well-known public health activist.

[39] James Love, 'Bayer CEO Marijn Dekkers explains: Nexavar cancer drug is for "western patients who can afford it"', Knowledge Ecology International, January 23, 2014 (https://www.keionline.org/22401).

Big Pharma used the regulators—the Federal Drug Authority in the US and the European Medicine Agency (EMA) in the European Union—to make it difficult for biosimilars, the equivalent of generics in biologics, to enter the market. Satyajit Rath describes in his introduction to Section 2, how Amit combined science with health needs of the people to examine the changes required in regulatory structures for providing access to cheaper biologics.

The Covid-19 pandemic has put public health and intellectual property rights back on the global agenda. Public health was important as long as infectious diseases were seen as threatening. As they were 'forgotten', so was public health in rich countries. In the case of hospitals, what drove the system was private profit for private hospitals. The same capitalist criteria were introduced as indices of 'efficiency' for public hospitals. The capitalist principle of maximizing efficiency called for reducing beds, equipment, and medical staff; or, in capital's terms, 'rationalizing' production and increasing 'efficiency'.

The other issue that will not go away either is that of intellectual property rights—or patents. With the great and urgent demand for Covid-19 medicines and vaccines, it's very much back on the global agenda. The provisions for compulsory licensing—used as a tool by the developing countries—can be used during the Covid-19 pandemic. Even if Trump wants Covid-19 vaccines or drugs for America first, any country can use the same compulsory licensing provisions to break the monopoly over a drug or a vaccine. This is in the Doha Declaration.

Recognizing the threat from compulsory licensing of Covid-19 vaccines or medicines, the clever sections in global capital mooted the idea of a voluntary patent pool. In the 73rd World Health Assembly (WHA) all countries except the US agreed that vaccines and Covid-19 medicines should be held in a voluntary patent pool, to which companies and institutions would assign their patents. Rather than a right during health emergencies as exists in the

Doha Declaration, this translates into a semi-charitable handout to countries by the patent holders. Even with the voluntary patent pool, it is unclear whether there would still be charges that need to be paid to the patent holders even if they are at concessional rates; or whether the concessions will extend only to certain selected regions. The sole holdout, even for this watered-down formulation of public good, was the US, which extolled the beauty of intellectual property.[40]

What happens when the hunger of capital enters the belly of the beast? In healthcare costs? For patented life-saving medicines? This is the question that Amit posed in the last People's Health Assembly held in Dhaka, Bangladesh, in 2018. What happens when that raging hunger rides piggyback on a virus—and slips into those countries where people thought infectious diseases belonged to their remote past? We know that the battle between microbes and us is continuous; as we evolve our defence, they also develop their offence. Pandemics have not only spread death and destruction, but they have also changed societies in fundamental ways. No, the world will not look the same once the Covid-19 pandemic is over. But will it lead to society confronting capital's greed against people's lives? That is the challenge before all of us; this is how history will judge us.

[40] The US was the *lone objector* to the patent pooling of Covid-19 medicines and vaccines, noting '... the critical role that intellectual property plays in incentivizing the development of new and improved health products' (https://geneva.usmission.gov/2020/05/19/explanation-of-position-covid-19-response-resolution/).

Section 1

MEDICINES FOR ALL

1. Medicines for All: A Reality Check, a Glimpse of Hope

KAJAL BHARDWAJ

Like many others, Kajal Bhardwaj joined the movement against patent monopolies—an important part of the struggle for public health—in the opening decade of the twenty-first century. Amit Sengupta represented the generation that had fought the patents and intellectual property rights battle, as part of the Left's and people's science movement against Big Pharma and the huge 'monopoly rents' it charges for the patents it holds. The two currents, the old and the new, met when India was forced to modify its 'process patent' regime to one of 'product patents'. The use of Section 3(d)—adopted by Parliament in 2005—to reject patents claimed on minor tweaks to the base chemical, pre- and post-grant opposition, as well as compulsory licensing: all this came about due to the intervention of the Left parties in Parliament, and the work of the National Working Group on Patent Laws, of which Amit was an active member.

Bhardwaj addresses not only past achievements, but future challenges that the larger people's health movement faces today. She also talks about the challenge of biologics, the emerging terrain of struggle against Big Pharma, and the importance of solidarity.

In its obituary for Amit Sengupta, the All India Peoples Science Network noted that issues related to public health, the Indian drug industry and intellectual property were 'a part of his core concerns, research and activities'. I want to focus on this aspect of Amit's work and on the challenges that lie ahead. Indeed, the intersections of trade, intellectual property and access to medicines remain among the most serious, enduring challenges in ensuring access to medicines for all.

In India we came up against this challenge in 2005, in complying with the World Trade Organization's Agreement on Trade-Related Aspects of Intellectual Property Rights (TRIPS). Amendments moved in Parliament by the United Progressive Alliance government would overturn over three decades of a patents regime that did not allow product patents on food or medicine. By then, Indian generic companies were supplying the developing world with affordable generic antiretroviral medicines to treat HIV, bringing prices crashing from $10,000 per person per year, to less than a dollar a day. The supply of cheap generic antiretrovirals catalysed HIV treatment programmes across the developing world; naturally, India's looming TRIPS deadline became the flashpoint for local and global protests.[1]

At the time, the Left parties played a key role in introducing critical amendments to the patents bill. These amendments included the introduction of the now famous Section 3(d), aimed at the prevention of evergreening—the practice by the pharmaceutical industry of filing for multiple, overlapping patents on the same medicine, for new uses and new forms of that medicine. In legal terms, Section 3(d) states that patents will not be granted for

> the mere discovery of a new form of a known substance which does not result in the enhancement of the known efficacy of that substance or the mere discovery of any new property or new use for a known substance ... Explanation—For the purposes of this clause, salts, esters, ethers, polymorphs,

[1] APN+, *Our Health, Our Right: The roles and experiences of PLHIV networks in securing access to generic ARV medicines in Asia*, available online (https://hivlawcommission.org/wp-content/uploads/2017/06/Our-Health-Our-Right-Securing-access-to-generic-ARV-medicines-in-Asia.pdf).

> metabolites, pure form, particle size, isomers, mixtures of isomers, complexes, combinations and other derivatives of [a] known substance shall be considered to be the same substance, unless they differ significantly in properties with regard to efficacy.

The National Working Group on Patent Laws, of which Amit was an important figure, worked with the Left parties to introduce not only 3(d), but also other amendments that finally became the new law. The Left faced criticism—some of it from unexpected quarters—for voting the amendments in once the provisions proposed by the Left were included. Amit was surprised at these reactions: 'I am a bit concerned about the shrill tone of opposition to the Act that is emanating today from some global NGOs and their Indian counterparts, and the Western media . . .' He pointed out that the TRIPS agreement was flawed. Anything done under the TRIPS framework 'will be worse than the 1970 Patents Act', he argued.[2]

The potential of Section 3(d) was soon obvious to all. People living with HIV jumped into the patent opposition battle wholeheartedly, challenging—successfully—patent applications on first and second line antiretrovirals.[3]

But the case that was going to decide the fate of the provision centred on imatinib—a breakthrough drug to treat chronic myeloid leukaemia. Novartis's first patent on this medicine was filed in 1992. The pharma giant had missed the TRIPS bus, so to speak. Our TRIPS obligations commenced in 1995. In 1997, Novartis filed a secondary or evergreening patent application for the beta crystalline form of imatinib mesylate. Indian generics

[2] V. Sridhar Siddharth Narrain, 'A tempered patents regime', *Frontline*, April 22, 2005 (https://frontline.thehindu.com/the-nation/article30204388.ece).

[3] 'People Living with HIV in India: The Struggle for Access', *Global Health Watch*, vol. 5, December 17, 2017 (https://phmovement.org/wp-content/uploads/2018/07/E3.pdf).

companies were already supplying affordable imatinib; and Novartis's previous attempts to stop them had delivered mixed results. Novartis's price was Rs 120,000 per month, while generic prices were in the range of Rs 8,000–10,000 per month. With a patent in hand, under India's TRIPS-compliant patents regime, Novartis hoped to finish off the Indian generics threat once and for all. But their patent application was opposed by the Cancer Patients Aid Association and several generics companies. The Patent Office found that this new version of imatinib failed the Section 3(d) test. Affronted, Novartis challenged Section 3(d), dragging cancer patients, the government and generics companies into nearly seven years of litigation.[4]

Novartis's intent to upend this critical public health safeguard met with a full-blown global campaign calling on them to drop the case. As Amit wrote, the case had 'implications for access to medicines not just for leukaemia patients but for a whole range of patients—located not just in India but in over a hundred countries in Asia, Latin America and Africa—who are today able to access cheaper drugs made by Indian companies'.[5] The Madras High Court upheld Section 3(d), stating that the provision was introduced to 'prevent evergreening; to provide easy access to the citizens of this country to life-saving drugs and to discharge [the] constitutional obligation of providing good healthcare to citizens'.[6]

Eventually, the case landed up in the Supreme Court where Amit was to play an unexpected role. Amit marshalled four other

[4] 'Novartis case: background and update—Supreme Court of India to recommence hearing', Lawyers Collective, September 6, 2011 (https://lawyerscollective.org/2011/09/06/126-novartis-case-background-and-update-supreme-court-of-india-to-recommence-hearing/).

[5] Amit Sengupta, 'Supreme Court Judgment on Novartis Case Vindication of Left's principled position in 2005', *Newsclick*, April 4, 2013 (https://www.newsclick.in/india/supreme-court-judgment-novartis-case-vindication-left's-principled-position-2005).

[6] *Novartis AG vs Union of India*, (2007) 4 MADRAS LJ 1153 (https://indiankanoon.org/doc/266062/).

colleagues (Prabir Purkayastha and K.M. Gopakumar among them) in writing to the Law Minister and raising concerns that one of the SC judges hearing the case may have a bias in the matter. The judge in question had attended conferences organized by the Intellectual Property Owners Association and had said in an article that pharma patent holders from developed countries 'must make all efforts to ensure that all countries are persuaded to enact proper laws'.[7] The five signatories to the letter knew they were courting contempt proceedings. A news report on their letter led to the judge recusing himself. Hearings in the matter began before a new bench of the Supreme Court in 2012, and stretched over several months. Novartis was now challenging the interpretation of Section 3(d), not its validity.

On 1 April 2013, the Supreme Court upheld the strict interpretation of Section 3(d) and held that Novartis's patent application failed the 3(d) test.[8] As the news of Novartis's defeat spread like wildfire across the globe, Amit used the opportunity to set the record straight on the origins and necessity of 3(d). While most commentators wrote about the journey of the provision from 2005 onwards, Amit was at pains to record the Indian resistance to the WTO, GATT and patents on medicines dating back to the late 1980s, and link that resistance to how Section 3(d) found its way into the patent amendments. A clearly jubilant Amit argued that the Supreme Court decision was a vindication of the Left's stand on the 2005 amendments. Arguing that the accusations of the Left selling out at the time were instances of radical posturing, he wrote:

> [I]t was only the Left that had firmly opposed the TRIPS

[7] 'SC judge under attack from health activists', *The Times of India*, September 6, 2011 (https://timesofindia.indiatimes.com/india/SC-judge-under-attack-from-health-activists/articleshow/9879869.cms).

[8] *Novartis AG vs Union of India*, (2013) 6 SCC 1 (https://indiankanoon.org/doc/165776436/)

> agreement under the WTO since the 1980s . . . it was only the Left in India—which made common cause with the domestic industry—which had taken a consistent position against a global patents system that forced countries like India to change their Patents Act. It was not an accident that India was the only country of significance that used the entire ten-year transition period before changing its law . . . That India was the last holdout was a consequence of its consistent position and its mobilization on the issue, that started right from the start of the Uruguay round of negotiations in 1986. It is interesting that many of the same NGOs and some of their vocal spokespersons now claim the 2005 Patents Act as a victory for 'civil society' and the Indian Act as a model Act. The Left has never claimed that the present Indian Act is ideal, but it can legitimately claim that it was the best that it could achieve given the political circumstances in 2005.[9]

A REALITY CHECK

That was six years ago. The heady days of the campaign to defend 3(d) have begun to fade, and the thrill of the hard-earned victory is already a distant memory. The case and the judgment have been consigned to textbooks. The words of the judges have been dissected in the harsh light of legal analyses, not the warm glow of an assured pathway to generic access for patients in India and across the developing world. A mere six years later, as changes and challenges to access to affordable generic medicines rapidly mount, was Section 3(d) and the judgment really the vindication Amit claimed it was?

Use of Section 3(d): In 2018, two studies were published on the Patent Office's use of 3(d). A study of the rejection of pharma patents found a significant uptick in rejections after the Supreme

[9] Sengupta, 'Supreme Court Judgment on Novartis Case Vindication of Left's principled position in 2005'.

Court judgment, a plateauing between 2014 and 2016, then a significant drop in rejections.[10] The second report was even more disheartening. Examining 2,293 pharma patents granted between 2009 and 2016, the report found that 72% of grants were for secondary or evergreening patents.[11] The studies paint a dismal state of affairs at the Patent Office. But is this just a matter of sheer incompetence?

One critical case is worth examining. Sofosbuvir is a new treatment against hepatitis C that offers a 98% cure, infamously priced at $1,000 a pill. Gilead's patent application was rejected with unfortunate timing, the same month US President Obama visited India in 2015. After some legal manoeuvring, the application ended up in the Patent Office again, this time before a new examiner who granted the patent. *The Caravan* ran an excellent investigation into the fate of the original patent examiner.[12] In recent years, the Patent Office has been told it must examine patent applications within eighteen months.[13] Patent examiner trainings take place in Japan, the EU and the US.[14] The US government has been relentless in

[10] Dr. Feroz Ali, Dr. Sudarsan Rajagopal, Mohamed Mustafa and Chinnasamy Prabhu, 'Rejected in India: What the Indian Patent Office got right on Pharmaceuticals Patent Applications (2009–2016)', AccessIBSA, December 2017 (https://accessibsa.org/media/2017/12/Rejected-in-India.pdf).

[11] Dr. Feroz Ali, Dr. Sudarsan Rajagopal, Dr. Venkata S. Raman and Roshan John, 'Pharmaceutical Patent Grants in India: How our safeguards against evergreening have failed, and why the system must be reformed', AccessIBSA, April 2018 (https://accessibsa.org/media/2018/04/Pharmaceutical-Patent-Grants-in-India.pdf).

[12] Mandakini Gahlot and Vidya Krishnan, 'What Happened to the Indian Official that Rejected the US Drug Company Gilead's Patent Application in 2015', *The Caravan*, May 10, 2016 (https://caravanmagazine.in/vantage/indian-official-rejected-gilead-patent-forced-out).

[13] 'Wait time for patent examination to be cut to 18 months by March 2018', *Business Standard*, April 28, 2017 (https://www.business-standard.com/article/economy-policy/wait-time-for-patent-examination-to-be-cut-to-18-months-by-march-2018-117042701106_1.html).

[14] *General Information on The JPO/IPR Training Program FY 2019 (for India)* (http://ipindia.nic.in/writereaddata/Portal/News/517_1_The_JPO-IPR_

its pressure on India's patents law through its Special 301 reports, its out-of-cycle reviews in 2014 and 2015.[15] An educated guess suggests that we are probably seeing the combined effects of these internal and external pressures on the Patent Office in its dismal application of 3(d). As the government's reluctance to strictly apply the health safeguards in the Indian patents law (Section 3[d], compulsory licensing) became more and more apparent, Amit noted, 'India is now perched on a slippery slope where decades of effort to promote a liberal IP regime, which allowed easier access to medical products, stands to be frittered away.'[16]

Access to affordable biologics: Pressure apart, Big Pharma is now increasingly using regulatory barriers, along with patents, to prevent generics competition particularly in the case of biologic medicines. In a report recently published by Third World Network, Amit deftly lays bare the challenges to accessing biosimilars.[17] The publication displays his genuine and infectious love for science, his quest to demystify it, and his determination to thwart attempts to monopolize science and scientific knowledge. Knowledge, as Amit would say, is public heritage. The report is the culmination of a four-year endeavour by Amit to demythologize biologic medicines, and highlight the next frontier in the battle to increase access to medicines.

Amit noted: 'The high prices of biologics are increasingly

Training_Program_FY_2019.pdf).

15 Amit Sengupta, 'Capitulation on IP: Reaching a Point of No Return?', *Newsclick*, October 27, 2014 (https://www.newsclick.in/india/capitulation-ip-reaching-point-no-return).

16 Amit Sengupta, 'India Assures the US it Will Not Issue Compulsory Licences on Medicines', *The Wire*, March 12, 2016 (https://thewire.in/health/india-assures-the-us-it-will-not-issue-compulsory-licences-on-medicines).

17 Refer to Satyajit Rath 'Biosimilars: Health Activism at the Leading Edge of Technology' in Section 2.

See also Amit Sengupta, *Biological Drugs: Challenges to Access*, Penang: Third World Network, 2018, available online (https://www.twn.my/title2/books/pdf/BiologicalDrugs-eng.pdf).

taking up a large share of the public health budget of many countries. In Brazil while biologics account for 4% by volume of drugs distributed through its National Health System, they account for over half of the ministry of health's expenditure on medicines.'[18] In the case of biologics—unlike that of chemical drugs—it is not possible to produce an exact replica of the original drug. Big Pharma has used this to push for regulatory requirements for biosimilars that effectively treat them as new biologic medicine. The report makes a series of recommendations calling for the removal of these regulatory barriers. In April 2019, a number of scientists made the same demand of the WHO, calling for a review of its biosimilar guidelines.[19] To the WHO's immense discomfort, Amit's report set the cat among the pigeons.

Big Pharma's dirty tricks: And what of Novartis and Big Pharma? Did their very public and very global loss in the Indian Supreme Court deter them from strong-arm litigation and lobbying tactics in developing countries? Halfway across the world, in Colombia, another legal battle on Novartis's 1998 patent for imatinib had a very different ending. The patent denied in 2003 was granted in 2012, and generics exited the market. The result: imatinib was sold for about $15,000 a year, twice the average Colombian worker's income, five times the lowest competitor price. Without competition from generics, the government would have to pay an extra $15 million a year supplying imatinib.[20] This led to serious consideration of the issuance of a compulsory licence. But after

[18] Amit Sengupta, 'People's Health Movement and Third World Network', submitted to the United Nations Secretary-General's High-Level Panel On Access To Medicines, February 28, 2016 (http://www.unsgaccessmeds.org/inbox/2016/2/28/yvtkspjtra6s965vwerl8mq67xfq4a).

[19] 'Revise Biosimilar Guidelines, Scientists Demand; WHO Says Not Now', *Health Policy Watch*, April 25, 2019 (https://www.healthpolicy-watch.org/revise-biosimilar-guidelines-scientists-demand-who-says-not-now/).

[20] 'Colombia battles world's biggest drugmaker over cancer drug', *Associated Press*, May 18, 2016 (https://www.foxnews.com/health/colombia-battles-worlds-biggest-drugmaker-over-cancer-drug).

meetings with the US Trade Representative, a memo from the Colombian embassy in Washington was leaked—and it recorded fears that US support for a peace deal with the FARC rebels would be seriously threatened if Colombia issued a compulsory licence on imatinib.[21]

Both Brazil and Argentina are also being sued by Big Pharma associations for their attempts to prevent evergreening.[22] In South Africa, Big Pharma drew up a $600,000 plan to thwart South Africa's patents-law reform process to adopt a full range of health safeguards. When their plan document was leaked, South Africa's health minister famously said, 'This document can sentence many South Africans to death. This is a plan for genocide.'[23]

The ever more complex trade and investment trap: Big Pharma's litigation and lobbying tactics are of course ably backed up by Free Trade Agreements (FTAs). The Regional Comprehensive Economic Partnership (RCEP) negotiations, launched in 2012, saw a significant push for TRIPS-plus provisions by South Korea and Japan.[24] The RCEP negotiations covered not only India, but also China and Thailand—three of the most important generics

[21] Thiru Balasubramaniam and Andrew S. Goldman, 'Constraints faced by developing countries and least developing countries (LDCs) in making full use of patent flexibilities', submitted by Knowledge Ecology International to the WIPO SCP, October 2017, available online (https://www.wipo.int/export/sites/www/scp/en/meetings/session_27/3rdparty_comments/kei.pdf).

[22] 'Big Pharma's Court Cases in Brazil & Argentina Threaten to Dismantle the National Laws Considered as Important Public Health Safeguards in the UN High Level Panel Report', *InfoJustice*, September 2016 (http://infojustice.org/archives/36928).

[23] 'Motsoaledi: Big pharma's "satanic" plot is genocide', *Mail & Guardian*, January 16, 2014 (https://mg.co.za/article/2014-01-16-motsoaledi-big-pharmas-satanic-plot-is-genocide/).

[24] 'India to resist Japan and South Korea's push for patent legislation at RCEP', *Economic Times*, June 12, 2015 (https://economictimes.indiatimes.com/news/economy/policy/india-to-resist-japan-and-south-koreas-push-for-patent-legislation-at-rcep/articleshow/47636517.cms?from=mdr).

manufacturers in the world. In late 2019, India announced it was opting out of the RCEP. The EU is pushing for the resumption of the EU–India FTA negotiations.[25] The US, in its FTAs, proposes ever-expanding monopolies—ten years of data exclusivity on biologic medicines in the US–Mexico–Canada trade agreement, and an anti-Section 3(d) provision in the Trans-Pacific Partnership Agreement. Fortunately, both proposals were ultimately rejected.[26] Meanwhile, Big Pharma is developing newer and more insidious ways of using this expanding trade and investment framework. In the Ukraine, with over two million people living with hepatitis C, access to sofosbuvir is critical. But Gilead excluded Ukraine from the voluntary licences it gave to Indian companies. After Gilead's patent application was rejected in the Ukraine, the health ministry registered a generic version. But Gilead claimed the registration violated the data exclusivity it had, and filed an investment dispute under the US–Ukraine Bilateral Investment Treaty (of $800 million), forcing the government to withdraw the registration for generic sofosbuvir.[27]

A broken compact: There is one other critical way in which we are in a very different situation today—what Amit called the 'broken compact' among the government, civil society and the generics industry. Eight years ago, Amit, in his heartfelt obituary for B.K. Keayla, recounted the journey that he and others from the

[25] 'EU FTA talks: India looking at ways to end stalemate, re-start negotiations', *The Hindu BusinessLine*, December 15, 2019 (https://www.thehindubusinessline.com/economy/eu-fta-talks-india-looking-at-ways-to-end-stalemate-re-start-negotiations/article30313313.ece).

[26] Carlos M. Correa, 'Intellectual Property in the Transpacific Partnership: Increasing the Barriers for the Access to Affordable Medicines', research paper submitted to South Centre, July 2017 (https://www.southcentre.int/wp-content/uploads/2017/07/RP62R_IP-in-TPP-Increasing-the-Barriers-for-the-Access-to-Affordable-Medicines_rev_EN.pdf).

[27] 'Gilead Pharma corp withdraws investment arbitration after Ukraine agrees to settlement of dispute over monopoly rights to market anti-viral drug', ISDS Platform, March 16, 2017 (http://isds.bilaterals.org/?gilead-pharma-corp-withdraws&lang=es).

health movement undertook with Keayla to establish the National Working Group on Patent Laws. Amit recalled that

> Keayla*ji* had broached the idea of setting up a working group to discuss the issue of patents and the negotiations in the Uruguay Round on a proposed agreement on intellectual property rights. He proposed a group that would include civil society organizations such as ours, the generic drugs/medicine industry, lawyers, academics, and trade unions in the pharma industry. The idea was novel—our first experience of Keayla*ji*'s ability to think out of the box. For some of us it was perhaps too novel to start with.
>
> We had never worked with the industry and viewed them as uncompromising enemies. This was the year 1988 when few in the drug movement had even heard about patents . . . This is how the National Working Group on Patent Laws was born.[28]

In some ways, 1 April 2013, the day of the Novartis judgment, may well have been the last day when the sheer force of that compact, institutionalized in the National Working Group, was visible. The government, the generic companies and cancer patients stood on the same side of the court room, waiting to hear the result of their epic legal battle against Big Pharma.

That three-decade-old compact is clearly broken. The relationship between Big Pharma and Indian generic companies has gone from an antagonistic one to one of camaraderie. There has been a significant buyout of Indian generics by multinational companies. There are contract-manufacturing tie-ups, marketing arrangements and, of course, voluntary licences. These licences are given bilaterally; or, in the case of HIV, hepatitis C and TB medicines, through the Medicines Patent Pool (MPP), an entity supported by a significant number of international civil society

[28] See Amit Sengupta's essay on B.K. Keayla in this section.

organizations. As Amit and a colleague from the People's Health Movement wrote when the plan for the MPP was being discussed at the global stage, 'the Patent Pool mechanism would ultimately be weighed on the consideration whether it strengthens or disarms the global struggle to secure sustainable, equitable and inclusive access to health products'.[29]

Over the past few years, it has become apparent that these sorts of licences allow MNCs to control virtually the entire global supply chain of key medicines, not through patents in each country, but simply by roping in the major Indian companies that supply internationally. Despite the restrictions on how and where generic medicines can be supplied, these Voluntary Licences have become the preferred option for Indian companies. It is no accident that today, the task of opposition to patents has been left to patients' groups and civil society organizations; generics companies are more focussed on their relationships with Big Pharma. Recently, the government's response to calls for a compulsory licence on bedaquiline, a new treatment for multi-drug resistant TB, has been to state that even here, the solution being sought was a voluntary licence.[30]

When Cipla took a voluntary licence from Gilead for sofosbuvir, Amit placed the development in the backdrop of the continually changing discourse on intellectual property protection in India. Noting that the victory on the patent amendments in 2005 was, in fact, out of step with the mainstream political consensus favouring neoliberal reforms, he wrote:

> Thirteen years ago, Cipla led the charge against Big Pharma

[29] 'PHM Letter to UNITAID Board on Patent Pool Plan', People's Health Movement, December 10, 2009 (https://archive.phmovement.org/en/node/2719.html).

[30] Vidya Krishnana, 'Extreme TB: Centre yet to push for cheaper versions of two crucial drugs', *The Hindu*, March 3, 2018 (https://www.thehindu.com/sci-tech/health/extreme-tb-no-licence-to-heal/article22920634.ece).

and changed the fate of millions of HIV/AIDS patients across the world by offering HIV/AIDS drugs at $1/40^{th}$ the price charged by them. That Cipla chose not to do so in 2014 and collaborated with Big Pharma illustrates the sea change in the legal, economic and political environment in the country over the last fifteen years.[31]

SOLIDARITY ... AND A GLIMPSE OF HOPE

In almost every presentation on this subject, Amit would speak of the spirit of the HIV movement. There was the spirit of the South Africans, who marched on the streets when Big Pharma sued Nelson Mandela for trying to expand access to generic HIV medicines in the 2000s. There was the spirit of solidarity forged in the wake of the epidemic. In an interview I conducted with Amit several years back, he said:

> After 1995, most of us had resigned ourselves to living with patents. HIV was an unusual disease in that it was devastating the North and the South. Frankly, had it affected only the South it would not have got the attention it has. With strong advocacy in the North, treatment for HIV got a major push. And then when it wasn't available to the rest of the world, groups in the North and the South took up the issue of treatment and patents. HIV has challenged the paradigm; it has questioned the patents system in a way no other issue has.

According to Amit, 'the solidarity of movements in North and South is what changed the global landscape for HIV.'[32]

Today, we can see a glimpse of a much greater North-South solidarity that is not just about affordable treatment for the South, but about affordable treatment for all. Section 3(d) and the Supreme

[31] Sengupta, 'Capitulation on IP'.

[32] APN+, *Our Health, Our Right.*

Court judgment have inspired something much larger than the backlash against Big Pharma and the developed world. Across the developing world, 3(d)-like provisions have been cropping up in patent laws, or in patent examination guidelines. Some version of restrictions on evergeening now exist in the Philippines, in Argentina, Israel, Thailand, Zanzibar, Samoa, Burundi, and Rwanda. Patent oppositions challenging secondary patents have been filed in Argentina, Brazil, China, Colombia, the Dominican Republic, South Korea, Russia, South Africa, Spain, Thailand, Ukraine and Vietnam—and even in the EU and the US.[33]

Despite concerns over pricing and the lack of R&D for neglected diseases, there was an assumption that the innovation, the inventiveness, of Big Pharma was beyond doubt—this became the alibi of the protections offered by the patents system. That myth has now been busted. What Section 3(d), the Supreme Court judgment, and every gesture of opposition in India did was question the very legitimacy of the patents being granted.

And this is not limited to developing countries. Study after study concludes that over 70% of patents granted in developed countries are 'secondary' or derivative patents. A recent study of the US's highest-grossing drugs found seventy-one patents granted per drug, with thirty-eight years of patent protection (blocking generic competition) sought by drugmakers for each of these top-grossing drugs. That is nearly double the twenty-year monopoly intended under US patent law.[34] Authorities overseeing market competition in developed countries are also increasingly taking note of how evergreening and patent thickets are anti-

[33] See the Patent Opposition Database (https://www.patentoppositions.org/en/search?utf8=✓&query=&facets%5Bdocument_types%5D%5B%5D =patent_opposition).

[34] 'Overpatented, Overpriced: How Excessive Pharmaceutical Patenting is Extending Monopolies and Driving up Drug Prices', IMAK website (https://www.i-mak.org/wp-content/uploads/2018/08/I-MAK-Overpatented-Overpriced-Report.pdf).

competitive.[35] So embedded is the recognition that patent quality has suffered, and that countries must take action, that when the US did propose the anti-Section 3(d) clause in the Trans-Pacific Partnership (TPP), it found only one ally—Japan—which tried to bring this provision into the RCEP negotiations as well. At the TPP negotiations, the US and Japan were opposed not just by the developing countries, but also by other developed countries.[36]

The illegitimacy of the system is sparking all manner of defiance, outrage and protest. And beyond HIV. Women living with cancer are spearheading the movement for access to generic medicines in South Africa. Their primary question: why is the breast cancer medicine, trastuzumab, on patent in South Africa till 2033 when the original patent was filed in 1985?[37]

In their desperation to access sofosbuvir, patients from developed countries have gone to some extraordinary lengths. They have imported the raw material and taken it to their pharmacists to be compounded. As Gilead attempted to scare desperate patients off this approach, researchers were quickly able to show that the compounded medicines had the same effectiveness as the formulated tablets.[38] Treatment activists and LGBTQI groups in the US and EU are raging against Gilead; the reason is the antiretroviral combination of tenofovir and emtricitabine. In the US, it's already off-patent and available for $6 a month for treatment. But the use

[35] 'The life cycle of pharmaceutical products', on the European Commission website (https://ec.europa.eu/competition/sectors/pharmaceuticals/cycle.html).

[36] 'Secret TPP treaty: Advanced Intellectual Property chapter for all 12 nations with negotiating positions', *WikiLeaks*, November 13, 2013 (https://wikileaks.org/tpp/static/pdf/Wikileaks-secret-TPP-treaty-IP-chapter.pdf).

[37] 'Global Day of Action Against Roche's Inhumanity #Rochegreedkills', Fix The Patent Laws (website), February 7, 2017 (https://www.fixthepatentlaws.org/global-day-of-action-against-roches-inhumanity-rochegreedkills/).

[38] 'Low-cost generic hepatitis C drugs match branded products in viral responses', InfoHep, April 16, 2016 (http://www.infohep.org/Low-cost-generic-hepatitis-C-drugs-match-branded-products-in-viral-responses/page/3050871/).

of these very same medicines for prevention of HIV costs $1,600 a month![39] In the Netherlands, a Dutch insurance company is suing AstraZeneca for patent evergreening which kept generics off the market, and forced patients to pay too much for Seroquel—a drug which helps people who suffer from schizophrenia, bipolar disorder, and major depressive disorders.[40] As Amit said in 2018, during the Fourth People's Health Assembly held at Savar, Dhaka, 'Finally, the hunger of capital has crossed borders into the belly of the beast—it haunts Europe, haunts North America as well.'[41]

The real vindication of Section 3(d) and the Novartis victory comes from the question mark it has placed on the legitimacy of most pharma patents. The illegitimacy of the patent system is no longer a matter of conjecture, or of activist posturing, or ideological beliefs. It is based instead on strong evidence. 'Small victories,' such as the Novartis judgment, Amit wrote, 'become inspirations for larger battles.'[42] The larger battle may well be upon us. And there lie the fruits—of the popular resistance and mobilization forged through solidarity and collective action—of the three decades of struggle that challenged corporate power.

Am I reading too much into these little acts of resistance, these small rebellions? Am I making a revolution out of a molehill?

Perhaps. But then, as Amit said, 'Treat optimism as a purposeful act of political resistance.'

39 'PrEP Could Reduce HIV Infection Rates. So Why Isn't It Cheaper?', *The Daily Beast*, July 24, 2018 (https://www.thedailybeast.com/prep-could-reduce-hiv-infection-rates-so-why-isnt-it-cheaper?ref=home).

40 'Health insurer takes pharma giant to court for "evergreening"', *DutchNews.nl*, September 20, 2018 (https://www.dutchnews.nl/news/2018/09/health-insurer-takes-pharma-giant-to-court-for-evergreening/).

41 'A Tribute to Comrade Dr. Amit Sengupta', *Peoples Dispatch*, December 7, 2018 (https://peoplesdispatch.org/2018/12/07/a-tribute-to-comrade-dr-amit-sengupta/).

42 Amit Sengupta, 'Two decades of struggle: The Glivec precedent', *HAIAP News*, August 2013, available online (http://www.haiasiapacific.org/wp-content/uploads/2019/02/TwoDecades-lof-StruggleGlivecNovartisHAIANews-2013Amit.pdf).

This is not Amit's story or even a story about Amit. Amit's prolific writing, his intellect and eloquence, all lend us the language and the lens with which to understand and describe just one part of the battle for access to medicines. This is part of a story of collective action, of solidarity, of the many friendships and decades of people's struggles that make up the health movement. This has been told—then written—in a moment of shock and devastation that makes one reach for the personal in the political, the individual in the collective, in a feeble attempt to recapture something that may be forever beyond our reach.

2. Generic Names Versus Brand Names

AMIT SENGUPTA

Writing in 1986, Amit Sengupta exposes the politics of profit behind the use of brand names for drugs, rather than their generic names. He explains how the commercial interests of pharmaceutical companies hinder the availability of low-priced medicines to the people. Using clear evidence, this essay brings out the scientific as well as economic reasons to promote generic names. Rebutting the arguments in favour of brand names, as advanced in the 1980s by the Organisation of Pharmaceutical Producers of India, the essay explains the political economy behind big business operations.

The movement for the use of generic names has come a long way since, though it took time to develop. The department of pharmaceuticals launched the Jan Aushadhi Campaign in April 2008, to provide generic medicines through Jan Aushadhi stores. In 2012, the government of India directed that all drugs be sold under their generic names. The health ministry has now issued directives that all drug companies have to carry the generic name of the drug, and doctors are to use the generic names in writing prescriptions. Amit's arguments on generics versus brand names still hold true. Indeed, they extend to the newly emerging biologic drugs field as well.

A drug has three names. The chemical name, a non-proprietary name, and, in most cases, a brand name. Thus, the drug which is sold by the brand names Crocin or Calphol in the market, has the chemical name N-acetyl-para-aminophenol or acetyl-para-aminophenol (referred to as APAP). And the third is the non-proprietary name, paracetamol, which is easier to remember and refer to, instead of the full chemical name.

The non-proprietary name of a drug is often referred to as the generic name. This is not exactly correct, as generic names actually refer to the different groups of drugs with similar properties, viz. sulphonamides, cephalosporins, etc. However, as non-proprietary names are generally referred to as generic names, I shall refer to them as such.

An overwhelming majority of drugs in the Indian market are sold by their brand names. The generic names are written in small type, and are virtually impossible to read. All promotions and marketing is on the basis of these brand names, and most doctors prescribe in brand names.

The controversy as to whether drugs should be marketed by their brand names or generic names has raged for years. The reasons for marketing in generics are, briefly:

1. Clarity: Generic names give information about the class of drugs. Thus, diazepam and nitrazepam are clearly related. But their brand names, Calmpose and Nitravit, are not. There have been cases of prescribers, when one drug has failed, unwittingly changing to another drug of the same group or even to the same drug, thinking that such different names must mean totally different drugs. On this the textbook of pharmacology by D.R. Laurence has this to say: 'Such occurrences are a criticism of the prescriber; but they are also a criticism of the system that allows such confusion.'[1]

Confusion over brand names is compounded by the fact that drug companies are so busy emphasizing the brand they almost never highlight the medicine's exact composition. That such confusions can be fatal is illustrated by this oft-quoted story:

[1] D.R. Laurence and P.N. Bennet, *Clinical Pharmacology*, 5th ed., Churchill Livingstone, 1980.

A dispenser received a written slip from the O.T. sister asking for 1 gm of Procaine (which is used for anaesthesia). Thinking Procaine to be similar to another drug, Percaine, the dispenser used crystals of Percaine and labelled the solution Procaine. The patient into whom the drug was injected had seven convulsions in fifteen minutes and died. This incident occurred in 1940 and was reported in *The Lancet*. Interestingly, in 1942 the makers of Percaine discarded the earlier trade name and started using the name Nupercaine. Ironically, the next year a woman died because now Nupercaine was mistaken for Novocaine (which is the brand name of Procaine).[2]

Examples of confusing brand names in the Indian market include the following:

Amiline	Psychotropic, anti-depressant
Amicline	Anti-amoebic
Lasix	Diuretic
Laxil	Laxative
Celin	Vitamin C
Ciplin	Anti-infective
Corbutil	Painkiller
Corbeta	Anti-hypertensive
Restin	Painkiller
Restyl	Sleeping pill

Such examples are endless; and the possibility of mistakes, even fatal ones, is enormous.

The type of names chosen by drug companies for their drugs is also a part of their hard-sell campaign. So we have names such as Neurophos, Neurobion, Calmpose and Serenace. These names try to convey the type of effects these drugs have or the conditions in which they are to be used. But as a single name can never

[2] Ibid.

convey full information, such names actually convey misleading impressions.

2. Economy: Drug prices are bound to come down if a switchover is made to generics. Many drug companies can afford to charge artificially hiked prices for their brands, as they have been able to create a 'brand loyalty', through aggressive promotional and marketing techniques over the years. It has been said, in a lighter vein, that doctors are almost equally divided in two camps over the superiority of Bactrim or Septran. It is, of course, well known that Bactrim and Septran are brand names for the same drug co-trimoxazole. Moreover, colossal sums are spent as promotional expenditure by the drug companies to build their 'brand image'. An estimated 33% of total outlay is spent by MNCs as promotional expenditure and administrative overheads. These costs get added onto the prices of the final products.[3]

Some examples of how brand names often mean high prices will be illustrative. Nalidixic acid—a drug used for urinary infections—is sold as Gramoneg by Ranbaxy, and Wintomylon by Win-Medicare. The respective prices for one tablet are:

Ranbaxy	Rs 1.48 for Gramoneg
Win-Medicare	Rs 3.15 for Wintomylon

Similarly, for Mebendazole, which is used to treat helminthic infection, the figures are as follows[4]:

Brand Name	*Company*	*Price (in Rs for 10 tablets)*
Idibend	IDPL	1.79
Mebendozole	Biddle Sawyer	2.13
Mebazole	Torrent	3.60
Mebex	Cipla	4.88
Besantin	Khandelwal	5.06

[3] Lovraj Kumar Committee Report, 1977.

[4] MIMS India, June 1986.

Emanthal	M.M. Labs	5.29
Wormin	Cadila	5.31
Eben	Gufic	5.50

Another classic example of how brand names mean higher prices: Metroni Drugs Pvt Ltd makes tinidazole and sells it to four companies who, in turn, market it under four different names[5]:

Brand Name	*Company*	*Price (in Rs for 10 tablets)*
Abdogyl	Biddle Sawyer	6.40
Amebomagma	John Wyeth	7.80
Fabizol	Unichem	8.90
Zil	Sarabhai	9.00

An even more blatant example of profiteering under the garb of brand names is that of Glaxo Laboratories. Glaxo markets two formulations, Betnelan and Betnesol, with exactly the same composition (betamethasone 0.5 mg). Betnelan is priced at Rs 2.08 for ten tablets, while Betnesol is priced at Rs 3.91 for ten tablets.

That prices do come down if generics are introduced is illustrated by the recent case of Britain. Britain has introduced compulsory prescription in generics for selected essential drugs by doctors attached to the National Health Scheme. This has resulted in a significant fall in drug prices in Britain. The industry has already started hitting back at the new regulation. G.D. Searle, a multinational company, has threatened to get rid of most of its British scientists. It claims that the government is preventing it from making sufficient profits, because one of its leading brands was 'blacklisted' from prescriptions in the National Health Scheme.[6]

3. *Medical education*: In the course of medical education, information about drugs is given in generics. All medical journals and textbooks stress generic names. Yet when a young doctor

[5] Ibid.

[6] *New Scientist*, January 23, 1986.

BOX 1.2.1

SPEAKING IN DIFFERENT VOICES: THE GOVERNMENT ON FIXED DOSE COMBINATIONS

Fixed dose combinations (FDCs) are two or more medicines combined in fixed proportion in a single dosage form (tablet, capsule, syrup, and so on). The development of FDCs has been a cause for concern as their irrational use is a threat to public health. The government has worked in divergent ways—enforcing strict adherence to rules for rational prescription on the one hand, and selling irrational FDCs from its Jan Aushadhi centres on the other.

When the Jan Swasthya Abhiyan (JSA) analysed 580 medicines supplied under the Pradhan Mantri Bharatiya Jan-Aushadhi Pariyojana (PMBJP), it found that more than 100 were FDCs, many of them irrational. This was a few weeks after the government signalled its intention to ensure rational prescription of medicines by sending out stern directives to doctors to prescribe by generic names.

Clearly, different wings of the government work at cross purposes. One requires strict adherence to rules regarding rational prescription; the other permits the sale of irrational FDCs in its own Jan Aushadhi outlets. Currently [2017], the government is also defending, in the Supreme Court, a ban on 344 FDCs that it had imposed, and which was challenged by drug companies and overturned by the Delhi High Court in December 2016.

We have different scenarios on the use of FDCs in India: rational use of rational FDCs, irrational use of rational FDCs, and irrational use of irrational FDCs. The problem is compounded by a dysfunctional drug regulatory system. The market is flooded with FDCs and almost 50% of drugs consumed are FDCs. Three factors appear to be responsible for the flood of FDCs in the Indian market:

1. Companies prefer to market FDCs not under price control, rather than single-ingredient drugs under price control.
2. 'Me too' marketing: Companies compete for a share of the market for the same class of drugs. In the guise of providing something 'new' to prescribers, they develop and market FDCs, often irrational, for commercial reasons. Sales are supported by sophisticated (and often unethical) marketing strategies.
3. An understaffed and inefficient drug regulatory agency allows irrational FDCs in the first place, then does not take action to ban them. The 59th report of the Parliamentary Committee on Health and Family Welfare pointed out that in 2012, the Central Drugs Standard Control Organisation (CDSCO) had, by various acts of omission and commission, failed to restrict the number of irrational FDCs. A glaring omission was pointed out—many FDCs were being marketed after receiving approval from State regulatory agencies, though marketing approval can only be provided by the CDSCO.

Every FDC needs to be treated as a new drug, and its safety and efficacy needs to be substantiated. But a large number of marketing approvals for FDCs did not meet this requirement. When the CDSCO imposed a ban on 344 FDCs in 2016, public health groups pointed out that these accounted for only a fraction of the FDCs being marketed.

Inappropriate use of FDCs poses a major threat to public health. They can lead to additional toxicity, limit the choices of prescribing physicians, increase treatment cost, lead to under- or overdosing. In the case of antibiotics, FDCs can contribute to more rapid development of antimicrobial resistance.

This text box is an edited version of an article by Amit Sengupta in The Hindu BusinessLine, *June 23, 2017. See also Patricia McGettigan et al., 'Use of Fixed Dose Combination (FDC) Drugs in India',* PLoS Med, *vol. 12, no. 5.*

begins prescribing, he has to make an immediate switch to brand names. In such a situation, the only information he has available about drug names is what is fed to him by drug companies. In many cases, a doctor does not even know the composition of drugs he is prescribing. Given the amount of misinformation and disinformation drug companies spread about drugs, such a situation often leads to disastrous consequences.

It is ironical then that resistance to a switchover from brand names to generic names often comes from doctors. The reasons are quite simple though. Having been 'indoctrinated' about brand names for so long, many doctors have lost the capacity to think in terms of generic names. So when a doctor wants to prescribe a tranquillizer, the name Calmpose comes readily to him, but the generic name diazepam eludes him. And in the absence of any unbiased, reliable source of drug information, a vicious circle is created. It is a sad commentary on the members of the medical profession who take pride in calling themselves 'men of science', that ultimately their output is determined by information pamphlets provided by drug companies, and not by their study of books.

4. Elimination of irrational drug combinations: Drug companies make the argument that generic names would be impossible to use when prescribing combination drugs. But that is precisely one of the advantages of going generic. Medical and scientific literature clearly indicates that an overwhelming majority of combination drugs marketed in India are either irrational, or both irrational and hazardous.[7]

[7] Fixed dose combinations can be either rational or irrational. A rational combination has a therapeutic logic for combining two or more drugs, fixed in a particular proportion by dosage. Irrational combinations combine two or more drugs without any therapeutic logic. For example, there is no therapeutic logic if (a) two or more drugs, not necessarily used together for a commonly encountered illness, are combined; or (b) if two or more drugs, used in the same illness, need their dosages changed independently, but are combined in fixed proportion. In such cases, combining the drugs in a fixed

Generic nomenclature will go a long way in changing a ridiculous situation in which 60,000 formulations flourish. When a doctor goes generic and realizes that a Santevini tonic contains eleven ingredients—most of them either useless or in unsuitable dosages—he will stop prescribing it.

BIOAVAILABILITY

Of all the arguments raised against generics, there is only one that has some scientific basis, and that is the question of bioavailability. Bioavailability means the exact amount of the active substance of a drug available for it to perform its therapeutic function in the body.

In addition to active ingredients, most formulations contain binding substances and additives which may alter the bioavailability of the active substance. The argument is that since these additives may differ for formulations by different companies, the bioavailability of the drug may differ.

This problem is likely to occur in a very small number of cases involving the prolonged treatment of chronic diseases, as in heart diseases, diabetes, TB or hypothyroidism. The solution lies in enforcing strict quality control measures, and in developing mechanisms by which drug formulations by different companies can be standardized. It is ridiculous to ask for the scrapping of a proposal which has so many obvious advantages, only because some mechanism to standardize formulations needs to be worked out.

The case for the use of generic names should be an open-and-shut one; different bodies have long favoured the use of generics. The Hathi Committee in 1975 did so and, in fact, prepared a list of thirteen drugs for immediate conversion to generics. The WHO has, at various forums, favoured the use of generics. Why then do brand names continue? The reason is simple. Drug companies, fired by their lust for profit, and given the enormous political clout

dose combination is considered irrational.—*Ed.*

they have come to acquire, have effectively managed to sabotage, so far, all efforts to go generic.

Pakistan is often touted by drug companies as an example of the failure of generic nomenclature. It is well known that drug MNCs actively sabotaged the 'generic experiment' in Pakistan. It is shameful that doctors there played the role of subordinate allies of drug MNCs.

OPPI DOCUMENT

The Organisation of Pharmaceutical Producers of India (OPPI) prepared a document on the generic versus brand name controversy. The arguments are so pathetic that they do not even merit a rebuttal. But a response must be made to some of the OPPI's points, or it will continue to raise them in order to obstruct the campaign for the abolition of brand names.

The OPPI document says that brand names ensure 'reliability of products' and total manufacture responsibility.[8] The point being made, obviously, is that big companies are more reliable and responsible. Just one example: out of a total of 218 reported cases of substandard production of drugs, 135 were from twenty-three multinationals.[9]

When drug companies talk of 'reliability' and 'responsibility', it must be remembered that in 1923, the League of Nations officially pulled up Hoffmann-La Roche, founder of Roche, for being involved in the trafficking of cocaine. The same Roche, and Bayer, two 'responsible' MNCs today, carried out experiments of psychotropic drugs on pregnant Jewish women in German concentration camps during the Second World War.

The document goes on to say that 'brands protect the doctor's rights to prescribe the medicine of choice to his patients'.[10] In fact, he does the opposite. Ephedrine—saline nasal drops—a

[8] OPPI document titled *Brand Names versus Generic Names.*

[9] UNI Economic Services, January 1981.

[10] Ibid.

drug useful in nasal bleeding and inflammation is not available in the market. In its place more expensive and less effective 'brand name' substitutes like Nasivion, Otrivin, Distem, Latazol flood the market. Often single drug topical ointments are not available, while combination formulations with steroids are freely available in the market. Such examples are endless.

Finally, the document makes the point that changing to generics will stifle the production of new drugs. First, the statement is untrue. Otherwise no drug research would be taking place in the Soviet Union, where brand names do not exist. More appalling is the audacity of such a statement from the OPPI, in view of the fact that big drug companies spend almost negligible amounts on R&D. In fact, the Lovraj Kumar Committee (1977) reported that the outlays of fifty-two MNCs on sale promotion and administrative overheads were 33%, as compared to a mere 0.8% on R&D. Just a handful of drugs are developed by drug companies in India. India, and indeed the entire Third World, are used as testing centres for drugs developed by MNCs in their parent countries.

The situation is aptly summed up in a textbook of pharmacology by D.R. Laurence: 'It is unlikely that the common sense system of one name for one drug will be achieved in the near future as it seems to be impossible to reconcile uniformity with commercial enterprise.'[11]

[11] D.R. Laurence, P.N. Bennett and M.J. Brown, *Clinical Pharmacology*, 8th ed., Churchill Livingstone, 1997.

3. Patent to Plunder

AMIT SENGUPTA

A landmark Supreme Court judgment of April 2013 upheld the Indian Patent Office's rejection of the Novartis patent application on Glivec. Writing a few months before the judgment, Amit Sengupta traced developments in the Indian patents regime, explaining how the introduction of Section 3(d) and 'health safeguards' in the 2005 Act helped the Indian domestic drug industry become a global force. Expensive patented drugs could be produced at much cheaper rates since the Patents Act made it difficult to patent medicines. There were pre- and post-grant opposition clauses in the Act; there was also the provision of compulsory licensing.

The Novartis case was an important battle against patent monopolies that have, in Amit's words, '... for too long, erased the benefits of scientific advances in healthcare across the world'. Amit explains the Novartis case—from the rejection of its patent application in 2006, through the Intellectual Property Appellate Board (IPAB) upholding the Indian Patent Office's 2009 decision citing Section 3(d), and Novartis's challenge to the IPAB's interpretation and application of Section 3(d) in the Supreme Court. He also documents the arguments against Novartis's Glivec International Patient Assistance Programme and demolishes its altruistic claims. Discussing the award of the first compulsory licence (CL) to Natco in India for sorafenib, a cancer drug, this article explains the importance of CLs for the availability of new drugs at affordable costs, not just in India, but in other developing countries.

The average life expectancy across the globe has increased from around thirty years a century ago to over sixty-five years today. This has been made possible, in large part, by modern medicine. Never before have humans had access to such an array of medicines and devices to treat and ameliorate illness. These advances have also created a new terrain of conflict. The knowledge required to promote health has expanded enormously; but, paradoxically, so have the attempts to restrict access to such knowledge.

The current regime of intellectual property rights (IPR) seeks to exercise monopoly control over the production and reproduction of knowledge. Consequently, products to treat a range of diseases are denied to those who need them the most—merely because they cannot pay for them. They are denied access, not because these medicines cannot be produced at a reasonable cost; but because a few corporations treat the knowledge as their property, and sell these medicines at exorbitant prices. They also use the monopoly created by patents to prevent other companies from producing and selling these drugs at much lower prices.

Nothing illustrates this better than the impact of the human immunodeficiency virus/acquired immune deficiency syndrome epidemic in Africa. In 2001, the annual cost of treating one HIV/AIDS patient was $10,000. Some African countries would have had to spend more than half their gross domestic product to procure medicines for those who needed them. The tragedy is that these medicines need not have been so expensive. In 2003, the Indian company Cipla finally began selling the same medicines at $250 per annum—at 1/40th the earlier cost. Even this price was high; the same drugs can be bought today at less than $100 for a year's supply.

Between 1972 and 2005, India had one of the most progressive patent laws in the world. And it was in this period that the domestic drug industry became a global force, and the third largest producer of drugs (by volume) in the world. In 1994, with the signing of the World Trade Agreement [Uruguay Round]—

which became the World Trade Organization (WTO) in January 1995—India acceded to a global patents regime. India's earlier law, the Patents Act, 1970, worked on a very simple principle. It argued that patents (a monopoly over the manufacture and distribution of a product) would not be allowed in the two most vital areas of human existence—food and health. New medicines could be manufactured by Indian companies without hindrance. This is why Cipla was later able to manufacture and supply HIV/AIDS medicines at a fraction of the earlier prices. Much of this enabling environment for Indian companies changed when India amended its Patents Act in 2005—after completing the ten-year transition period allowed when India signed the WTO agreement.

But while amending the Patents Act to conform to the obligations set by the WTO agreement, the parliament introduced a number of 'health safeguards'. These were designed to mitigate the impact of a patents regime that denied Indian companies free access to available knowledge. Two recent developments are now poised to test the ability of the domestic law on patents—after the 2005 amendments—to actually secure access to medicines.

The Indian law faces a challenge from the Swiss drug maker Novartis. At the heart of the challenge lies the vital anti-leukaemia (blood cancer) drug called imatinib mesylate. The drug was introduced in 2001 and quickly became the key drug used to treat a form of leukaemia called chronic myeloid leukaemia (CML). The drug is the difference between a healthy life and a death sentence for patients suffering from CML.

Imatinib mesylate has been patented in many countries by Novartis, which sells the drug under the brand name Glivec (or Gleevec). The patent application for Glivec was rejected in 2006 by the Indian Patent Office, which upheld the contention of Indian generic companies and of the Cancer Patients Aid Association that Glivec was not a new drug, and did not merit grant of a patent.

Novartis persisted in its efforts and appealed to the Intellectual Property Appellate Board (IPAB). In June 2009, the IPAB upheld the decision of the Patent Office. Simultaneously, Novartis filed two writ petitions in the Madras High Court, one challenging the decision of the Patent Office, and the other challenging Section 3(d) of the Patents Act. In the latter case, Novartis claimed that the section was in violation of India's obligations to the WTO. The Madras High Court rejected both these appeals. It pointed out that domestic courts could not be asked to give an opinion on international treaties and obligations; and that Novartis should take its complaint to the disputes settlement mechanism in the WTO. Novartis has never done so, and clearly Section 3(d) does not violate international obligations.

It is important to understand why courts and the Patent Office have repeatedly turned down Novartis's request for a patent. The original patent on Glivec was filed by Novartis in 1993 for the amorphous molecule of the chemical imatinib mesylate. An amorphous salt is what exists in nature and is a mixture of different variants. In the late 1990s, Novartis filed a fresh patent for the beta variant of the molecule, which is already present in the amorphous salt patented earlier. It also claimed that the beta variety was better absorbed in the body and was more stable. The 1993 patent was not recognized in India as Indian law at the time did not allow the patenting of medicines.

When the law was changed in 2005, Novartis applied for a patent on the beta variety of the salt. The Patent Office refused the patent on a number of grounds. It said that under Section 3(d), a slightly modified version of a known molecule could not be patented. Section 3(d) stipulates that trivial changes in existing molecules cannot be candidates for fresh patenting. Such trivial patenting (known as 'evergreening') is an old ploy used by drug companies to extend their monopoly. Companies first apply for a patent for the basic molecule, then attempt to extend the life of their monopoly by applying for fresh patents after a few years on a slightly different version of the original molecule.

The Patent Office also said that the patent application did

not fulfil two necessary criteria for patenting—novelty (that is, it should be a new compound); and inventive step (that is, it should involve an inventive change not anticipated by someone well-versed with the technology). Both the Patent Office and the IPAB invoked Section 3(d) to deny Novartis's appeal.

Novartis is now arguing its case in the Supreme Court through a special leave petition challenging the IPAB's interpretation and application of Section 3(d) to its patent application, and final arguments on the case are to commence on 10 July 2012.[1] Instead of challenging Section 3(d), Novartis now argues that the section has not been properly interpreted. The section says that minor variations in an existing molecule cannot be patented unless there is a 'significant' enhancement in the 'efficacy' of the medicine. 'Novartis claims that since the beta variant is better absorbed (by about 30%), it constitutes a significant enhancement. Novartis's panel of expensive lawyers is led by Gopal Subramaniam, who was the Solicitor General of India (and hence technically responsible for leading the government's defence) when Novartis first approached the Supreme Court.

CLAIMS OF ALTRUISM

How much would Novartis gain if its patent were to be upheld? The arithmetic speaks for itself. A month's supply of Glivec costs Rs 120,000—way beyond the means of more than 99% of Indians. Remember the drug has to be taken throughout the life of the patient. Yet the same drug is sold by several Indian companies at Rs 8,000 for a month's supply—1/15th of what Novartis charges. At the heart of Novartis's battle is a \$4-billion-plus global market for Glivec—about Rs 20,000 crore, equal to the entire Union health budget of India for 2010–11.

Novartis claims that price is not an issue in India because 'eligible' patients are covered by a programme called GIPAP—

[1] The case was decided against Novartis.—*Ed.*

Glivec International Patient Assistance Programme. The only problem with Novartis's spin on the issue is wrong arithmetic. Novartis claims that it supplies the drug free of cost to about 11,000 leukaemia patients in India. The Cancer Patients Aid Association estimates that there are over 100,000 patients in India who suffer from chronic myeloid leukaemia, and that 20,000-odd new patients are added every year. (The disease has an annual incidence of 1–2/100,000 population a year.) Studies also show that the disease strikes earlier in life in India—in a younger age group—than in Europe and North America.

Novartis has regularly claimed credit for its GIPAP programme. How altruistic is the GIPAP? The programme was launched in 2002, and Novartis claims that it reaches 35,000 patients in eighty countries. In 2003, *The New York Times* carried an investigative report that blew the lid off the claims of altruism.[2] The report, as well as another report from Argentina, document how Novartis has used the GIPAP first to create a demand for Glivec, then pressure governments and health management organizations to reimburse its cost. The report stated: 'In wealthier countries like South Korea, Hong Kong and New Zealand, Novartis, meanwhile, has encouraged patients who have received free drugs to become advocates, pressing public health systems to pay high prices for the drug. One company document declared that drug donations along with media campaigns and legal tactics were part of a concerted plan to win reimbursement for Glivec.'

Novartis says that it is not fighting the case to make money, but to uphold the principle that it deserves credit for its investment

[2] Stephanie Strom and Matt Fleischer-Black, 'Drug Maker's Vow to Donate Cancer Medicine Falls Short', *The New York Times*, June 5, 2003 (https://www.nytimes.com/2003/06/05/business/drug-maker-s-vow-to-donate-cancer-medicine-falls-short.html); and an Argentinian report: Silvia Garcia, 'The worst kind of deceit: Fraud by Novartis and Max Foundation targets patients', *El Medico*, no. 191 (July 30, 2006), the English translation can be found here: http://www.healthyskepticism.org/global/news/int/hsin2006-07.

in research to develop the drug. What Novartis does not tell us is that Glivec was granted 'orphan drug'[3] status in the US and was, therefore, eligible for tax rebates equal to half the cost of clinical testing (the major cost of drug development).

Brian Druker, one of the scientists involved in developing imatinib while working in the Oregon Health and Science University Knight Cancer Institute, commented in a signed article in *Livemint* in 2007:

> My work in Oregon on a therapy for CML [chronic myeloid leukaemia] was primarily funded by public sources, particularly the National Cancer Institute. My persistence with scientists at Ciba-Geigy (now Novartis) helped to keep the development of imatinib on their agenda despite uncertainty from product managers. As imatinib progressed through early and late clinical trials and demonstrated outstanding results, scientific and media interest in our discovery increased. The approval of imatinib by the FDA [the US Food and Drug Administration] in May 2001 for use in CML was the culmination of a ten-year project for me, something I had dreamed of since medical school.[4]

And still, Novartis laments that it is not being given due credit for its 'original' research.

INDIA BREAKS A PATENT

In March 2012, the Indian Patent Office issued a compulsory

[3] A drug adjudged to be commercially unviable without certain incentives, as the condition it treats has a low incidence in the population. The incentives are generally lower taxes, R&D subsidies, extended market protection and other benefits.

[4] Brian Druker, 'Don't abuse patents: scientists', *Livemint*, August 15, 2007 (https://www.livemint.com/Opinion/26rbSkGiTxNYKobbO568kL/Don8217t-abuse-patents-scientists.html).

BOX 1.3.1

SECTION 3(D)

Section 3 of the Indian Patents Act, 1970, lists 'what are not inventions'. The relevant subsection (d) after it was amended in 2005 reads:

> ... the mere discovery of a new form of a known substance which does not result in the enhancement of the known efficacy of that substance or the mere discovery of any new property or new use for a known substance or of the mere use of a known process, machine or apparatus unless such known process results in a new product or employs at least one new reactant.
>
> Explanation: For the purposes of this clause, salts, esters, ethers, polymorphs, metabolites, pure form, particle size, isomers, mixtures of isomers, complexes, combinations and other derivatives of known substance shall be considered to be the same substance, unless they differ significantly in properties with regard to efficacy.

Before 2005, subsection (d) read thus:

> ... the mere discovery of any new property or new use for a known substance or of the mere use of a known process, machine or apparatus unless such known process results in a new product or employs at least one new reactant.

licence (CL) to the Indian generic drug company Natco Pharma Ltd for Bayer's anti-cancer drug sorafenib. The licence was issued under Section 84 of the Patents Act, and it has broken Bayer's monopoly over the drug. Natco can now manufacture and sell the drug in India.

Sorafenib has been shown to extend survival rates among those suffering from hepatocellular carcinoma (liver cancer) and renal cell carcinoma (a form of kidney cancer). At present, Bayer's version of the drug costs a patient Rs 280,000 a month. Natco will make the drug available at a cost of Rs 8,800 a month, a 97% reduction on Bayer's price.

The decision has been followed by reverberations across the world. A range of people working on public health and access to medicines issues have welcomed the decision of the Indian Patent Office. The fact that this is the first CL issued in India is a major step, and it can set a precedent for many more CLs in the future.

The CL on sorafenib not only helps cancer patients who require the drug, but is also a step towards building domestic manufacturing capacity and knowhow in a new range of anti-cancer drugs. Sorafenib is one of the first in a group of new drugs that specifically target cancer cells. Similar drugs with better results are likely to be available over time, and it is important that generic manufacturers develop the capacity to manufacture these.

Patents are supposed to represent a balance between the rights and obligations of a patent holder. Patent laws are required to ensure that the products of new research are available to the largest number of people, while providing a fair return to the innovator. Compulsory licensing is a key instrument incorporated in patent laws to maintain this balance. It allows regulators to break the monopoly of a patent holder by allowing a third party to use the patent, in situations where the patent holder abuses the monopoly right to deny access to its innovation to a very large number of people.

The 2005 Patents Act provided broad grounds for issuing a CL, including (a) when the reasonable requirements of the public with respect to the patented invention have not been satisfied, or (b) it is not available to the public at a reasonably affordable price, or (c) the patent is not being worked. By pricing its drug at almost Rs 3 lakh for a month's treatment, Bayer was denying access to the drug to thousands of cancer patients in the country.

DECISIVE BATTLE?

The two developments have several long-term implications for India's domestic drug industry. Novartis is challenging the very heart of the Indian Patents Act, and its attempt to balance the rights of patent holders with the Indian people's need for affordable treatment. Section 3(d) of the Act has been used several times by the Indian Patent Office to deny patents for other similar trivial inventions, especially in the case of HIV/AIDS medicines. If the section is diluted or overturned, all these cases will be reopened. Also, it will open the door for a flood of applications, many of which were not filed by companies because of the existence of Section 3(d).

The case has implications for leukaemia patients, but also for a whole range of patients who are now able to access cheaper drugs made by Indian companies. These patients are located in India as well as in over a hundred countries in Asia, Latin America and Africa. For example, over 80% of all patients in developing countries who consume HIV/AIDS medicines are able to do so because Indian companies supply them these medicines at affordable rates. This is a case that Novartis must not win because it is not about corporate pride. It is a case that sets corporate greed against the lives of millions across the world.

It is useful to recall that the Madras High Court, while rejecting Novartis's appeal, had said: 'We have borne in mind the object which the Amending Act wanted to achieve, namely, to prevent evergreening; to provide easy access to the citizens of this country to life-saving drugs and to discharge the constitutional obligation of providing good healthcare to its citizens.'

The first grant of a CL in India has clear implications for the availability of new drugs at affordable costs, in India and in many developing countries. Compulsory licence provisions exist in the laws of most countries, but they are rarely used. As a result, only a few countries have issued CLs since 1995. Most of these have been for HIV/AIDS medicines, and almost all have been for use by the government, or in situations where a government has declared a national emergency (as in the case of the HIV/AIDS epidemics in Africa). The US and the European Union, acting at the behest of their pharmaceutical industries, have brought extreme pressure to bear upon governments in developing countries to dissuade them from issuing CLs.

What is extremely significant in the case of the sorafenib CL in India is that it is a rare instance when a general CL has been issued, not bound by 'government use' provisions, or provisions allowed only in cases of 'extreme urgency' or 'national emergency'. This has the potential to expand the scope of CLs, both in terms of the kind of drugs for which they can be issued in the future, and the conditions under which they are issued.

Further developments in these areas will be closely watched. They will determine whether India can continue to be known as the 'pharmacy of the South'—with the ability to produce and market new drugs at prices people in most countries in the developing world can afford. We may well be watching the decisive battle against patent monopolies that have, for too long, erased the benefits of scientific advances in healthcare across the world.

4. Two Decades of Struggle: The Glivec Precedent

The 2013 Supreme Court judgment denied Swiss multinational Novartis's claim of a patent on the anti-leukaemia drug Glivec (imatinib). With this important judgment in the background, Amit Sengupta discusses the long and tortuous course leading to the enactment of the Indian Patents Act of 2005.

THE URUGUAY ROUND

In 1986, a new round of negotiations was initiated under the General Agreement on Tariffs and Trade (GATT), otherwise known as the Uruguay Round of negotiations. In the Uruguay Round, developed countries introduced a number of issues on the agenda. These were related to intellectual property (IP) rights, investment and services—hitherto not considered trade issues.

Initially, developing countries led by India and Brazil were able to stall the introduction of these new issues,[1] while the US continued to press for their inclusion. The latter's position was dictated by the state of the US economy. Having lost its competitive edge in the manufacturing sector, and with its agricultural exports threatened by state-subsidized agricultural exports from Europe, the US was keen to open up the services sector—especially for financial services. At the same time, the US had an interest in protecting its IP-dependent industries where it still had an advantage, specifically

[1] S.P. Shukla, 'From GATT to WTO and Beyond', Working Paper No. 195, United Nations University-World Institute for Development Economics Research, Helsinki, Finland, 2000, pp. 14–15.

in pharmaceuticals, software and audio-visual media.[2]

India had a clear interest in not agreeing to these new demands. India's pharmaceutical sector had flourished in the wake of its 1970 Patents Act—which did not allow product patents on medicines and agrochemicals. India only allowed process patents on pharmaceuticals, and had leveraged this to develop capacity in process technologies.

By the beginning of 1989, the resistance from developing countries broke down. The enormous pressure by the US resulted in the two main holdouts changing their position. India went to the extent of replacing its chief negotiator at GATT, S.P. Shukla, because of his strong opposition to the inclusion of IP issues in the negotiating agenda.[3]

The significance of the negotiations was not clear to most popular movements and civil society groups in different parts of the world. A key to the development of the resistance in India was the formation of the National Working Group on Patent Laws (NWGPL). In spite of its relatively small numbers, the NWGPL was highly influential in shaping opposition to the Trade-Related Aspects of Intellectual Property Rights (TRIPS) Agreement, from the late 1980s. It was composed of a group of former civil servants, lawyers, scientists, representatives of the domestic pharmaceutical industry and representatives of trade unions in the pharmaceutical industry.[4]

The NWGPL was not a mass movement, but it became a catalyst for advocacy and mobilization. It was the principal source of evidence-based arguments against the proposed regime on IP. Strong support from the domestic industry found resonance

[2] Ibid., pp. 20–21.

[3] Sherry S. Marcellin, *The Political Economy of Pharmaceutical Patents: US Sectional Interests and the African Group at the WTO*, Farnham, England: AshgatePublishing, 2010, p. 87.

[4] For more information about the formation of the NWGPL, see Amit Sengupta's essay on B.K. Keayla in this section.—*Ed.*

among a wide range of political actors. Over the next decade, the NWGPL organized a Forum of Parliamentarians, which had representation from virtually the entire political spectrum. Several political and social movements, non-governmental organizations and mass organizations in India formed alliances against the GATT negotiations. Many subsequent developments had their roots in the popular mobilizations between 1990 and 2005.

TORTUOUS PATH

From 1991, the path towards the final formulation of India's Patents Act was also increasingly informed by the formal introduction of neoliberal reforms. Earlier, the government and its spokespersons had argued that India was forced to concede to the US and the EU countries during the Uruguay Round of the GATT negotiations. Now, there was an attempt to argue that strong IP protection would promote India's domestic interests. However, popular sentiment remained hostile to bringing intellectual property within GATT or bringing in a stronger patents regime at the domestic level.

The TRIPS Agreement, which became a part of the WTO agreement, provided a three-stage, time-bound framework for developing countries. A 'mailbox' facility[5] and exclusive marketing rights were introduced from 1995; provisions on rights related to the duration of patent protection, compulsory licensing, and reversal of burden of proof, by 2000; and product patent protection in all fields from 1 January2005.

The political instability in India, post-1996, meant that further discussions on amendments to India's 1970 Act resumed only in 1998 after the installation of the Bharatiya Janata Party

[5] Countries which had not yet granted product patents had to provide a mailbox in which patent applications could be filed during the transition period, before product patents were introduced. The mailbox provision allowed applicant companies to establish their filing dates, while permitting countries to defer the grant of patents.

(BJP)-led National Democratic Alliance (NDA) government. The Indian Parliament enacted two legislations through the Patents (Amendment) Acts of 1999 and 2002, which addressed the first two requirements of the TRIPS Agreement.

After assuming office, the NDA government adopted the same neoliberal agenda while engaging with public policy on a range of issues.[6] The NDA government then circulated the draft Third Patents (Amendment) Bill in 2003, but it could not be discussed because of the change of government in 2004.

In 2004, there was a clear consensus between the two principal parties in India—the Congress and the BJP. The United Progressive Alliance (UPA) government circulated an almost unchanged version of the NDA's Third Patents (Amendment) Bill draft. In the then political spectrum, only the Left parties (along with some regional parties) stood firmly against the draft Bill. But towards the end of 2004, the BJP began voicing opposition to the draft Bill. While this is in the realm of speculation, the BJP's *volte-face* had little to do with any opposition to the substance of the Bill, given that this was identical to the Bill they had circulated. It had more to do with an intent to embarrass the UPA government. With support for the bill now unsure, the UPA government decided to beat the deadline of 31 December 2004 by promulgating an ordinance on 26 December 2004 (The Patents [Amendment] Ordinance 2004).

PATENTS ORDINANCE OF 2004

Once ratified by Parliament, the Ordinance would have made it impossible for Indian companies to continue producing cheaper versions of new drugs. In early 2005, with the BJP engaged in a bitter tussle with the Congress in Bihar and Jharkhand over the formation of ministries, it became clear that the Ordinance would

[6] See, for example, David P. Arulanantham, 'The Paradox of the BJP's Stance Towards External Economic Liberalisation: Why a Hindu nationalist party furthered globalisation in India', Asia Programme Working Paper, Chatham House, London, 2004.

be defeated in Parliament. The Congress was now forced to seek the Left's support.

In the consequent negotiations between the Left and the government, the Left, for the most part, depended on advice provided by people associated with the NWGPL. These negotiations also allowed other interested parties to suggest new language. Finally, several important amendments were made to the 2004 Ordinance,[7] including the insertion of Section 3(d), which has been the subject of much discussion after its use by the Supreme Court to strike down the appeal by Novartis, in 2013.

The negotiations were held in the backdrop of protests across the country, as well as in different parts of the world—all demanding that the 'pharmacy of the South' should not be jeopardized. By 2005, the global Access to Medicines campaign was a powerful force, and organizations such as Médecins Sans Frontières and others were able to organize support across the globe. Protest letters were sent to the Prime Minister, including one where the co-signatories included Jim Yong Kim, the present World Bank chief, and then director, Department of HIV and AIDS, WHO.[8]

IMPORTANT AMENDMENTS

While there has been considerable focus on Section 3(d) of the amended Act, many important amendments to the 2004 Ordinance were adopted. These include:

1. Restrictions on Patentability: The amendments clarified that an 'inventive step' means a feature of an invention that 'involves technical advances as compared to the existing knowledge or having economic significance or both'. It incorporated a new definition for 'new invention':

[7] International Centre for Trade and Sustainable Development (ICTSD), 'Indian Parliament Approves Controversial Patent Bill', *Bridges Weekly Trade News Digest*, vol. 9, no. 10 (2005).

[8] Martin Khor, 'A Victory for Patients' Access to Medicines', Global Trends Series, Third World Network, 2013.

> . . . any invention or technology which has not been anticipated by publication in any document or used in the country or elsewhere in the world before the date of filing of patent application with complete specification, i.e., the subject matter has not fallen in public domain or that it does not form part of the state of the art.[9]

It also provided a definition for 'pharmaceutical substance' as being 'a new entity involving one or more inventive steps'.

2. Restoration of Pre-grant Opposition to Patents: The amendments restored all the original grounds in the previous Act for opposing grant of a patent, and also provided that 'the Controller shall, if requested by such person for being heard, hear him'. The time for filing such opposition was extended from three to six months.

3. Export to Countries without Manufacturing Ability: The amendments clarified that a country could import from India if it 'by notification or otherwise allowed importation of the patented pharmaceutical product from India'.[10]

4. Continued Manufacture of Drugs with Applications in Mailbox: The amendments clarified that Indian companies already producing drugs that were the subjects of mailbox applications, could continue to produce them after payment of a royalty, even if the drug was, subsequently, granted a patent.

5. Time Period for Considering Compulsory Licence Application: Concerns that the process of granting compulsory licences could take too long were addressed by specifying that the 'reasonable time period before the Patents Controller considers issuance of a compulsory licence when such a licence is denied by the patent holder shall not ordinarily exceed six months'.

9 The Patents (Amendment) Act, 2005, No. 15 of 2005, available online (http://www.ipindia.nic.in/writereaddata/Portal/IPOAct/1_69_1_patent_2005.pdf).

10 Patents Act, 92A(1). Ibid., p. 14.

6. *Export by Indian Companies of Patented Drugs*: The amendments provided that when patented drugs are produced under compulsory licence in India 'the licensee may also export the patented product'.

Several of the amendments are being used today by different groups to try and safeguard access. In particular, the pre-grant opposition provisions have been used extensively by domestic companies and civil society groups. Combined with restrictions on patentability, the provisions have allowed many important drugs to be kept off-patent. Further, a number of drugs introduced in the transition phase (1995–2005) were not patented, as the amended Act allowed generic companies to manufacture and sell drugs introduced in this period.

The language for Section 3(d) was provided by the Indian Drug Manufacturers' Association. The Left parties had asked for a more stringent definition of patentability by limiting the grant of patents for pharmaceutical substances to 'new chemical entities' or to 'new medical entities involving one or more inventive steps'. Section 3(d) was a compromise, and the government had agreed to refer the matter to an expert panel.

Subsequently, the government constituted a Technical Expert Group under the chairmanship of R.A. Mashelkar, former director general, Council of Scientific and Industrial Research. The Group, in its report in 2007, stated that restriction of patents to new chemical entities would be incompatible with the TRIPS Agreement. Evidence surfaced that parts of the report had been plagiarized from a study by the UK-based Intellectual Property Institute, funded by Interpat, an association of twenty-nine drug companies including Novartis.[11] The report was withdrawn and press reports indicated that Mashelkar had resigned from the committee.[12] Yet, the same committee resubmitted a new version—

[11] T.V. Padma, 'Plagiarised Report on Patent Laws Shames Indian Scientists', *Nature Medicine*, vol. 13, no. 4 (2007), p. 392.

[12] Ibid.

with the same conclusions—in 2009. These recommendations were expeditiously accepted by the government.

VINDICATION OF STRUGGLE

The Supreme Court judgment in the Novartis case thus needs to be read not just as an instance of the application of one section (Section 3[d]) of the Indian Patents Act. The judgment is important as it vindicates the entire process that led to health safeguards being incorporated in the Indian Act.

The judgment, in fact, refers clearly to this process by noting (in para 26)[13]:

> ... to understand the import of the amendments in clauses (j) and (ja) of section 2(1) and the amendments in section 3 it is necessary to find out the concerns of Parliament, based on the history of the patent law in the country, when it made such basic changes in the Patents Act. What were the issues the legislature was trying to address? What was the mischief Parliament wanted to check and what were the objects it intended to achieve through these amendments?

The judgment is a vindication not just of a legislative process, but of popular resistance and mobilization—in India and across the world—that challenged corporate power. Small victories such as this become inspirations for larger battles.

[13] The text of the final judgment is available online (https://indiankanoon.org/doc/165776436/).

5. B.K. Keayla: A Personal Reminiscence

AMIT SENGUPTA

In this heartfelt reminiscence, Amit Sengupta pays tribute to Bal Krishan Keayla, a member of the Hathi Committee. Keayla was one of the strong figures behind the formation of the National Working Group on Patent Laws, which laid the ground for the global access campaign against patents and intellectual property. Amit Sengupta summarizes how the National Working Group and the Forum of Parliamentarians were formed under Keayla's able guidance. He acknowledges Keayla's insights on the issues of patents and intellectual property, as well as his ability to bring together people and constituencies to work on these issues.

It was twenty-two years ago, but the day is still fresh in my mind. Amitava Guha of the Federation of Medical and Sales Representatives' Associations of India, and I, made our way with hesitant steps into the corporate office of Ranbaxy in Nehru Place. We were curious about why a director in Ranbaxy would want to meet two anti-corporate activists. That is how I first met B.K. Keayla, then director, Corporate Environment, in Ranbaxy. We had gone prepared for a fifteen-minute meeting and left after two hours. Keayla*ji* (as he was soon known in our circles) captivated us with his thorough knowledge of the pharmaceutical industry, and his deep commitment to the need to sustain the domestic generic industry. We came away with sheaves of data on multinational corporations operating in India, their sins of omission and commission. We also came away with the feeling that we had met someone whom we wanted to meet again and again.

Later, we pieced together Keayla*ji*'s history. He had spent much of his life in the government, and had retired as Commissioner of Payments. He was associated with the Hathi Committee in 1974—the committee which had charted the path for the generic industry to develop in India. We kept going back to him, because he always had some new insight to offer about the pharmaceutical industry. We developed a relationship that is hard to define—that of very dear friends, though Keayla*ji* was a year older than my father. He was a mentor, a colleague and, above all, a marvellous human being. When we first met him, Keayla*ji* was nearing seventy, but had the kind of energy and patience all of us envied. Those were the heady days when self-reliance was not a bad word even within the government, and India was battling it out in the negotiations in the Uruguay Round of the General Agreement on Tariffs and Trade.

Dinesh Abrol, my colleague in the Delhi Science Forum, mentioned the issue one day. Keayla*ji* had broached the idea of setting up a working group to discuss the issue of patents and the negotiations in the Uruguay Round on a proposed agreement on intellectual property rights. He proposed a group that would include civil society organizations such as ours, the generic drugs/medicine industry, lawyers, academics, and trade unions in the pharma industry. The idea was novel—our first experience of Keayla*ji*'s ability to think out of the box. For some of us, it was, perhaps, too novel to start with.

We had never worked with the industry and viewed them as uncompromising enemies. This was the year 1988 when few in the drug movement had even heard about patents. But Keayla*ji* persuaded us as only he could—we were later to repeatedly sample his unique ability to work across sectors and bring together people. This is how the National Working Group on Patent Laws was born.

GUIDING THE GROUP

The first meeting of the group was in Ranbaxy's boardroom—it was the first time some of us had been in any boardroom. I remember looking around the room. Dinesh Abrol and Usha Menon, my colleagues in the Delhi Science Forum, were there. Mira Shiva from the All India Drug Action Network, Amitava Guha from the FMRAI, Ashok Rao of the Confederation of Officers' Associations of Public Sector Undertakings, B.S. Chimni from Jawaharlal Nehru University, senior journalist Balraj Mehta, several stalwarts from different generic companies, Keayla*ji*, perhaps some others I am forgetting now—all were there. But who would have thought that history was to be created? For the national working group did create history. It initiated a process that today reverberates across the world in the form of the access campaign on medicines. But twenty-two years ago, in the plush carpeted office in Nehru Place, perhaps only Keayla*ji* had a true sense of what we were setting out to do.

The next two years were a blur of activity, with Keayla*ji* marshalling his troops like a general. A prolific writer himself, Keayla*ji* egged on everyone around him to match him. The national working group produced scores of documents on intellectual property rights and the various positions India took in the Uruguay Round. Others joined—eminent lawyer Rajeev Dhawan, Biswajit Dhar, and more. Justice Krishna Iyer and Nitya Anand from the Central Drug Research Institute became our chairpersons. Keayla*ji* was our convenor, and remained so till the end. It was a heady battle as we familiarized ourselves with unknown concepts, brushed up on the law and on the nuances of international negotiations. We received two jolts in the space of a year. In 1989, India made a U-turn in the GATT negotiations and agreed to negotiate the Trade-Related Aspects of Intellectual Property Rights (TRIPS). It had one happy fallout for us. S.P. Shukla, then our ambassador to GATT, refused to go along with the change in position by the Indian government and was called back to India. In a trice, Keayla*ji* recruited him into the national working group.

The second jolt came in the form of a change of guard at Ranbaxy—and their consequent withdrawal of support to the working group. Keayla*ji* had left Ranbaxy, and overnight we were left without a space to operate from. For about a year we functioned from the small office of the Delhi Science Forum, but Keayla*ji* remained unfazed. He subsequently organized an office for the working group in Okhla, where our operations shifted. Remember this was before the day and age of computers and the Internet. All communications were drafted by Keayla*ji* and sent out through the postal system, and followed up with his telephone calls.

INVOLVING THE POLITY

By the early 1990s we realized that India was on a slippery slope in the GATT negotiations, and would agree to a TRIPS agreement. What followed was a master stroke by Keayla*ji*. He formed the Forum of Parliamentarians that united all non-Congress parties, and also mobilized a few from the Congress. Only Keayla*ji* could have brought together Ashok Mitra, George Fernandes, and Murli Manohar Joshi on one platform. Keayla*ji* remained a diehard optimist till the end, and with an almost demonic zeal, the national working group organized a series of events that were designed to create public awareness in India and across the world. The working group organized a series of consultations, both Indian and international, and lobbied incessantly with Indian lawmakers. Keayla*ji* and his flock in the National Group on Patent Laws (of which we were part) were instrumental—in at least a small way, if not more—in laying the ground for the global access campaign against patents and intellectual property. The deed was done on 31 December 1994, and India, along with others, signed on to the World Trade Organization (WTO) agreement. Keayla*ji*'s zeal did not flag, and he exhorted all of us to battle on. He fought the 1999 amendment to the 1970 Act that provided for Mailbox applications, the 2002 amendments, and finally the 2005 amendments. It needs to be put on record that it is not an accident India was the last holdout and made use of the full ten years of the transition period, finally amending its Act in 2005. It was not an accident that many public health safeguards were incorporated in the 2005 Act, including some that are held out as examples to be emulated. Behind all such small victories was Keayla*ji* (and those he was able to get to move and act). Always, he urged on everyone, always he believed that things can change. In between, he was also asked by the WHO regional office to advise a number of Asian countries on how their patent laws could best reflect national interests.

Even after 2005, when his health began to fail and many of us thought it was time to move on, Keayla*ji* did not give up. He battled the Patent Office on its draft manual for patent examiners, and took up cudgels against the proposed bill on the private utilization of public-funded intellectual property.

It is an unreal feeling that I shall never again hear his voice on the phone urging me to attend the next meeting of the national group. But all of us who were touched by his work know that his spirit lives on among us. That smiling benevolent presence that urged us along when we, decades younger than him, had almost given up. When Keayla*ji* and I travelled together outside India, he would tell his family not to worry because I was with him as a doctor. Unfortunately, when he passed away, I was 1,500 kilometres away. But I know Keayla*ji*. If he could read this he would say: I have lived a full life and given my best—it is now up to all of you to take it forward.

Section 2

NEW OPPORTUNITIES AND CHALLENGES: BIOLOGICAL DRUGS

1. Biosimilars: Health Activism at the Leading Edge of Technology

SATYAJIT RATH

Amit's role in the field of biosimilars brings out the kind of health activist he was. He saw the importance of biosimilars for public health and how they can they be made accessible to people, particularly in the Third World or the global South. Being a physician in the health activist movement is not what made him unusual; there are many of them. He was unusual in being more than a health activist—he was also a social and economic justice activist. To him, these were integrated issues. While this perspective is a commonplace one for non-physicians in health activism, it is perhaps not as common among physicians. The second unusual thing about Amit was that, even among those with some understanding of health activism, and involvement in its social and economic justice aspects, Amit had an unusually nuanced sense of the technological issues mediating their integration. The third component that Amit brought to health activism was an insider's awareness of the last three to four decades of discourse on intellectual property issues, and its intersection with health, social and economic justice.

The biologics and biosimilars issue is a striking example of these three aspects of Amit's health activism. In looking at health activism, social and economic justice activism, technology and intellectual property, he understood enough to see the future importance of biologics to public health. He understood, perhaps earlier than many of us, that biologics would assume growing importance in the matter of people's access to medicines and, therefore, for health activists.

What I say here may overlap greatly with what he has written about biologics, since we talked a fair amount about it and thought along similar lines. Nonetheless, let me say something about this peculiar class of medicines called biologics. These are medicinal entities, compounds, 'molecules', manufactured by using living cells rather than made synthetically, using chemistry. Why can't we make them chemically? Simple compounds are easily made using chemistry. As the compounds become more complex, all the reactions necessary to build larger and larger molecules (and at industrial scale) have to be worked out. That's a lot of steps, to the point that we may not be able to do it at all reliably on an industrial scale. Also, as the number of steps increases, the costs tend to increase greatly. Since biological systems are geared to effect this kind of synthesis, why not let them handle the manufacture?

A question that comes up at this stage is, are vaccines also biologics? When we discuss biologics, or when Amit discusses biologics, we don't really mean vaccines. Why? The explanation relates to how vaccines work. A vaccine works to protect you against a disease, not by acting on the disease itself, but by provoking your body into making a response that works on the disease. This is the sense in which vaccines are not 'drugs'. The biological response of our bodies to a vaccine is the drug and not the vaccine itself.

The other class of biologics, drugs, come from the signalling molecules that various parts of the body use for communication. A certain set of signals can generate a certain set of responses in the body, and if we know the biological molecule that triggers an appropriate response, that biological molecule is potentially a drug, which we can make and use. These signalling molecules are biological molecules, and they are usually also large in the chemical sense.

So, we now have two categories of biologics as drugs. One is that of vaccines which get our bodies to make useful biological responses. The other is that of those biologics that are essentially molecules of the body itself. Therefore, while technically biologics can be either vaccines or drugs, when it comes to medicines, we are talking of only the biologics as drugs. Amit was among the earliest working within the tripartite framework of public health, social and economic justice, and property rights, to see that biologics could not be handled well within the pre-existing framework.

One problem is that biologics are very large molecules, which means that they're difficult to manufacture chemically using industrial chemistry. Hence, we use biological systems to manufacture them. This means there is an entirely different technology for their manufacture, distinct from that of manufacturing small molecules. New kinds of regulation are needed. Now, it could be said that this biologics technology is akin to fermentation technology, and we've known fermentation for a long time. We make antibiotics with it, after all. Aren't biologics just more of the same? There is an element of truth in this, but inadequate to the whole case. Fermentation technology is traditionally dependent upon a small number of robust yeast or bacterial cultures. Biologics are quite different; they can be and are made from many different cell cultures. So, the range of technologies required for biologics manufacture has broadened hugely over the years. This has implications for how the industry will work, how regulation will work, and in turn for the accessibility of biologics to patients.

Further, most of our fermentation technology outcomes are small drugs like antibiotics. Biologics, on the other hand, are large molecules. And there's a chemical and a legal problem with large molecules.

The chemistry problem we have seen: biologics are hard to manufacture. The reason is that every time you add a building block to this large molecule, you're not quite sure you have fitted it in right. As the blocks multiply, uncertainties multiply about the shapes of these molecules and their final structure. In fact, the final structure is more of a statistical idea, rather than a certainty. This chemical problem creates an enormous problem in regulatory terms, since new chemical entities are patented on the basis of a known and defined structure. An interesting question arises: strictly speaking, are biological macromolecules patentable at all, if their structure is not definitively 'knowable' in the legal sense?

Another difficulty at the regulatory level is that, with a definite structure for a drug, you can set up a whole range of safety-related regulatory requirements that depend simply on the demonstration of its structure. Since that particular structure has been tested and found to be safe, if somebody else makes it, even by a different process, so long as it is of demonstrably the same structure, it is safe. But in the case of biologics, uncertainty over their structure makes these regulatory issues uncertain as well.

In addition, the intellectual property space of biologics is restricted, in part because they have come out of fairly complex and cutting-edge fundamental research, and are almost invariably licensed out of publicly-funded research to pharmaceutical companies—the ones with deep enough pockets to complete the remaining technological optimizations and fulfil the regulatory requirements. This allows the companies to make major profits, and means that biological drugs are not available at a reasonable price to ordinary people. Again, with their deep pockets, these companies have used the regulatory uncertainties for biologics—which we were talking about—to their own advantage. With their support, regulatory authorities across the world have insisted on a whole range of safety- and efficacy-testing steps to deal with the uncertainties in the structure of biologics. This makes it difficult for a biogeneric industry to introduce a generic alternative quickly and cheaply even after a biological drug goes off-patent. All of this means that biologics are expensive, restricted to a few companies, and take a fair amount of time to come into the market.

Amit had a range of responses to this. These responses were

related to the fact that the discovery stream of traditional small-molecule drugs, which the pharmaceutical industry as a whole has been exploiting steadily for the past fifty years, has been drying up. Over the past few years, the only growing source of drugs has been in the area of biologics. Amit saw that biologics were creating a unique landscape, and raising unique possibilities. He also saw that with biologics likely to become more and more prominent, people's health activists needed to think about and frame an approach to this class of drugs. As was his way, Amit not only saw the issues but pushed effectively for substantive responses to them.

More specifically, here's what has ended up happening. First, since the structures of biologics are somewhat uncertain, regulatory requirements have become (as might be expected) far stricter and more onerous. In intellectual property terms, both vaccines and biologic drugs face similar issues. Both have similar uncertainties in terms of their structure and need to be looked at similarly from the point of view of 'intellectual property protection'. Sceptical of the claims of big manufacturers, Amit was enthusiastic about going to battle with them on such claims.

In regulatory terms, however, vaccines and biologic drugs are quite different beasts. Vaccines are expected to provoke a response, not work directly on the disease. Drugs on the other hand are expected to work directly on disease and are emphatically not expected to provoke a response from the immune system. So, does a vaccine provoke an immune response? If the answer is yes, seen in regulatory terms, that's a good thing. Does a biologic drug provoke an immune response? If yes, that's a drug allergy and it's a bad thing. In consequence, vaccines and drugs have been treated quite differently in regulatory terms.

Along with these regulatory issues, certain possibilities also began to emerge over the past decade, directly affecting the issue of future biological drug accessibility. In the background was the fact that many of the original patents to biologics began to expire, which meant that there was a potential (and increasingly an actual) market for biogenerics manufacturers. Even some of the large companies began to position themselves as biogenerics manufacturers. This raised the general issue of how to regulate biogenerics, in the context of the older issue of regulating generics that people like Amit and health and economic justice activists across the world, including in India, have been struggling with. What are the most productive ways of dealing with profiteering pharma companies? They make small 'tweaking' adjustments and evergreen their patents as the original patents begin to expire. Given the inherent structural uncertainty of biologics, one can imagine that 'tweaking' could acquire a whole new dimension, creating a major evergreening opportunity in biogenerics.

But there's also something else that began to emerge from a decade of experience in how biologics are regulated and how they work, in which Amit saw remarkably interesting, even counter-intuitive, possibilities for people's health activism. One of our major problems with traditional small-molecule drugs concerns their 'side effects'. We worry about them, and with good reason. How do drugs have side effects? Say, a small molecule works on a biological pathway that results in a 'therapeutic effect'. It also has the potential of causing many off-target effects, meaning that, being a small molecule, it can affect other biological pathways as well, and the consequences of that are quite likely to be what we see as side effects. Interestingly, a possibility emerged that biologics may pose less of a problem in this respect. Since biologics are large molecules, and in fact are quite frequently molecules of the body itself, they may work on the pathway they are designed for, and not have 'off-target' effects. As a result, they may paradoxically have fewer off-target side effects than small-molecule drugs.

This was merely a possibility, and we do not frame regulatory processes based on such 'possibilities'. But a decade of empirical knowledge has also begun to suggest this is so, and an extremely interesting regulatory path begins to emerge, with major consequences for the accessibility of biologics. So far, we had been worrying about their structural uncertainties, and therefore thinking about more stringent regulation. Now, we begin to think that these uncertainties may not matter in the practical sense, because this shape variation may simply mean differences in the potency of therapeutic effects, rather than increasing worries about off-target side effects. The regulatory regime for the off-target effects of small molecules can then be different from that of large molecules. This is counter-intuitive and obviously has potential consequences for accessibility. As a movement, we are still in the process of thinking through these issues, in large part through a process that Amit nucleated the past two years about how we should address the issue of biogenerics.

Let me give an example. When people with cancer receive chemotherapy, one of the side effects of chemotherapy is that the bone marrow is damaged and therefore their red- and white-blood-cell production is damaged. How do you re-stimulate the generation of these cells? The body uses large protein molecules that stimulate the bone marrow to re-grow and start making these cells again. Across a whole range of cancer chemotherapies, it has become commonplace to supply patients with these protein hormones as biologics, to stimulate blood-cell production from the bone marrow. Patents for these biologics have been expiring, and there are biogenerics in the market. How should we regulate the biogenerics? Do biogenerics have to go through the entire process that the original biologic went through because we are worried about structural uncertainties? How much do we have to worry about safety? How much should we worry about off-target effects? This technical landscape is part regulatory, part scientific and is intrinsically connected to the accessibility issue. Amit was deeply in his element in being able to navigate with nuance across all of these domains.

So, an argument began to emerge that we should worry primarily about testing for the potency of these biogenerics. Does the new biogeneric that anyone manufactures work or not? And perhaps we should not worry too much about off-target effects in these biogenerics, because we already know from the original that there aren't too many of those. What is the main off-target side effect likely in the case of these large-molecule biologics that are made outside the body and then put into the body? If the body reacts to it immunologically, it effectively generates an allergy. So, we should test for allergy in the regulatory process. Even there, it has become increasingly apparent from the evidence that we only need test for certain kinds of inadvertent modifications; in their absence, allergies may not be a major problem. In effect, what we are talking about is the creation of a relatively abbreviated and therefore rapid pathway for follow-up biogenerics, which would then be accessible faster and cheaper without compromising safety.

This is an argument that Amit anchored. We all worry while walking this path because safety is a core issue that we keep in mind all the time. But the evidence begins to look more and more as though this were a supportable position. All of this occurs amid the framework of Amit's trivalent landscape, of public health activism, social and economic justice, and intellectual property issues.

Finally, we should note a specific example in this domain, to underline just how complex it is and how many issues still confront us. This issue is a special category of biologics, namely, monoclonal antibodies (or 'mAbs', as they are commonly called). What are mAbs, and in what way are they peculiar? The example we looked at earlier, of bone marrow-stimulating biologics, involves molecules that normally do that work in our bodies. The molecule is the same in each and every one of us. If we find the gene that codes for the molecule, we can use it to make the protein molecule at an industrial scale, and the resultant 'biologic' will not only work in everybody, it will be the same as the molecule everybody already has in them (we will simply be giving them much more of it).

On the other hand, as we noted earlier, if we are given a vaccine, we will 'make' an immune response to it, meaning that we will make antibodies against the vaccine, and the antibodies will work against the disease. In fact, what we make is a whole collection of mAbs. Hence some of these mAbs will act effectively on specific diseases, and so work as 'drugs'. So, if we can identify the gene/s that code/s for such mAbs, we can make and start administering the antibody itself. The mAb is thus a biologic drug.

However, there is a catch. Let us say that we give me a vaccine and find a mAb that works on a certain target. A year later, we vaccinate me again, and find a second mAb that does the exact same thing. Or, we vaccinate someone else and make a similar mAb that does the same thing. We now have three mAbs that work on the same target. The catch is, each of them is quite different in structure from the other two! So, do we have only one biologic, or do we have three? In a strict reading of the original 'new chemical entity' (NCE) definition in the 'intellectual property rights' context, their amino acid composition and sequences are different, so they are different NCEs, and therefore different drugs. This is how regulatory authorities have been treating this issue. However, mAbs are extraordinarily specific in what targets they work on. As a consequence, mAbs will have very few off-target effects, although they do have a specific category of them, namely allergies. So, should we think about them in different regulatory terms? Can we create a regulatory framework for them that specifically tests for potency and for potential allergic risks only? These are the cutting-edge issues at the interface of emerging technologies, regulatory policies and health activism that need to be addressed for biologics.

Is the regulatory framework evolving for biologics, particularly biogenerics? Yes and no. It is evolving, but private-sector pressure and the otherwise risk-averseness of the state regulatory apparatus makes change a very slow and uncertain process. Last year, Amit put together a consultation in Geneva with the Third World Network (TWN). It got many people together who were all thinking innovatively about these issues, and it focused on how these issues would modify universal access to these new medicines. Again, it is a testament to Amit's sheer connectedness that people from so many disparate domains got together to discuss the issues. As a result, there have been a series of consultations with the WHO on what is possible and what's not. None of these are settled matters, but it is the kind of nuanced, deeply intricate activist engagement that Amit excelled in. We will see how far it goes, but wherever it goes, it will be a tribute to his vision in getting this kind of group together and initiating efforts that rigorously address emerging technologies from a public health perspective.

So what are the reasons for the very high prices of biologics, and even biogenerics? Biologics are costly for a range of reasons. Firstly, they depend on increasingly expensive publicly-funded research and they are being generated in a global neoliberal context where governments insist on revenue returns from publicly-funded research. This is deeply attractive at the individual level also to the scientists involved, so publicly-funded research centres are now profit-making entities. As a consequence, these are expensive 'intellectual property' for the companies that acquire the licences to make biologic drugs, which in turn makes the drugs expensive. That's one reason. In fact, the intellectual property protections for many of these molecules are still at their zenith; as a result many of them are simply monopolies, and that may be the largest reason for the steep prices. Therefore, public health activism needs to challenge the 'intellectual property' status of these drugs.

A second reason is that the technologies are expensive, because they involve living systems that are much more intricate and, therefore, more expensive at the manufacturing level than the old chemical technologies, whether in resource terms or those of skill and knowledge. As a result, the number of companies willing to invest in an industrial-scale technology of this kind is limited and that creates a manufacturing bottleneck, with an impact on prices. Therefore, public health activism needs to engage with alternative means of bringing these manufacturing technologies into operation for biogenerics.

A third issue is that the overwhelming majority of these molecules are large proteins we can't swallow in a pill, because our digestive system is designed to digest proteins large and small. Since biologics are proteins (some large, some not so large), they get digested in the gut if they are swallowed. If they get digested, they lose structure. If they lose structure, they lose function. Thus, they are not absorbed from the gut as biologically 'active' functioning proteins. They cannot be taken as pills to be swallowed but must be injected directly into the body, so that they bypass gut digestion. If they have to be injected, that creates the need for a hospital-based infrastructure—which adds its own layers of complexity and expense. The broader concerns of public health activism in healthcare delivery address this aspect.

Finally, the regulatory processes also add to the costs. On the one hand, they are not drastically different between small molecules and large molecules. But the structural uncertainties of biologics create even more stringent regulation for them. Added to this is the idea that any new agent should be 'non-inferior' to the existing one/s. This idea relates, among other matters, to our worries about side effects. Proving 'non-inferiority' means that an actual comparison needs to be made, which adds to the expense since the 'original' biologic drug is even more expensive than, say, an 'original' small-molecule drug. However, with the differences between the 'side-effect' landscapes of small-molecule drugs versus biologics, it may be argued that this is not a sensible requirement.

Thus, there's an entire range of reasons for the costliness of biologics. And Amit was looking at each one of these and attempting both to address the nuances involved and to integrate them.

It is thought that regulatory systems do not easily recognize the concept of 'biosimilars'. Again, the difficulty arises because the regulatory authorities would be most comfortable seeing essentially identical chemical molecules in large-molecule biogenerics just as they do in small-molecule generics. For example, once 'aspirin' goes off-patent, anyone can make the same chemical compound as a generic, and it is easy to prove that it is the exact same compound. As a result, it is easily put into the market. The regulatory worry is that large-molecule drugs cannot be definitively shown to be the same thing structurally. Therefore, so risk-averse regulatory thinking goes, should we not treat it as a new entity that has to go through the entire gamut of regulatory procedures as a new molecule? It is in this context that the effort Amit led is putting together a different perspective of major public health importance; that an abbreviated regulatory process would lead to equally safe products, yet faster and cheaper access for the people. That is the argument being made, among others, to the WHO. This is tactical, because if the WHO can be persuaded, and it changes its guidelines, then individual countries will be easier to convince. Amit would have been in the thick of this advocacy, and all his colleagues are going to miss him badly going forward.

Let me put it in the sort of hard-headed empirical perspective that Amit was most comfortable with. He would have said: Listen, we are not worrying about whether biologics ought to be the future or not. What the last few years show us is that, for better or worse, biologics are going to be a major part of the future. If that's the case, then it behoves the people's health movement to engage with it. This was Amit: a combination of passionate commitment and the hard-headed pragmatism with which that commitment gets work done.

2. The Growing Importance of Biologics

AMIT SENGUPTA

Biological drugs (commonly referred to as 'biologics' or 'biopharmaceuticals') are complex molecules produced through biological processes. They target diseases which, hitherto, had very limited or no available treatment options—including several types of cancers, autoimmune diseases and other non-communicable diseases. These drugs are different because they are produced in living cells.

Biologics are larger in size and more complex than the small-molecule drugs manufactured using chemical synthesis processes. Biologics have several potential advantages as they can, theoretically, be tailored to hit specific 'targets' in the human body.

The global list of top-selling drugs is increasingly populated by biologics (see Table 2.2.1). Revenues being generated by biological drugs are huge: the projected global sales of the top-selling biologic, AbbVie's Humira (adalimumab)—a drug used to treat autoimmune disorders such as rheumatoid arthritis—in 2018 are US$20 billion, equal to about two-thirds of the entire pharmaceutical market in India in 2017.

The penetration of biological drugs in standard treatment practices is still comparatively lower than older small-molecule drugs, due to their high costs. Treatments that are currently available are limited to a small number of diseases and the need for an appropriate health system needed to supervise treatment with biologics.

Table 2.2.1: Top 10 best-selling drugs in 2015 and the share of biologics

Drug	*Company*	*Ingredient*	*Indication*	*Biologic*	*2015 sales (million USD)*
Humira	AbbVie	Adalimumab	Autoimmune disorders	Yes	14,012
Harvoni	Gilead	Ledipasvir + sofosbuvir	Hepatitis C	No	13,864
Rituxan	Roche	Rituximab	Non-Hodgkin's lymphoma	Yes	7,327
Lantus	Sanofi	Insulin glargine	Diabetes	Yes	7,088
Avastin	Roche	Bevacizumab	Various cancers	Yes	6,951
Herceptin	Roche	Trastuzumab	Breast cancer	Yes	6,799
Remicade	Johnson & Johnson	Infliximab	Autoimmune disorders	Yes	6,561
Prevnar	Pfizer	Streptococcus pneumoniae vaccine	Vaccine	No[1]	6,245
Januvia/ Janumet	Merck	Sitagliptin	Diabetes	No	6,014
Revlimid	Celgene	Lenalidomide	Multiple myeloma	No	5,801

Source: 'Pharmaceuticals: Going large', *The Economist*, January 3, 2015 (https://www.economist.com/node/21637387/print).

However, in some therapeutic areas, treatment with biologics is already quite significant, especially in high-income countries as can be seen below:

- In Europe, by 2010, about 19% of rheumatoid arthritis patients were treated with biologics.[2]

[1] While vaccine manufacture is through a biological process, they are not classified as biologics (see Satyajit Rath's piece in this section).—*Ed.*

[2] Pedro A. Laires et al. 'Patient's Access to Healthcare and Treatment in Rheumatoid Arthritis: The views of stakeholders in Portugal', *BMC Musculoskel-*

- In 2014, there were 3.1 million patients in the US being treated with one of seven top-selling biologics available in the country.[3]
- In 2015, the World Health Organization (WHO) included two new biological drugs[4] in its list of Essential Medicines apart from two other older ones.
- The fastest-growing segment of the market for biological drugs—the recombinant glycosylated proteins segment—is projected to grow annually at 25% by 2018.
- Within this, the monoclonal antibody segment alone will have an estimated compounded annual growth rate of 41.9% from 2013 to 2018.
- In the US, the growth of biologics between 2013 and 2014, increased by 32.4%, while spending on traditional small-molecule drugs increased by just 6.8%.
- In the US, over half the revenues in 2016 was generated from biologics[5] and eight of the ten top-selling drugs were biologics.[6]
- The anticipated percentage growth rate of biologics and biosimilars far exceeds that of the more established small

etal Disorders, no. 14 (2013), p. 279 (http://www.ncbi.nlm.nih.gov/pmc/articles/PMC3849024/).

3 'Biosimilars in the United States: Providing more patients greater access to lifesaving medicines', The Biosimilars Council, 2017, available online (http://biosimilarscouncil.org/wp-content/uploads/2017/09/Biosimilars-Council-Patient-Access-Study-090917.pdf).

4 Gilberto Lopes, 'Biosimilars in Emerging Markets: India and Russia', *ASCO Connection* (blog), July 11, 2016 (https://https://connection.asco.org/blogs/biosimilars-emerging-markets-india-and-russia).

5 'Generating Value in Genetics: Finding the next five years of growth', McKinsey and Company, May 2013, available online (https://www.mckinsey.com/~/media/mckinsey/dotcom/client_service/pharma%20and%20medical%20products/pmp%20new/pdfs/generating%20value%20in%20generics_final.ashx).

6 'The Economic Impact of Biosimilars in the US', Generics and Biosimilars Initiative, July 29, 2016 (http://www.gabionline.net/Biosimilars/Research/The-economic-impact-of-biosimilars-in-the-US).

molecules: the biologics are set to increase their total market share from 16.6% in 2015 to 22.2% in 2021.[7]

The growing commercial importance of biological drugs is also evident from the rise in patenting activity related to these drugs.

In 2009, biological drugs accounted for 60% of the patents filed by the top ten pharmaceutical companies.[8] Abbott had as much as 80% of the patent filings between 2007 and 2009 focused on biologics.[9]

Recent interest in biological drugs is also driven by the fact that several top-selling biologics have gone or will go off-patent between 2013 and 2018. These include blockbusters such as Rituxan/MabThera, Remicade, Herceptin, Humira, Avastin, Synagis, Erbitux and Lucentis.

While many of the discoveries of new biological drugs continue to originate in specialized biotech companies, the drugs are increasingly developed by leading multinational pharmaceutical companies (hereinafter referred to as 'Big Pharma') which had traditionally concentrated on developing traditional small-molecule drugs. The Big Pharma have enlarged their share through acquisitions of smaller biotech companies.

Currently, biologics contribute significantly to the revenues of

[7] *Pharma & Biotech. 2017: Review of Outsourced Manufacturing*, Results Healthcare,
2017, available online (http://resultshealthcare.com/wp-content/uploads/2017/01/Results-Healthcare_Pharma-Biotech-2017-Review-of-outsourced-manufacturing_Whitepaper.pdf).

[8] A. Jack, 'Fall in Number of Patents Filed by Big Pharma', *Financial Times*, March 18, 2012 (https://www.ft.com/content/0912c0ea-70f9-11e1-a7f1-00144feab49a).

[9] Alex Philippidis, 'Higher Percentage of Large Molecules Compared to Small Molecules Makes it to Market', *Genetic Intelligence and Biotechnology News*, April 9, 2012 (http://www.genengnews.com/keywordsandtools/print/3/26751/).

Big Pharma. They accounted for 22% of the Big Pharma companies' sales in 2013, and this is projected to rise to 32% by 2023. Some of the leading companies poised to benefit from growing sales of biological drugs include Abbott, Roche, Bristol-Myers Squibb, Merck, Eli Lilly and Sanofi.[10]

[10] 'FirstWord Lists: The 100 bestselling pharmaceutical brands', *FirstWord Pharma*, April 18, 2016 (https://www.firstwordpharma.com/node/1375342).

3. How Biological Drugs Differ from Small-Molecule Drugs

AMIT SENGUPTA

Biological products include a wide range of products such as vaccines, blood and blood components, gene therapy, and genetically engineered products. What we term as biologics in medicine is a subset of such biological products and refers to products that are genetically engineered with tools such as recombinant gene technologies. They are complex, large molecules[1] unlike the small chemical molecules that we use as conventional drugs.

What is the difference in complexity between conventional small-molecule drugs (SMDs) and the large complex molecules that are biologics? Conventional small-molecule chemicals have a molecular weight typically between 100 and 900 Da. Dalton (Da) is atomic mass, and is a measure of complexity of the molecule. In contrast, biologics are much larger, complex and heterogeneous proteins with more variable molecular weight, commonly ranging from 18,000 to 145,000 Da.[2]

1 'What Are "Biologics" Questions and Answers', US FDA website (https://www.fda.gov/about-fda/center-biologics-evaluation-and-research-cber/what-are-biologics-questions-and-answers).

2 Huub Schellekens, 'Biosimilar Therapeutics—What do we need to consider?', *NDT Plus*, vol. 2, suppl. 1 (2009), pp. i27–i36 (doi: 10.1093/ndtplus/sfn177).

Table 2.3.1: Differences between biologics and small-molecule drugs

Characteristic	*Small-molecule drugs*	*Biological drugs*
Size of molecule	Small	Large
Drug production	By chemical synthesis	By genetic engineering methods Produced in cell lines
Product characterization	Well characterized	Difficult to characterize the product as they tend to be produced as diverse mixture of molecules which are very slightly different from one another
Purification, contamination possibility	Easy to purify Contamination can be generally avoided, is easily detectable and often removable	Lengthy and complex purification process High possibility of contamination, detection is harder and removal is often impossible
Laboratory analysis	Easily analysed with routine laboratory tests	Current physico-chemical analytical methods or bioassays cannot detect all product variations
Susceptibility to environmental or process changes	Not affected by environmental changes or any changes in the steps of the production process, hence the product is more important than the production process	Highly susceptible to the slightest changes in the environment, cell strains or the manufacturing process, hence it remains the most essential aspect of manufacturing
Immunogenicity	Low immunogenicity	Generally immunogenic

Biologics can be produced through: a) biological processes that do not involve the creation of a new cell (to produce the product), or b) recombinant technology that can splice the DNA of two different organisms (see Chapter 4, Box 2.4.1). The major innovation of the last two decades, has been the development of genetically engineered products. It must be remembered, though, that biological drugs had been produced before genetically engineered technologies became available, including, for example, vaccines[3] and antibiotics such as penicillin. However, in this paper we are limiting our analysis largely to biological drugs developed through genetically engineered technologies.

Biological drugs differ in many ways from small-molecule drugs. Biologics are extremely sensitive to the manufacturing process and the starting material. As the starting material are living cells in the case of new biological products, it is impossible to have exactly similar starting cells. Moreover, very small changes in the manufacturing process can bring about changes in the final product. It is impossible for a company producing a follow-on biological product to completely replicate a large, complicated biomolecule, since it doesn't have access to the specific methods and conditions that the original company had in synthesizing and characterizing the compound.[4] This has implications for the development and manufacture of follow-on products.

Here it may be noted that even in the case of the original product, there are variations in the product between batches and even within the same batch. Current analytical methods cannot fully predict the structural properties of a biological drug (called 'characterization') though the body's immune system can detect alterations in products missed by analytical methods. This is, however, changing rapidly as more sophisticated methods of

[3] Rath's piece in this section deals with the difference between vaccines and biologics.—*Ed.*

[4] Bob Stembridge, 'Unique Solutions to Biosimilar Patenting', Thomson Reuters, 2015.

analysis are developed to characterize the large complex molecules of which biologics are composed.

The relative uncertainty about the structural characteristics of biologics has led to a reluctance to refer to follow-on products of biologics—that is, similar biologics manufactured by someone other than the originator company—as generics. The biologics industry has introduced the notion that since it is impossible to manufacture an exact replica, follow-on products should be called biosimilars and not generics or biogenerics. Many see this as a ploy to restrict the use of follow-on products by creating doubts in the minds of regulators and prescribers.

The complexity of the manufacturing process for biologics is several orders of magnitude higher than that for SMDs. Further, biological drugs have high immunogenicity—that is, their ability to produce an immune response in the body is of a higher order than SMDs. This places limitations on the use of biologics in settings where patients cannot be adequately supervised while on biological medicines. Biological medicines come in the form of injectables, further limiting access to these in resource-poor healthcare systems.

4. Recombinant Technologies in the Manufacture of Biological Drugs

AMIT SENGUPTA

In the case of drugs developed through recombinant technologies, there were two waves of biologic drug discoveries: recombinant versions of human endogenous molecules (i.e. hormones and enzymes found inside the human body) were developed in the 1980s; and more complex products, such as monoclonal antibodies, in the late 1990s.[1]

Recombinant biological products include: a) recombinant non-glycosylated proteins; b) recombinant glycosylated proteins; and c) recombinant peptides. Recombinant non-glycosylated proteins include insulin, granulocyte colony-stimulating factor (G-CSF), interferons and human growth hormone; recombinant glycosylated proteins include erythropoietin, monoclonal antibodies and follitropin; and recombinant peptides include calcitonin and glucagon. Of these, the new generation of drugs for cancer and autoimmune diseases comprises those that are characterized as monoclonal antibodies (the convention for such drugs is to use an International Non-proprietary Name (INN) ending in the three letters 'mAb').

To create mAbs, researchers inject mice with an antigen from

1 Bruno Calo-Fernández and Juan Leonardo Martínez-Hurtado, 'Biosimilars: Company strategies to capture value from the biologics market', *Pharmaceuticals*, vol. 5, no. 12 (December 2012), pp. 1393–408 (doi:10.3390/ph5121393).

human cells. They then harvest the antibody-producing cells from the mice and individually fuse them with a myeloma cell (cancerous B cell) to produce a fusion cell known as a hybridoma. Each hybridoma then divides to produce identical daughter cells or clones—hence the term 'monoclonal'—and antibodies secreted by different clones are tested to identify the antibodies that bind most strongly to the antigen. Large quantities of antibodies can be produced by these immortal hybridoma cells. Because mouse antibodies can themselves produce an immune response in humans, which would reduce their effectiveness, mouse antibodies are often 'humanized' by replacing as much of the mouse portion of the antibody as possible with human portions. This is done through genetic engineering.[2]

RENEWED INTEREST IN BIOLOGICAL MEDICINES

There is, at present, renewed interest in the biologics market, and as a consequence biotech companies are attracting large amounts of funding. According to a PricewaterhouseCoopers (PwC) and National Venture Capital Association (NVCA) report, over US$2.1 billion was invested in biotech companies in the US in the second quarter of 2015. Four of the five quarters up till then were among the top record-setting quarters for the past ten years, in terms of the magnitude of venture capital funding made available to biotech companies.

When more capital is channelled into a particular area as compared with historical norms, questions around bubbles and over-funding get raised. The question that may be asked is whether there is indeed a funding and valuation bubble in the biotech sector. The growing pool of capital available today could dissipate quickly if market sentiment turns against the biotech sector.[3]

[2] 'Biological Therapies for Cancer', US National Cancer Institute official website, n.d. (https://www.cancer.gov/about-cancer/treatment/types/immunotherapy/bio-therapies-fact-sheet).

[3] Bruce Booth, 'The Venture Funding Boom in Biotech: A few things it's not',

The question is valid if one scans the history of the promise of the biotech revolution. Delivery on the promise of biotechnology has been slow and previous failures would suggest the need for caution. The last time the biotech industry was able to garner current levels of funding was around 2000, when companies promised, and investors believed, that genomics, particularly after the decoding of the human DNA sequence, would revolutionize drug discovery. However, biotech stock prices eventually collapsed when genomics did not yield the promised bonanza.[4]

The current enthusiasm around biotech drugs needs to be tempered by the knowledge that we are yet to see biological drugs that have truly revolutionized therapy in many areas. Most available therapies utilizing biological drugs are clustered around autoimmune disorders such as rheumatoid arthritis, ankylosing spondylitis, Crohn's disease, ulcerative colitis and psoriasis, and around some forms of cancer. In the former case (autoimmune disorders), while treated patients have seen significant improvement in quality of life, the new biologic-based treatments do not target life-threatening diseases of an immediate nature. Cancer therapies available in the form of biologics are yet to provide dramatic results—rather, in most cases they effect an incremental increase in survival rates. In fact, in the recent past, it is small-molecule drugs such as imatinib (for chronic myeloid leukaemia) and sofosbuvir (for hepatitis C) that have provided dramatic therapeutic breakthroughs.

An associated issue is that of the cost of biologics, including of follow-on versions (called 'biosimilars' or 'biogenerics'). The US market (and to a certain extent the EU market) is fuelling the

Forbes, July 23, 2015 (http://www.forbes.com/sites/brucebooth/2015/07/23/the-venture-funding-boom-in-biotech-a-few-things-its-not/#4d-b49959439c).

4 Andrew Pollack, 'Riding High, Biotech Firms Remain Wary', *The New York Times*, January 18, 2015 (http://www.nytimes.com/2015/01/19/technology/riding-high-biotech-firms-remain-wary.html?_r=0).

Table 2.4.1: Classification of recombinant biological products

Non-glycosylated proteins	Insulin, interferons, granulocyte colony-stimulating factor (G-CSF), human growth hormone
Peptides	Calcitonin, glucagon
Glycosylated proteins	Erythropoietin, follitropin, monoclonal antibodies

Source: 'Biosimilars Market Product & Application (Oncology, Blood Disorders)—Global Forecast to 2018', *PR Newswire*, November 26, 2013 (https://www.prnewswire.com/news-releases/biosimilars-market-product-recombinant-non-glycosylated-proteins-insulin-filgrastim-somatropin-glycosylated-monoclonal-antibodies-erythropoietin-peptides-glucagon-calciton-in--application-oncology-blood-disorders-233468431.html).

growth of the biologics sector, but the ability of even these markets to sustain the growth of such high-cost therapies is uncertain unless new breakthrough drugs become available.

This is not to suggest that the predicted growth of the biologics (and biosimilars) market is a mirage or a funding-induced bubble, but to predicate future projections on a bigger realization of the promise of biotechnology towards promoting better outcomes in a larger range of diseases.

The current optimism around the biotech sector is being driven by two factors. As mentioned above, the fastest-growing segment of the biologics market is the recombinant glycosylated proteins segment—projected to grow annually at 25% by 2018.

One of the drivers of this growth is the investment by drug manufacturers in developing biosimilar versions of monoclonal antibodies (over fifty biosimilars of monoclonal antibodies are in the pipeline). This interest is further strengthened as patents on many top-selling biological drugs have expired or are set to expire soon. Other fast-growing products (other than monoclonal antibodies) include follitropin (to treat infertility) and erythropoietin (especially useful in treating anaemia secondary to chronic kidney failure). Optimism around biological drugs is also

BOX 2.4.1

WHAT ARE RECOMBINANT TECHNOLOGIES?

Biotechnology involves biological processes that have been manipulated or modified in some way by modern science. A major industrial application of biotechnology is in the development and preparation of biological medicinal products using genetically engineered bacteria, yeast, fungi, cells or even whole animals and plants. Some of these biological medicines were originally extracted from tissues and secretions, often of human origin and in relatively small amounts. With the advent of recombinant DNA technology, the preparation of large amounts of highly purified and characterized materials became possible. These include products modified by pegylation—treatment of a complex biomolecule with polyethylene glycol to stabilize it—or changes in DNA sequences, fundamentally changing the manner in which biological substances like these were produced and standardized.

See 'Biotherapeutic Products' on the WHO website (https://www.who.int/biologicals/biotherapeutics/biotherapeutic-products/en/)

being fuelled by the high prices commanded by the top-selling drugs.

Big Pharma was not involved in and did not benefit from the success of innovative biotech companies in the late 1990s, but the pharmaceutical giants have recently acquired some of those successful biotech companies to shore up their capabilities in the biotech sector. The mega-mergers of Pfizer and Wyeth, Roche and Genentech, and Merck and Schering-Plough are examples of recent acquisitions by Big Pharma. However, the rate of introduction of new biologics has slowed from the peaks in the late 1990s. One reason for this deceleration is that innovative biotech companies had patented and developed products saturating the currently available approved indications, and regulatory agencies require new products to show better efficacy than the existing ones.

BOX 2.4.2

WHAT ARE MONOCLONAL ANTIBODIES?

Monoclonal antibodies, or mAbs, are laboratory-produced antibodies that bind to specific antigens expressed by cells, such as a protein that is present on the surface of cancer cells but is absent from (or expressed at lower levels by) normal cells.

The slowdown in introduction of new biologics is driving interest in biosimilars. Big Pharma, which missed the bus earlier, is now entering the biosimilars market. This is an attractive option for Big Pharma, given that a number of biologic blockbusters have lost or are soon to lose market exclusivity. Top biotech innovator companies are also entering the biosimilars market. For example, Amgen, the largest biologics manufacturing company globally, signed a deal in July 2016 with Japanese firm Daiichi through which Amgen secured an exclusive agreement to commercialize nine biosimilars in Japan.[5] Earlier in 2016, Amgen had announced plans to launch in the US its biosimilar version of AbbVie's Humira (adalimumab), the world's biggest blockbuster drug.[6]

Established innovative biotech companies fund their research and development (R&D) operations through the revenues obtained from their biologic blockbusters, the majority of which were patented during the wave of biologic drug discoveries of the late 1990s. The strategic decisions of mega generics companies and Big Pharma to enter the biosimilars market are therefore a real

[5] 'Amgen and Daiichi Sankyo Announce Agreement to Commercialise Biosimilars in Japan', Amgen news release, July 13, 2016 (http://www.amgen.com/media/news-releases/2016/07/amgen-and-daiichi-sankyo-announce-agreement-to-commercialize-biosimilars-in-japan/).

[6] S. Lawrence, 'Amgen partners with Daiichi on biosimilars after positive FDA panel', *FierceBiotech*, July 14, 2016 (http://www.fiercebiotech.com/biotech/amgen-partners-daiichi-biosimilars-after-positive-fda-panel).

threat to the survival of innovative biotech companies.[7]

Companies such as Teva, Sandoz and Hospira, the largest generics companies, are already commercializing biosimilar hormones, cytokines and enzymes (e.g. insulin, EPO, interferon, G-CSF and imiglucerase). Among monoclonal antibodies, the three most targeted products for biosimilars are rituximab, infliximab and adalimumab, due to their high worldwide sales and approvals for multiple indications. Various key industry players in the generics market have started working on the manufacturing and clinical trials of mAbs. Bioexpress Therapeutic (Switzerland) has sixteen biosimilar candidates of mAbs in the pipeline. Other major companies that have invested in the production of mAbs are Gene Techno Science (Japan), Celltrion (South Korea), Zydus Cadila (India), Biocon (India) and Samsung Biologics (South Korea). Across countries, China and India are considered attractive destinations for R&D outsourcing by foreign biosimilar manufacturing companies that are looking to reduce their growing R&D costs and increase the number of drug applications and approvals.

[7] Calo-Fernández and Martínez-Hurtado, 'Biosimilars: Company strategies to capture value from the biologics market'.

5. Why are Biologics and Biosimilars So Expensive?

AMIT SENGUPTA

In the case of small-molecule drugs (SMDs), the generic equivalents become available soon after the patents on these drugs expire (or in situations where the patent is not recognized in a particular territory). Unlike the SMDs, there is no effective competition in the market for biologics even in situations where the patents on the originator molecules have expired or are not granted. The complex structures of biologics and their dependence on relatively complex manufacturing processes involving living cells or biological processes introduces barriers to competition in the market. Thus, in addition to intellectual property-related barriers—similar to what we see in the case of SMDs—early introduction of biosimilars faces *additional* technological and regulatory barriers.

As a result, biologics are extremely expensive and consequently not easily accessible to patients, especially in low and middle-income countries (LMICs). For example, one vial of adalimumab (for the originator product Humira from AbbVie) would cost about US$1,000—almost equivalent to the average annual wage in a low-income country. The high prices of biological drugs place a major burden on the public health budget of many LMICs which have introduced these drugs. For example, in 2015 biological drugs accounted for 35% of the pharmaceutical market in Colombia. Similarly, in Brazil, while biological drugs account for *4% by volume* of drugs distributed through its National Health System, they account for *over half of the Ministry of Health's expenditure* on medicines.[1]

The entry of biosimilars into the regulated markets of the EU and the US has also been very slow; biosimilars in 2014 accounted for less than 0.5% of the market for biological medicines.[2]

Even though biosimilar versions of many top-selling biological drugs are now being produced by non-originator companies, there are various factors that limit access to these. Current regulatory regimes require clinical trials to be done to establish that the biosimilar matches the potency, safety and efficacy of the originator. This requirement, together with the costly manufacturing processes, escalates the development costs for biosimilars. The estimated cost for development of a biosimilar is between US$75–250 million, *one order of magnitude* higher than the cost of development for generic SMDs.[3]

Unlike the case of the small-molecule generic industry, many multinational pharmaceutical companies are also entering the area of biogeneric manufacture. The latter have a stake in keeping the prices of biosimilars comparatively high, hence repeated industry-led assertions that introducing biosimilars will lead to only a modest drop of 10–50% in prices.[4] While different estimates exist regarding the cost of developing a biosimilar, the US Federal Trade

[1] F. Barry, 'Filgastrim Biosimilar is first Latin Copy Biologic, Says Brazil', *BioPharma Reporter*, November 24, 2015 (https://www.biopharma-reporter.com/Article/2015/11/24/Filgrastim-biosimilar-is-first-Latin-copy-biologic-says-Brazil).

[2] Emma Dorey, 'How the Biologics Landscape is Evolving', *The Pharmaceutical Journal*, November 17, 2014.

[3] Calo-Fernández and Martínez-Hurtado, 'Biosimilars: Company strategies to capture value from the biologics market'.

[4] A.W. Mulcahy, Z. Predmore and S. Mattke, 'The Cost Savings Potential of Biosimilar Drugs in the United States', Rand Corporation, n.d., available online (https://www.rand.org/content/dam/rand/pubs/perspectives/PE100/PE127/RAND_PE127.pdf)

Commission estimates the cost to be in the range of US$100–200 million. The development time is between 8–10 years (in contrast to 2–3 years for small-molecule generics). According to the industry, the high investment and risk involved in producing biosimilars would lead to a drop of the prices of these drugs by only about 10–35% compared with the cost of the originator biologic.[5]

These assertions are, however, belied by other evidence—for example, the version of adalimumab produced by India's Zydus Cadila (Exemptia) led to an 80% price reduction.[6] In Europe, price drops in the range of 45–70% are already being seen in segments where there is competition from biosimilars.

Some analysts[7] now say that the cost of developing a biosimilar is nearer US$60 million, and not US$100–200 million as claimed. Of this, it is projected that US$7–15 million is the typical cost of analysing the originator molecule over a period of four years. Steinar Madsen,[8] the Director of the Norwegian Medicines Agency says that the cost of manufacture of a biologic is significantly less than the market cost of the drug. It is under discussion that regulatory regimes will, in the near future, largely forgo the need[9] to

5 Dorey, 'How the Biologics Landscape is Evolving'.

6 'Zydus Cadila Launches Biosimilar of AbbVie's Humira in India', *Economic Times*, December 9, 2014 (https://m economictimes.com/industry/healthcare/biotech/pharmaceuticals/zydus-cadila-launches-biosimilar-of-abbvies-humira-in-india/articleshow/45432274.cms).

7 Dan Stanton in his article quotes industry figures such as Richard Dicicco, Chairman of Harvest Moon, on the costs of developing biosimilars. 'Number of Biosimilar Developers Growing as Costs Plummet, Say CPhI Experts', *BioPharma Reporter*, October 21, 2015 (https://www.biopharma-reporter.com/Article/2015/10/21/Number-of-biosimilar-developers-growing-as-costs-plummet-say-experts).

8 Steinar Madsen, 'Learning From the Norwegian Experience With Biosimilars', *American Journal of Managed Care*, November 15, 2017 (https://www.centerforbiosimilars.com/conferences/smi-2017/learning-from-the-norwegian-experience-with-biosimilars).

9 'A Shift In Regulatory Thinking—Are confirmatory phase III studies redundant for biosimilars?', Neuclone website, September 24, 2018 (https://neu-

conduct expensive Phase III trials before biosimilars are approved, drastically cutting the cost of development of biosimilars.

clone.com/a-shift-in-regulatory-thinking-are-confirmatory-phase-iii-studies-redundant-for-biosimilars/).

6. Technology and Intellectual Property Rights Barriers for Biosimilars

AMIT SENGUPTA

The introduction of generic drugs for small-molecule drugs (SMDs)[1] led to competition and a huge drop in prices, significantly enhancing access. A classic example is that of HIV medicines. Prices dropped by *97.5%* in the early 2000s after the introduction of generics by Indian companies. This hasn't happened in the case of biological drugs. For biologicals, the complexity of the molecule, their three-dimensional structures, and dependence on production in living cells make it difficult to make exact copies.

Conventional generics—generics for SMDs—are considered therapeutically equivalent to a reference molecule, once pharmaceutical equivalence (identical active substances) and bioequivalence (comparable pharmacokinetics or movement of the drug in the body) have been established. Generally, stringent clinical efficacy and safety studies are not required. In contrast, regulatory bodies demand clinical trials to confirm safety and efficacy for biosimilars before providing marketing approval. The argument is that the effects of a biological drug depend on its structural stability. Factors causing physical and chemical instability alter the three-dimensional structure and folding pattern of proteins, and may lead to changes in their immunogenic

[1] Copies of originator SMDs manufactured by non-originator companies.

properties[2]—adding a new layer of complexity in testing for safety.

It needs to be underlined that all medicinal products developed through biological processes do not pose the same level of complexity. In fact, 'similar' versions of biological drugs have been in the market for over five decades. One example is the case of penicillin, which is produced through fermentation technology. Likewise, vaccine manufacture is now undertaken by a number of companies other than the originator company. More recently, there have been several versions of human insulin available in the market. The discussions below on the challenges to biosimilar manufacture pertain to more recent biological drugs that use genetic engineering and recombinant DNA technology, especially for the production of monoclonal antibodies. These challenges are particularly relevant as the recent biologics of therapeutic importance fall in this category.

TECHNOLOGICAL BARRIERS TO MANUFACTURE OF BIOSIMILARS

A biosimilar has been defined as a biological medicine that has been proven to have a high similarity to a reference biological medicine (also referred to as the originator or original biological medicine). A biosimilar's *primary* amino acid sequence matches that of the reference biological medicine, with differences only in clinically inactive components. Biosimilars are approved by regulatory authorities to meet standards for similarity in quality, efficacy and safety to the reference biological medicine.[3]

The manufacture of biologics using recombinant technology

[2] Krishna Undela, 'Biogenerics or Biosimilars: An overview of the current situation in India', *International Journal of Medical and Pharmaceutical Sciences*, vol. 1, December 2011, pp. 1–10 (https://www.researchgate.net/publication/236894615_Biogenerics_or_Biosimilar s_An_overview_of_the_current_situation_in_India).

[3] *International Union of Pure and Applied Chemistry (IUPAC) Compendium of Chemical Terminology*, 2nd ed., Cambridge Healthcare Institute.

requires several stages of cell culture and purification, processes which are confidential to the company developing the product. As it is not possible for companies producing biosimilars to directly access this know-how, their manufacturing process differs from that of the originator; and there may be a higher structural variability of the product. For example, different cell lines could alter the three-dimensional structure of the final product. These alterations can, theoretically, lead to undesired immunogenic responses[4] that either inactivate the therapeutic effects of the drug or even cause adverse effects.

It must be kept in mind, however, that all biological products are inherently variable due to the fact that they are produced from living organisms. This variability exists—even when the originator company manufactures the drug—within batches, from batch to batch, and when production processes are improved or changed. Thus, what is rarely acknowledged is that different batches of biologics from the originator companies also differ.[5] This is what Steinar Madsen of the Norwegian Medicines Agency says about biologics: 'All biologics are biosimilars,' a well-kept 'secret' of the biotechnology industry.

INTELLECTUAL PROPERTY RIGHTS BARRIERS

Patents constitute the first-level barrier to the entry of biosimilars. Biological drugs are protected by patents on both products and processes, trade secrets and data exclusivity.

In the case of SMDs, it is easy to find alternate processes to create the same molecule, the route that the Indian generics industry took.

[4] Calo-Fernández and Martínez-Hurtado, 'Biosimilars: Company strategies to capture value from the biologics market'.

[5] Anna Rose Welch, 'The Norwegian Biosimilar Phenomenon: From biosimilar to "biogeneric"', *Biosimilar Development*, July 26, 2016 (http://www.biosimilardevelop ment.com/doc/the-norwegian-biosimilar-phenomenon-from-biosimilar-to-biogeneric-0001).

Table 2.6.1: Patent expiry of top-selling biologics (global sales >US$4.5 billion)

Drug	*Ingredient*	*Company*	*Indication*	*Patent expiry*	
				EU	*US*
Humira	Adalimumab	AbbVie	Autoimmune disorders	2018	2016
Lantus	Insulin glargine	Sanofi	Diabetes	2014	2015
Enbrel	Etanercept	Amgen	Autoimmune disorders	2015	2028
Remicade	Infliximab	Johnson & Johnson	Autoimmune disorders	2015	2018
MabThera	Rituximab	Roche	Cancers; autoimmune disorders	Expired	2018
Avastin	Bevacizumab	Roche	Cancers	2019	2019
Herceptin	Trastuzumab	Roche	Breast cancer	2014	2019
Avonex/ Rebif	Interferon Beta -1A	Biogen/ Pfizer	Multiple sclerosis	2015	2016
Copaxone	Glatirameracetate	Teva	Multiple sclerosis	2017	2014
Neulasta	Pegfilgastrim	Amgen	Adjunct to cancer chemotherapy	2015	2015
Lucentis	Ranibizumab	Genentech	Macular degeneration	2016	2016

Source: https://ppri.goeg.at/sites/ppri.goeg.at/files/inline-files/1030_StrandI_Vulto.pdf.

Due to the large-molecule nature of biologic products, *product patent* protection is often narrower for biologics than for small-molecule drugs. However, the significant molecular size of biologic products makes it easier to 'invent around' an existing patent, thus narrowing the extent of coverage by a product patent.[6] *Process patents* here act as a major barrier to the introduction

[6] Steven Globerman, ed., *Intellectual Property Rights and the Promotion of Biologics, Medical Devices, and Trade in Pharmaceuticals*, Fraser Institute, October 14, 2016, available online (https://www.fraserinstitute.org/studies/intellectual-property-rights-and-the-promotion-of-biologics-medical-devices-and-trade-in-pharmaceuticals).

of biosimilars, as the processes involved could also be protected under patents through such means.

Much of the recent interest in biosimilar development is being driven by the fact that several top-selling biologics have recently lost patent exclusivity, or are poised to lose it soon. The combined value in 2015 of eight top-selling biologics losing exclusivity protection from patents or other measures between 2015 and 2020 in the US, France, Germany, Italy, Spain and the UK, was US$110 billion.[7] This includes one of the world's biggest-selling drugs of all time, AbbVie's Humira (adalimumab), which had sales of €10.8 billion in five EU countries and the US, and which loses exclusivity in the EU in 2018 and in the US in 2016.

Similarly, Amgen and Pfizer's Enbrel (etanercept), which is used in the treatment of a number of chronic inflammatory conditions and which earned €6.9 billion in the EU and the US, has lost exclusivity in the EU. Sanofi-Aventis's diabetes drug Lantus (insulin glargine), which had sales of €8.7 billion in the EU and the US last year, lost exclusivity in the EU in 2014 and in the US in 2015.[8]

An estimated thirty companies are actively developing biosimilars, particularly for infliximab, etanercept, rituximab and adalimumab.[9]

Even after originator biologics lose patent exclusivity, *trade secrets* can continue to create barriers to the entry of biosimilars. Most small-molecule drugs can be easily manufactured once their chemical structure is known. Due to the complexity of producing biologics, companies guard the specifics of their manufacture and methods for scaling-up production, as trade secrets. Trade

[7] Zachary Brennan, 'IMS: Biosimilars could save up to $110B in EU, US through 2020', *Regulatory Focus*, March 29, 2016 (https://www.raps.org/regulatory-focus%E2%84%A2/news-articles/2016/3/ims-biosimilars-could-save-up-to-$110b-in-eu,-us-through-2020).

[8] Ibid.

[9] Ibid.

secrets are cheaper, they do not involve either disclosure or a costly process of filing and maintaining patents. They also last well beyond the patent period, the examples being Coca Cola's still secret 130-year-old formulae for its coloured carbonated drink and Wyeth's 75-year-old Premarin from mare urine.[10]

The second set of barriers come from process patents that seek to patent not the final product but the manufacturing processes themselves. There are also platform patents—where the basic tools such as CRISPR are sought to be patented.[11]

Product and process patents force biosimilar manufacturers to develop their own methods of manufacture and subsequent validation (to show similarity with the originator when applying for marketing approval), often at great expense. One of the major expenses for a biosimilar manufacturer is to procure the originator drug itself in the extensive trials prescribed under most regulatory regimes.

The biotech industry sources also assert that product and process patents are inadequate, or less effective compared to SMDs. They demand protecting—as intellectual property—the innovator firm's safety and efficacy data. Hence, data exclusivity provisions are necessary to enhance protection for innovator drugs.[12] Such provisions are 'TRIPS-plus', i.e. not required by the World Trade Organization's Agreement on Trade-Related Aspects of Intellectual Property Rights (TRIPS).

The importance assigned to data exclusivity provisions by innovator biotech companies was evident in the protracted negotiations on the issue during the discussions on the Trans-Pacific Partnership (TPP) free trade agreement. The US (among

[10] Jacob S. Sherkow, 'Protecting Products Versus Platforms', *Nature Biotechnology*, vol. 34, 2016, pp. 462–65 (https://www.nature.com/articles/nbt.3553).

[11] Ibid.

[12] K.M. Lybecker, 'The Biologics Revolution in the Production of Drugs', Fraser Institute, July 2016 (https://www.fraserinstitute.org/sites/default/files/biologics-revolution-in-the-production-of-drugs.pdf).

others) bargained very hard for the introduction of a special protection period of twelve years' exclusivity for biologics,[13] which was opposed even by Australia and New Zealand.[14] The final agreement requires countries to implement one of two options: (1) give eight years of market exclusivity from the date the biologic is approved in the country concerned; or (2) give five years of market exclusivity from the date the biologic is approved in the country concerned and other measures to deliver a comparable market outcome. It is argued by a number of TPP governments, such as Australia, New Zealand, Chile and Singapore, that the provision does not require countries to grant more than five years of biologic exclusivity.

[13] 'Piggy-backing to Market? TPP negotiations bring data exclusivity periods of biologics into public spotlight', Baldwins, September 7, 2015 (https://www.baldwins.com/news/piggy-backing-to-market-tpp-negotiations-bring-data-exclusivity-periods-of).

[14] Australia: 'TPP outcomes: biologics', Deptt. of Foreign Affairs and Trade (https://www.dfat.gov.au/trade/agreements/not-yet-in-force/tpp/Pages/outcomes-biologics); New Zealand: 'Trans-Pacific Partnership. Intellectual Property: Fact Sheet', Ministry of Foreign Affairs and Trade (http://tpp.mfat.govt.nz/assets/docs/TPP_factsheet_Intellectual-Property.PDF); Chile: 'Transcript of the Trans-Pacific Partnership Atlanta Ministerial Closing Press Conference', Office of the US Trade Representative (https://ustr.gov/about-us/policy-offices/press-office/speechestranscripts/2015/october/transcript-trans-pacific); Singapore: 'Singapore's demands complicate TPP—U.S.-India statement wide-ranging—EU nods to TTIP secrecy concerns', *Politico*, November 26, 2014 (https://www.politico.com/tipsheets/morning-trade/2014/11/singapores-demands-complicate-tpp-us-india-statement-wide-ranging-eu-nods-to-ttip-secrecy-concerns-212543).

7. Current Regulatory Barriers for Biosimilars

AMIT SENGUPTA

While the early introduction of cheaper biosimilars faced hurdles regarding intellectual property and technology, the regulatory barriers imposed by regulatory agencies in different countries are, currently, the most significant. Rather than facilitating access, the WHO's conservative approach has had a chilling effect on the early introduction of biosimilars.

Since the late 1990s, non-originator biological products have been known by different names such as follow-on biologics, biogenerics, and biosimilars. Generally speaking, these nomenclatures are closely linked to the regulatory pathways followed for the approval of these products. Interestingly, regulatory pathways for non-originator biological products were recognized in many Asian countries (India, South Korea, etc.) as early as the 1990s, much before regulatory pathways existed in the EU and the US. Thus non-originator biological products were available in countries such as India *a decade or more* before their entry into the European market.

The regulatory pathway initially followed in Asian countries was different from the biosimilar regulatory pathway broadly advocated by the international conference on harmonization (ICH). The ICH was a closed regulatory standard-setting body founded by drug regulatory authorities of the EU (European Medicines Agency—EMA), Japan (Ministry of Health, Labour and Welfare—JMHLW) and the US (Food and Drug Administration—US FDA) *with the originator pharmaceutical industry associations* of those countries: the European Federation of Pharmaceutical Industries' Associations—EFPIA; the Japan Pharmaceutical Manufacturers Association—JPMA; and the Pharmaceutical Research and Manufacturers of America—PhRMA). Not surprisingly, the positions that the ICH promotes are reflective of the interests of originator companies.[1]

Biosimilars, including monoclonal antibodies, received regulatory approval in India and South Korea much before the developed-country markets. To date, India has approved more than fifty 'similar biologic' products for its market. In contrast, the more stringent requirements of ICH-aligned countries (largely developed countries) have limited approvals to much lower numbers. Till 2015, Australia had approved eight; Japan seven; and Canada three.[2] The EU had approved about twenty-four, while the US approved its first biosimilar for filgrastim in 2015. In June 2013, the first approval for a biosimilar monoclonal antibody was granted in the EU for infliximab.[3]

The Indian guidelines for the introduction of biosimilars were modified in 2012. Prior to 2012, the guidelines were less onerous on biosimilar manufacturers. (See Table 2.7.1 for important divergences between the pre-2012 regulations in India and the WHO guidelines.) The 2012 guidelines in India were modelled on the then existing EMA guidelines and the WHO guidelines,[4]

[1] 'WHO: Alliance with industry raises concerns over medicine regulation', Third World Network Info Service on Health Issues, May 20, 2014 (http://www.twn.my/title2/health.info/2014/hi140502.htm).

[2] Cheryl Scott and S. Anne Montgomery, 'Biosimilars and Biobetters Offer Unique Benefits—and Risks', *BioProcess International*, June 16, 2015 (http://www.bioprocessintl.com).

[3] 'Biosimilars Approved in Europe', Generics and Biosimilars Initiative, February 2, 2018 (http://www.gabionline.net/Biosimilars/General/Biosimilars-approved-in-Europe).

[4] C. Ohly, 'The New India Guidelines on Similar Biologics: Regulatory and market authorization requirements', *Spicy IP* (https://spicyip.com/2012/10/

drastically reducing the divergences. The guidelines were further modified in 2016.[5]

THE WHO'S GUIDELINES AND RESOLUTION AT THE WHA

In 2009, the WHO Expert Committee on Biological Standardization adopted guidelines on evaluation of similar biotherapeutic products. These guidelines drew heavily from the broad positions advocated by the ICH; and since then, there has been a major push for the adoption in other countries of biosimilar guidelines modelled on the ICH's positions and EU guidelines. The 2009 WHO guidelines require 'head to head' comparability of the non-originator product with the originator product.

The EU guidelines have been modified since and are now much less onerous. The principles underlying the approach to biosimilars included in the WHO guidelines are:[6]

- Full quality dossier, including comparisons with original
- Limited preclinical dossier including pharmacokinetics comparison with original
- Clinical similarity where hard clinical endpoints[7] are not needed
- Extrapolation possible
- Post-marketing safety studies including immunogenicity

---

guest-post-new-india-guidelines-on.html).

5 'India Updates Its Similar Biologics Guidelines', Generics and Biosimilars Initiative, November 10, 2017 (http://www.gabionline.net/Guidelines/India-updates-its-similar-biologics-guidelines).

6 See Huub Schellekens, 'Who needs biosimilars?: The arguments for a separate pathway for biologics', (https://e-b-f.eu/wp-content/uploads/2018/05/bcn2012-S21.-1_schellekens.pdf).

7 Hard clinical endpoints are, for example, parameters like survivability rate. Since such studies involve small numbers with a large variation in the patients and the progress of the disease, hard end points are not very useful. Hence, clinical similarity is used instead of hard endpoints.

Table 2.7.1: Pre-2012 Indian guidelines and WHO guidelines

Pre-2012 Indian guidelines	*WHO guidelines*
Comparative PK/PD is not mandatory	Comparative PK/PD is required
Comparative CT is not mandatory	Comparative CT is required
Extrapolation to other indication can be obtained	Extrapolation to other indication can be approved only if the mode of action is similar
Immunogenicity is not mandatory but expected	Immunogenicity is mandatory
Note: PK: pharmacokinetic; PD: pharmacodynamic; CT: clinical trials	

Source: H. Malhotra, 'Biosimilars and Non-Innovator Biotherapeutics in India: An overview of the current situation', *Biologicals*, vol. 39, 2011, pp. 321–24 (https://www.sciencedirect.com/science/article/pii/S1045105611000832).

Demonstration of similarity with the originator demanded by the regulator requires comparative clinical trials with the originator product. A significant proportion of the biosimilar development cost is due to the need of purchasing the expensive originator product. Further, the burden of proof on similarity also increases the duration of biosimilar development. These onerous regulatory requirements delay the introduction of biosimilars and prevent a significant drop in prices even when biosimilars are introduced.

Thus, regulatory requirements represent one of the most significant barriers to affordable access to biological products. Also, even with the smaller clinical trials that are demanded by current regulations, biosimilar sponsors face challenges in identifying clinical sites, recruiting investigators who understand their unique development issues and who attract a sufficient number of participants.[8]

[8] J. Wechsler, 'Biosimilar Trials Differ Notably from Innovator Studies', *Applied Clinical Trials*, November 1, 2016 (http:// www.appliedclinicaltrialsonline.com/biosimilar-trials-differ-notably-innovator-studies).

WHO GUIDELINES

The WHO guidelines have been criticized by analysts for their 'similarity proof requirement': Biosimilars regulatory guidance should be reviewed in light not only of the scientific and regulatory experience gained over time, but also of the needs and interests of national health systems and pharmaceutical markets in low-resource countries. Stringent regulatory authorities such as EMA have already begun to waive requirements for comparability exercise at clinical level under appropriate circumstances. This approach is supported by academic experts who argue that non-comparative clinical trials are sufficient for regulatory purposes, and call for pragmatic approaches focused primarily on the patient's clinical outcomes and on scientific principles, using the 'state-of-the-art tools'.[9]

In 2014, reflecting the concerns on non-availability of biological products at affordable prices, the WHO's governing World Health Assembly (WHA) adopted a resolution that urged member states:

> ... to work to ensure that the introduction of new national regulations, where appropriate, does not constitute a barrier to access to quality, safe, efficacious and affordable biotherapeutic products, including similar biotherapeutic products.[10]

The resolution further requested the WHO Director-General:

[9] B. Milani and S. Gaspani, 'Pathway to Affordable, Quality-based Sources of Pegylated Interferon Alpha for Treating Hepatitis C', *Generics and Biosimilars Initiative Journal*, vol. 2, no. 4 (2013), p. 194 (http://gabi-journal.net/pathway-to-affordable-quality-assured-sources-of-pegylated-interferon-alpha-for-treating-hepatitis-c.html).

[10] 'Sixty-Seventh World Health Assembly, Resolutions and Decisions Annexes', Geneva: World Health Organization (hereinafter WHO), p. 68 (http://apps.who.int/gb/ebwha/pdf_files/WHA67-REC1/A67_2014_REC1-en.pdf#page=25).

> … to convene WHO's Expert Committee on Biological Standardization to update the 2009 guidelines, taking into account the technological advances for the characterization of biotherapeutic products and considering national regulatory needs and capacities and to report on the update to the [WHO] Executive Board.

However, WHO does not seem to have followed the spirit of the WHA resolution. Instead, it has, on its website, issued certain 'clarifications' in the form of Q&As.[11] Thus, WHO has not actually updated its 2009 guidelines. It has issued several reports by its Expert Committee on Biological Standardization which continue to *strengthen* the obligations of biosimilar manufacturers laid out in the 2009 guidelines.

A report by the expert committee issued in 2016 recommends reappraisal or re-registration of products introduced in situations where the WHO guidelines were not followed.[12] The 2016 report recommends that:

> Attention should be paid to any key differences between national requirements and the WHO Guidelines—such as the lack of a head-to-head comparability exercise for an SBP [similar biotherapeutic product]. The NRA [national regulatory authority] should provide manufacturers with a critical dataset for the re-registration of such products. Changes in regulatory requirements may be needed, as well as amendments to the legal framework of the country concerned, to enable such new requirements to be implemented.

[11] 'WHO Questions and Answers: Similar Biotherapeutic Products', WHO, December 2017, available online (https://www.who.int/biologicals/QA_for_SBPs_HK_12_Dec_2017_(2).pdf?ua=1).

[12] 'WHO Expert Committee on Biological Standardization, Sixty-sixth Report', WHO Technical Report Series No. 999, available online (http://www.who.int/biologicals/expert_committee/WHO_TRS_999_corrigenda_web.pdf).

EUROPEAN GUIDELINES

In October 2014, the EMA finalized new regulatory guidelines on biosimilars in the EU.[13] The guidelines update its October 2005 guidelines on biosimilarity (developed based on ICH standards), which officials said had become outdated. The new guidelines, it is claimed, would clarify how companies can establish biosimilarity between their follow-on biologic and the original biologic product approved by the EMA. The guidelines also include a discussion regarding the 'principles of establishing biosimilarity'. The EMA recommends a 'stepwise approach' meant to build upon rigorous data at every stage of the evaluation process. The EMA explains:

> If the biosimilar comparability exercise indicates that there are relevant differences between the intended biosimilar and the reference medicinal product making it unlikely that biosimilarity will eventually be established, a stand-alone development to support a full Marketing Authorization Application (MAA) should be considered instead . . . Clinical data cannot be used to justify substantial differences in quality attributes.[14]

Essentially, what this stepwise approach involves is an assessment of similarity at every step. If, at any step, the divergence in similarity is seen to be too large, the similar molecule will be treated as a new molecule requiring submission of a full dossier.

US GUIDELINES

At the end of March 2010, the US enacted the Biologics Price Competition and Innovation Act (BPCI). The BPCI defines

[13] The EMA guidelines can be accessed on their official website: http://www.ema.europa.eu/ema/ index.jsp?curl=pages/regulation/general/general_content_000408.jsp&mid=WC0b01 ac058002958c.

[14] See the 'Guideline on similar biological medicinal products', EMA website, available online (http://www.ema.europa.eu/docs/en_GB/document_library/Scientific_guideline/2014/10/WC500176768.pdf).

a biosimilar product as '(A) ... highly similar to the reference product notwithstanding minor differences in clinically inactive components', adding that there exist '(B) ... no clinically meaningful differences between the biological product and the reference product in terms of the safety, purity, and potency of the product'.[15]

As regards interchangeability between originator products and biosimilars, the Act says that the interchangeable product must meet all the same requirements as a reference product and in addition have the same route of administration, dosage form and strength as the reference product.[16] In many states in the US, an interchangeable may be substituted for the reference product without the intervention of the healthcare provider who prescribed the reference product, as this is governed by state pharmacy laws. The US FDA states in this respect: 'Once a biosimilar has been approved by FDA, patients and healthcare providers can be assured of the safety and effectiveness of the biosimilar, just as they would for the reference product.'[17]

The FDA's definition of interchangeability can create two kinds of biosimilars interchangeability, one at the pharmacy level, and others at the healthcare level—the clinics or hospitals where most biologics are administered. As the bulk of biologics are not bought at the pharmacy, the real battle over interchangeability is at the level of doctors, hospitals and clinics.

There are no fundamental differences between the EU and US guidelines concerning the non-clinical and clinical testing strategies. However, extrapolating immunogenicity data from

15 S.J. Lemery, F.J. Esteva and M. Weise, 'Biosimilars: Here and Now', *ASCO Educational Book*, vol. 36, 2016, pp. e151–e157 (https://ascopubs.org/doi/full/10.1200/EDBK_155954).

16 See the US FDA FAQ on 'Prescribing Biosimilar Products', available online (https://www.fda.gov/media/108103/download).

17 See a more elaborate US FDA FAQ on 'Prescribing Biosimilar and Interchangeable Products' (https://www.fda.gov/Drugs/DevelopmentApprovalProcess/HowDrugsareDevelopedandApproved/ApprovalApplications/TherapeuticBiologicApplications/Biosimilars/ucm580430.htm#sub).

one indication to another is allowed in the US but not in the EU. The European Commission issued a directive in 2012 requiring biological products to be identified by brand name and not by International Non-proprietary Name (INN). However, the US FDA is less precise in this context, saying only that the naming and labelling of the drug should facilitate decision-making by the prescribing healthcare professional.[18]

[18] Tobias Blank, 'Safety and Toxicity of Biosimilars—EU versus US regulation', *Generics and Biosimilars Initiative Journal*, vol. 2, no. 3 (2013), pp. 144–50 (doi: 10.5639/ gabij.2013.0203.039).

8. Biosimilars: The Struggle Over Regulatory Requirements

AMIT SENGUPTA

The key issue in discussing the regulatory requirements of biosimilars is the value of comparative clinical trials to show clinical equivalence, once a high degree of physical, chemical and biological structural similarity is established. The comparison[1] of quality characteristics between the biosimilar and the reference product will always show differences. It is further argued that there are many reasons to question the usefulness of comparative pharmacokinetic trials.

> The assays to determine product levels are often too imprecise; the relation between pharmacokinetic parameters and clinical effect of biologics is unclear; the dose-response curve of therapeutic proteins is often bell-shaped (meaning that widely differing protein levels have the same clinical effect); and the acceptance range for pharmacokinetics parameters between biosimilar and reference product are difficult or impossible to predefine and justify ... Dropping the obligation to do the comparability exercise will make it easier to develop more

[1] Sengupta, 'People's Health Movement and Third World Network Submission', UN Secretary General's High Level Plan on Access to Medicines.

complex biosimilars, such as monoclonal antibodies (mAbs) and vaccines.[2]

Advances in analytical methods today with robust non-clinical data should reduce the need for extensive clinical comparison.[3]

The role of regulatory agencies is also critical in the uptake of biosimilars in clinical practice. In the EU, different countries have differing approaches to the issue of interchangeability between biologics and biosimilars. Most EU member states do not explicitly authorize the substitution of biologicals from different manufacturers, and a number have gone as far as banning this practice.[4] However, Norway has emerged as a leader in the introduction of biosimilars in the EU, led by Dr Steinar Madsen of the Norwegian Medicines Agency.

Europe saw the approval of Omnitrope, its first biosimilar, in 2006. Shortly thereafter came the rise of what Madsen referred to as the 'biosimilar resistance'. EU countries encountered numerous claims that biosimilars were inferior products and, therefore, that 'switching' (that is, interchangeability between higher-cost biologics and lower-cost biosimilars) should not be permitted. However, Norway encouraged switching and the results were often

[2] H. Schellekens and E. Moors, 'Clinical Comparability and European Biosimilar Regulations', *Nature Biotechnology*, vol. 28, pp. 28–31; see also F.X. Frapaise, 'The End of Phase 3 Clinical Trials in Biosimilars Development?', *Bio Drugs*, August 2018.

[3] H. Schellekens et al., 'Safety and Efficacy of Biosimilars in Oncology', *The Lancet*, vol. 17, no. 11 (November 11, 2016), pp. E502–E509 (http://www.thelancet.com/pdfs/journals/lanonc/PIIS1470-2045(16)30374-6.pdf); also see Christopher Webster and Gillian Woollett, 'A Global Reference Comparator For Biosimilar Development', *BioDrugs*, August 2017 (https://www.ncbi.nlm.nih.gov/pubmed/28526943).

[4] 'Biosimilars and interchangeability', Generics and Biosimilars Initiative, November 13, 2015 (http://www.gabionline.net/Biosimilars/Research/Biosimilars-and-interchangeability).

dramatic. In Norway the biosimilar infliximab (Remsima) has a 92.9% market share (April 2016). Other Scandinavian countries have followed suit; in Denmark, the biosimilar of infliximab has 96% of the market, and in Finland 88%. In the absence of similar strategies in Sweden, biosimilars account for just 33.5% of the market.[5]

Likewise, in the US, a number of states have passed legislation that requires a biosimilar to be deemed to be interchangeable by the FDA, before a pharmacist can automatically substitute a biosimilar for a biologic. No interchangeable biosimilars have been approved in the US as yet.[6]

In 2015, the Australian regulatory authorities made the world's first recommendation to allow clinicians and pharmacists the option of substituting expensive biologic medicines at the chemist's if there is a cheaper replacement or biosimilar available that has been determined by experts to be a safe, equally effective treatment. The recommendation does not require that pharmacists notify physicians or patients of a substitution, nor does it specify that pharmacists must keep a log of the substitution.[7]

How biosimilars are named also has an impact on the willingness of physicians to switch between branded biologics and biosimilars. In the case of small-molecule drugs, generic equivalents are given the same international non-proprietary name (INN) as the innovator drugs. But there is no uniformity regarding this across various regulatory regimes for biological products.

The WHO's INN Expert Group has proposed the use of a biological qualifier (BQ), separate from the INN scheme, to

[5] Welch, 'The Norwegian Biosimilar Phenomenon'.

[6] Zachary Brennan, 'IMS: Biosimilars could save up to $110B in EU, US through 2020', *Regulatory Focus*, March 29, 2016 (https://www.raps.org/regulatory-focus%E2%84%A2/news-articles/2016/3/ims-biosimilars-could-save-up-to-$110b-in-eu,-us-through-2020).

[7] R. Hernandez, 'Australia Allows Pharmacy-Level Substitution of Biologics', *BioPharm International*, June 24, 2015 (http://www.biopharminternational.com/australia-allows-pharmacy-level-substitution-biologics).

identify the source of a biological substance to 'enable substances to be traced in different licensing systems, whether classified as 'similar biological substances' or not.[8] Consisting of four random consonants and an optional two-digit checksum, the BQ is proposed as an identifier that follows the non-proprietary name of each biologic and biosimilar product. This recommendation is in fact contrary to the recommendation of an informal consultation in 2006 convened by WHO. This consultation recommended: 'INNs should be based, as now, on considerations of molecular characteristics and pharmacological class. No specific process should be introduced for naming biosimilars.'[9]

Biosimilar manufacturers argue that distinct names will impede the adoption of biosimilars.[10] Currently, WHO has shelved the proposal on BQs, but it could be resurrected at a later date at the behest of some WHO member states which choose to side with industry.

The resistance towards substitution of originator biologics with biosimilars, including in the medical profession, stems from the notion that given the unique characteristics of biological drugs, copies in the form of biosimilars simply will not be able to match the performance of the originator. However, some recent research seems to suggest that biosimilars appear to be as good as the originator biologics. A recent study reviewed data from nineteen studies conducted through April 2016, which compared biologic and biosimilar versions of tumour necrosis factor-alpha

[8] *International Nonproprietary Names (INN) for biological and biotechnological substances (a review)*, Geneva: WHO, 2016, available online (https://www.who.int/medicines/services/inn/BioReview2016.pdf?ua=1).

[9] See the 'WHO Informal Consultation on International Nonproprietary Names (INN) Policy for Biosimilar Products', INN Working Document, September 2006, available online (https://www.who.int/medicines/services/inn/BiosimilarsINN_Report.pdf).

[10] S. Li and I. Royzman, 'Final WHO Biosimilar Naming Proposal Resembles FDA Approach', *Biologics Blog*, February 3, 2016 (https://www.biologicsblog.com/final-who-biosimilars-naming-proposal-resembles-fda-approach/).

(TNF-α) inhibitors. These treatments suppress the over-activity of the immune system in rheumatoid arthritis, inflammatory bowel disease (such as Crohn's disease) and psoriasis. They include well-known biologics—Amgen's Enbrel, AbbVie's Humira, and Johnson & Johnson's Remicade. The findings, published in the *Annals of Internal Medicine*, suggest that the biosimilar forms of TNF-α inhibitors are just as safe and effective as their biologic counterparts.[11]

THE WAY FORWARD: THE POTENTIAL ROLE OF BIOLOGICAL DRUGS

The analysis of the ecosystem that informs access to biological drugs, including biosimilars, leads us to the following conclusions and recommendations:

- The potential role of biological drugs in promoting real therapeutic advances needs a deeper analysis. However, current evidence suggests that they will play an increasingly major role in the future in advancing therapeutic outcomes for several autoimmune and degenerative diseases and in cancer treatment.
- Biological drugs are extremely expensive. Their high prices are a reflection of not only the complex production process, but also protected monopolies in the biotech sector. Further, unlike in the case of small-molecule drugs (SMDs), the anticipated drop in prices after introduction of biosimilars is conventionally pegged at only around 30%. There are no clear technical reasons why price drops cannot be much sharper.
- Regulatory barriers (i.e. onerous requirements for regulatory approval) are key factors preventing introduction of equivalent but cheaper follow-on products of same efficacy. The current

[11] S. Guzowski, 'How do Biosimilars Compare with Brand-Name Biologics?', *Drug Discovery and Development*, n.d.

regulatory regimes and the underlying WHO guidelines are not in sync with advances in the science of biological products. Insistence, by regulatory agencies and in the WHO guidelines, on head-to-head comparisons, including comparative pharmacokinetic studies, between innovator products and follow-ons is no longer justifiable. Moreover, it is possible to obviate the need for expensive and difficult-to-design clinical trials given better techniques for characterization of follow-ons, which could be combined with animal studies. Regulatory regimes and guidelines, including the WHO guidelines, need to be revised taking the above into account.

- Given monopolies enjoyed by originator biologics and their very high market prices, there appears to be little incentive available to reduce the cost of manufacture of biological products through introduction of more efficient technologies. On the other hand, the manufacturers of follow-on products appear better placed to introduce more efficient and cheaper technologies.
- Intellectual property protection, just as in the case of SMDs, promotes monopolies and prevents the early introduction of follow-on biologics. Process patents and trade secrets are major barriers to the introduction of biosimilars. In addition, the biotech industry is more aggressive in demanding data exclusivity rules. All these act as multiple layers of barriers to the early introduction of cheaper biosimilars.
- The proposed introduction of 'Biological Qualifiers' to be tagged on to INNs for biosimilars is unjustified and WHO should not pursue this proposal.
- It is necessary to harmonize rules and allow for interchangeability between innovator products and biosimilars which have received regulatory approval. This would make the uptake of biosimilars in clinical practice easier.

Section 3

HEALTH FOR ALL

1. Deconstructing Dominant Paradigms and Envisioning an Alternative in Health

INDRANIL

It was a sultry September afternoon in 2018, the day before the Third National Health Assembly at Rabindra Bhavan in Raipur. Amid the usual chaotic activity just before a major national event, Amit and I passed each other in front of the stage. We paused to look at Dr Ajay Khare's photo as it was mounted on the backdrop. We exchanged a glance, sighed and moved on to attend to the mundane. It was Amit's idea to have the stage of the assembly named after our beloved comrade Dr Ajay Khare. No one could have imagined that it would be Amit's last NHA.

As we come to terms with Amit's sudden death and the void it has left in our lives and movements, can we sketch a portrait of his intellectual journey? Many of his best contributions were anonymous, writing and other work done for the various movements he was part of. He took every writing project seriously, whether it was for a renowned journal on public health, a booklet to demystify complex developments for activists working on the ground, or the volumes of the People's Health Movement's great work—the *Global Health Watch* (*GHW*).[1]

Amit took sides without a qualm, and with pride and purpose. He exposed the neoliberal design to privatize public systems, stood by the working class in their struggle for labour rights, and fought

[1] *Global Health Watch*, vol. 5 (https://www.ghwatch.org/node/45529).

for health rights; his arguments backed by evidence and his passion backed by conviction. The rigour of his mind and the courage of his positions opened young minds to a deeper understanding of the intricacies of global health. He always stood by young people, encouraged them to take on new challenges, and ensured that they had their turn at leadership positions. He did not hesitate to reach beyond organizational structures to ensure that new energy was represented in the movement, while staying out of the limelight himself. He never gave up on us. When our written work was not handed in on time, or was of inadequate quality, he would quickly transform it into readable material.

Amit was not a great fan of academicians sitting in ivory towers. He wanted to break the myth that knowledge can be produced only in universities and institutions; or that it is confined to classrooms, books and journals. He devoted his life to building an alternative way of creating scholarship—by staying deeply rooted in people's struggles, learning from the lives and experiences of people, and linking these lessons to developments taking place around the world. The *GHW* remains brilliant testimony to his kind of intellect and scholarship. Its purpose has been to develop an alternative to the dominant health discourse, with the collective taking precedence over the individual.

This section on health includes six papers by Amit. His intellectual outlook was greatly influenced by the Marxist concept of political economy as he dealt with complex issues of international health politics. His work on health systems and international health deciphers the links between medical science as a human activity, and the particular characteristics of a society in which it is produced.

The paper 'Health in the Age of Globalization'[2] traces the economic and political developments associated with the rise of neoliberalism, and demonstrates how structural adjustment

[2] Amit Sengupta, 'Health in the Age of Globalization', *Social Scientist*, vol. 31, no 11–12 (2013), pp. 66–85. See Chapter 2 in this section.

programmes (SAPs)—adopted and promoted at the behest of the International Monetary Fund (IMF) and/or the World Bank (WB)—led to sharp increases in destitution and inequality. One of the casualties has been public health, and Amit clearly brings out the inherent contradiction between the 'principal tenets of public health and neoliberal economic theory'.

The neoliberal health-sector reforms had two key elements: macroeconomic stabilization policies and SAPs. Macroeconomic stabilization essentially means that the government must reduce its deficit to allow the market to work freely, so that prices are determined by market forces. The understanding is that if the government borrows and invests, it creates barriers to private investment ('crowding out'). A series of policies prescribed by the IMF included reduction in government deficit by cutting back public investment; liberalization of trade by reducing tariffs and taxes on import and export; withdrawal of subsidized provision of goods and services from a wide range of sectors, including healthcare, so that any restrictions on the free movement of prices and smooth functioning of the market are removed.

SAPs are sector-specific reforms intended to infuse market principles in areas where the state has a considerable presence, through measures like user charges, contracting out of services, shifting from direct provisioning to insurance-like mechanisms, and injecting market principles into the functioning of the public sector. The implicit understanding is that the market is superior to the state, and the latter should facilitate and steer the free flow of market resources, rather than being directly responsible for service provision. Thus, health-sector reforms brought about major shifts in the basic philosophy about the government's role in healthcare. Typically, neoliberal policies do not promote welfare, and this has translated into the progressive abolition of welfare rights related to economic security, health services and education.[3]

[3] Sengupta, 'Health in the Age of Globalization'.

At the national level, restrictions on and the restructuring of subsidies became a major issue of policy debate. Government subsidies were categorized into three groups: public goods, which deserve complete government intervention; merit goods, where the provision of subsidies would be based on societal judgment; and purely private goods. Among the sectors relevant to the second group were public health, sewerage and sanitation. The third category was that of 'non-merit' services. Here, provision is based on the principle of commercial rivalry, and the exclusion of non-payers is possible. It was emphasized that a strict reduction of subsidies in these services would be required and user fees would be introduced. Among the health services, all curative care was considered a 'non-merit' service.

What followed from this understanding of public good was the idea that an essential package of health services be publicly funded, on the basis of cost effectiveness and the positive externalities[4] of these interventions—an approach called 'selective primary-level care'. This was a marked departure from the primary healthcare (PHC) approach emerging from the Alma-Ata Declaration. Amit quotes extensively from the *World Development Report* (*WDR*) 1993, one of the most influential and widely quoted documents, to deconstruct its arguments. The *WDR* recommended that 'Poorer countries must, of necessity, define their essential packages more narrowly'.[5]

The state was to gradually withdraw from funding services other than a small group—including preventive healthcare, family planning and immunization, which are broadly of the nature of

[4] A 'positive externality' is where the benefits of consumption are not restricted to those who utilize a service. For instance, if a person spends money to kill mosquitoes in her compound, the neighbours also benefit. Or, if you treat a person with TB early, the treatment prevents further spread of the disease. In such situations, where people may prefer not to pay but expect others to pay, it becomes the obligation of the state to sustain services.

[5] 'Investing in Health', in *World Development Report, 1993*, New York: OUP, 1993, p. 57.

a 'public good'. The other integral part of the package was the promotion of private-sector participation in the health sector, especially in areas which are comparatively more profitable like super-speciality hospitals; contracting out clinical and non-clinical services, and introducing user charges for various outpatient and inpatient services for the non-poor.

Several of Amit's writings bring out the perils of neoliberal health-sector reforms for people in the global South. In his piece on universal health coverage (UHC) he points out that in the poorest thirty-seven countries, public per-capita spending on health had shrunk by half in the 1980s.[6] Public spending on health had never been high in most low-income countries. During the reforms period this declined further. Reductions in public spending on health in low- and middle-income countries were felt directly by publicly-run services. By the turn of the millennium the overall situation as regards healthcare in most low- to middle-income countries was characterized by a crumbling public health system with poor infrastructure, falling morale among health workers and diminishing resources. The private sector penetrated the vacuum created by the retreat of public services. This was especially true in the case of secondary and tertiary care services, where profit opportunities for the commercial sector were greater. A large section of people living on the border of poverty and destitution suffered considerably, facing delayed care, untimely deaths and a rise in catastrophic health expenditure.

To tide over the situation of crumbling health systems in developing countries and a rising burden of household healthcare costs, by the mid-2000s, international institutions espoused UHC. There was a renewed call for increased public spending on health to finance different types of demand-side financing

[6] D. Sanders, 'The Medicalization of Health Care and the Challenge of Health for All', Background Paper 3 for PHA I, 2005 (http://phm.phmovement.org/pipermail/phm-exchange-phmovement.org/attachments/20010826/c8862696/attachment.pdf).

mechanisms—such as health insurance—to ensure financial protection. The underlying belief appeared to be that once finances were secured, the provisioning of health services could be taken care of by the existing mix of private and public sector. The use of the term 'coverage' rather than 'care' symbolizes the move away from concerns of health-systems design and towards financing. Amit's work continuously exposed the politics behind the rhetoric of UHC. In dissecting the ideological foundations of UHC, Amit argues that the international agencies are trying to pursue a particular agenda under the guise of UHC, where the government's role is that of a financing source and a 'strategic purchaser' of care organized on market principles.

The importance of public healthcare services is not part of this narrative and the state is confined to the role of a system manager. Advocates of UHC emphasize the role played by governments in strategically 'purchasing' care to improve 'efficiency'. The *WHO Bulletin* argues: 'Countries cannot simply spend their way to UHC. To sustain progress, efficiency and accountability must be ensured. The main health financing instrument for promoting efficiency in the use of funds is purchasing, and more specifically, strategic purchasing.'[7]

Amit recognizes that UHC is a step forward to the extent that it represents an explicit recognition of three important aspects of public health: the financial catastrophe of healthcare costs, the need to go beyond a selective package of services, and the need for state intervention in healthcare as an area of market failure. UHC recognizes that 'market failures' are a feature of private healthcare that is detrimental to the interests of patients. Second, UHC recognizes that even clinical healthcare services are an area of market failure due to the uncertainty of outcomes in the services purchased, high levels of information asymmetry, the

[7] J. Kutzin, 'Anything Goes on the Path to Universal Health Coverage?', *Bulletin of the World Health Organization*, vol. 90, no. 11 (November 1, 2012), pp. 867–68.

lack of alignment of incentives for provider and patient, and also due to the nature of professional power which leads to under-consumption of healthcare.[8] The UHC discourse recognizes the need to have state interventions to ensure access to health services.

Amit was probably among the first few to recognize and put forward the inherent contradictions of UHC. UHC uses the framework of public choice theories, where the failure of individuals to exercise choice is countered by building intermediate agencies/institutions that can make the purchase on behalf of people. Thus, though UHC provides the possibility to exercise this option, i.e. of making pro-people choices, it is frequently the case that this power to make choices is used to foster monopoly, aggregating services for that purpose, so that people's choices get even more restricted than in free markets. Financial pooling through UHC could make it easier to develop comprehensive public systems; instead it is used to route public expenditure through private providers, especially towards monopoly in a time of global recession.[9]

Amit points out in several of his writings that the dominant approach of UHC is in sharp contrast to the vision of primary healthcare (PHC) envisaged in the Alma-Ata Declaration of 1978. PHC called for the building of health systems that would provide comprehensive care. These would be integrated, organized to promote equity, and driven by community needs.[10] Instead UHC envisages healthcare, as Amit puts it 'as bits and pieces of a jigsaw puzzle', connected only by a common financing pool and by the regulation of an array of private and public providers in response

[8] Kenneth J. Arrow, 'Uncertainty and the Welfare Economics of Medical Care', *The American Economic Review*, vol. 53, no. 5 (1963), pp. 941–73.

[9] Amit Sengupta, 'Universal Health Coverage: Beyond Rhetoric', Occasional Paper No. 20, Municipal Services Project, IDRC, November 2013 (https://www.municipalservicesproject.org/sites/municipalservicesproject.org/files/publications/OccasionalPaper20_Sengupta_Universal_Health_Coverage_Beyond_Rhetoric_Nov2013_0.pdf); also see Chapter 5 in this section.

[10] *Global Health Watch: An alternative world health report*, vol. 1, 2005–2006, Bangalore: People's Health Movement, 2005, p. 56.

to numerous market failures. Such a model, through a combination of pooled funds and private provision, becomes a convenient way for private capital to extract profits from public resources. With the state intervening to pool healthcare funds in one basket (the locus of collection may range from primarily tax-based to a combination of employee, employer and government contributions), new avenues for profit-making are opened up through the medium of insurance companies and health management organizations.[11]

Pooling of funds provides an effective demand (i.e., purchasing power) for the healthcare industry in settings where most people live in extreme poverty. It also opens up a new and lucrative private market: the administration of health insurance funds which introduces a new layer of competition to the system. Not only do public and private service providers compete, we also see competition between public and private insurance plans. Furthermore, private companies are offered a series of advantages in order to break the 'monopoly' of public institutions.[12]

The roots of such a design may be traced back to the 'Medicaid' scheme in the US, introduced during the 1960s, where the government provided subsidies to enrol the poor into private health insurance schemes. Some early initiatives in the late 1990s and early 2000s—especially in Latin America where reforms were based on public-funded health insurance schemes—shaped the UHC agenda across the globe. Mechanisms adopted in Chile, Colombia and Mexico, for example, shared certain key features: increases in national healthcare expenditures, both public and private; and a market logic centred on 'individual care' conceived as a 'private' good. Notably, the World Bank played a key role in consensus-building around reforms that were to become precursors to UHC, much before the WHO formally adopted it as

[11] Sengupta, 'Universal Health Coverage: Beyond Rhetoric'.

[12] A.C. Laurell, 'Can Insurance Guarantee Universal Access to Health Services?', *Social Medicine*, vol. 5, no. 3 (2010), pp. 137–38.

part of its policy plank.[13] There remains limited evidence that these schemes have been successful in improving financial protection and bringing about health system efficiency.

Amit points out that developing countries' experiences with health insurance and private provisioning have been ineffective in improving financial protection, quality of care, equity or efficiency. He argues that such strategies have disastrous consequences for people's health while destroying the institutional scaffolding of public and collective health.

India has witnessed a plethora of public-funded health insurance schemes introduced both at the national and state level.

The consequences of private sector-led growth are well documented, both in India and around the world. A large number of studies on state (or public) funded insurance in India, and on the centrally-funded Rashtriya Swasthya Bima Yojana suggest that cashless insurance mechanisms fail to reduce out-of-pocket expenses.[14] The experience of the OECD group of developed countries shows that the cost of care is increasing faster than growth of GDP, as every day a larger share of resources is invested to finance healthcare while entitlements get gradually curbed. Global experience suggests that most of the developing countries do not have the capacity or the willingness to regulate the private health sector and especially corporate hospitals, a point repeatedly emphasized by Amit.

[13] J. Kutzin, 'Towards Universal Health Care Coverage: Health, nutrition and population', Discussion Paper, Washington, DC: World Bank, July 2000.

[14] S. Selvaraj and A.K. Karan, 'Why Publicly-Financed Health Insurance Schemes are Ineffective in Providing Financial Risk Protection', *Economic and Political Weekly*, vol. 47, no. 11 (2012), pp. 61–68. A. Ranjan, P. Dixit, I. Mukhopadhyay and T. Sundararaman, 'Effectiveness of Government Strategies for Financial Protection Against Costs of Hospitalization Care in India', *BMC Public Health*, vol. 18, 2018, p. 501 (online ISSN: 1471–2458). S. Nandi, H. Schneider and S. Garg, 'Assessing Geographical Inequity in Availability of Hospital Services Under the State-Funded Universal Health Insurance Scheme in Chhattisgarh State, India, Using a Composite Vulnerability Index', *Global Health Action*, vol. 11, no. 1 (November 2018).

The private sector is highly amenable to induced demand for unnecessary provisioning of services, the drive towards more technology, intensive and over-emphasis on diagnostics, and, above all, high cost of care. One of the reasons why the private sector needs to employ such unethical practices is the failure to achieve economies of scale for the investments made on capital-intensive equipment and diagnostics. One of the ways to achieve economies of scale is to plan on an epidemiological basis and develop systemic norms of cooperation among providers, so that they share the load and ensure a continuum of care. Public-owned-and-managed district health systems with clear referral links are the main feasible approach by which many nations have achieved this goal. But if the reliance is solely on a demand-side financing of private providers, then this possibility is lost.

Amit was an eternal optimist and believed strongly that a more caring world is possible. He brought his optimism to bear on documenting pockets of resistance and alternatives to neoliberal design. In the piece titled 'Creating, Reclaiming, Defending Non-Commercialized Alternatives in the Health Sector in Asia' he attempts to map out some of the important experiments in the public domain, initiatives which are sustainable and have advanced health equity. The alternatives include large national initiatives as well as experiments conducted by non-government actors in the areas of comprehensive primary care, secondary hospitalization care and specific aspects of service delivery.

In calling to strengthen the public system as an alternative to profit-oriented market-based healthcare delivery, Amit asks that the public system be re-imagined as one which attempts to provide the best services possible to all, while addressing the special needs of those most vulnerable. Such a system can only be built, he argues, by keeping popular needs at the centre, with people's participation in planning and implementation—a system which is accountable to people. For the public sector, it cannot be business as usual—it has to reform, and do so on a theoretical foundation completely different from what was pushed under the New Public

Management and Health Sector Reform of the 1990s. The change of emphasis from reform to strengthening health systems represents this, in part, but it is a concept that has to be built on.

Amit worked tirelessly to build global evidences, through his writings, including those in *GHW*, to suggest that public-private partnerships (PPP) have been either unsuccessful or have brought disastrous consequences to people and health systems. Several national governments and local bodies have rolled back PPPs and de-privatized public systems, withdrawn user charges and reclaimed public spaces. These initiatives have come through mass movements where citizens and workers affected by the corporatization and privatization of hospitals have come together to halt PPPs or de-privatize services. It is important to build strong people's movements, defend and reclaim public systems and make them pro-people.

However, the battle to rebuild the public sector with a PHC approach cannot be fought in isolation. In the current context of neoliberalism, the possibilities of rejuvenating government health services are bleak. Under the present regime, where the exploitation of labour is taking place in highly advanced and pervasive ways, the state still plays its role in generating demand. But only in a manner which doesn't interfere with the process of production or price setting. That is why artificial means of demand generation like cash transfer, voucher schemes, insurance and other market guarantee schemes are promoted; which allow the market to operate freely and plunder people's savings. This is why healthcare, food and nutrition, and water services, are packaged, as the epitaph of universal and comprehensive public provisioning is being written in unprecedented haste. We should continue to fight the battle to uproot the basic structures of capitalist exploitation with passion and rigour—a cause Amit devoted his life to. We must show the same spirit Amit demonstrated throughout his life.

Lal salaam, dear comrade!

2. Health in the Age of Globalization

AMIT SENGUPTA

The advent of neoliberal economic policies has had a severe impact on the distribution of resources and wealth, and on various other aspects of collective life—as evidenced by increasing health inequities. The following paper, from 2003, traces the economic and political developments associated with the rise of neoliberalism and demonstrates how the structural adjustment programme, adopted and promoted at the behest of the IMF/World Bank, brought about a sharp rise in destitution and inequalities. One of the casualties has been public health, and Amit clearly brings out the inherent contradiction between the 'principal tenets of public health and neoliberal economic theory'. The paper was written in the aftermath of the formation of the People's Health Movement (PHM) at Dhaka. The People's Health Charter was formulated as an alternative vision of Health for All.

Globalization is not a new phenomenon, neither is it necessarily an evil force. However, what we see today in the garb of globalization is something that is unique and unprecedented. Notwithstanding the rhetoric, globalization has come to mean the legitimation of neo-imperialist loot. Globalization, as practised today, does not encourage a free flow of goods, ideas and people across the globe. On the contrary it perpetuates and increases monopoly control over resources, technology, knowledge and capital. The tools used are multinational corporations and finance capital, aided by the institutions of globalization—the International Monetary

Fund (IMF) and the World Bank (WB), with the World Trade Organization (WTO) functioning as the lawmaker who constantly changes the rules of the game to favour the rich and the powerful. We need to make a distinction between this form of globalization and true globalization—which would mean unhindered flow of technology, knowledge and resources to those corners of the globe which need them most. The globalization that we see today is global only in regard to the vastly increased ability of imperialism to interfere in governance and decision-making in sovereign nations. What we have is not interdependence, but increasing dependence on a few who control productive resources and capital.

This kind of globalization is plagued with a fundamental contradiction—in an age when restrictions on information flow and the flow of goods, services and capital are sought to be removed, there is a greater concentration of wealth and knowledge in a few hands. Such concentration is manifest in growing inequalities. More than a decade back UNICEF took note of the initial signals:

> In many countries poverty, child malnutrition and ill-health are advancing again after decades of steady retreat. And although the reasons are many and complex, overshadowing all is the fact that the governments of the developing world as a whole have now reached the point of devoting half of their total annual expenditures to the maintenance of the military and the servicing of debt.[1]

Such appeals obviously went unheeded and in the last decade of the past millennium actual per capita incomes fell in over eighty countries.[2] This is what is unique about the present phase—the fact that the consequences of current policies are being felt at an unprecedented scale. Such wide-ranging reversals of social and

[1] United Nations Children's Fund (UNICEF), *The State of the World's Children*, UN, 1990.

[2] *Human Development Report 1999*.

economic gains have never happened in the history of human civilization.

IMF/WORLD BANK-DICTATED POLICIES

The seeds of this process were sown a quarter of a century back when the International Monetary Fund introduced its infamous structural adjustment programmes (SAPs) in the poor countries of Latin America, Africa and Asia. In brief, the SAP was designed to:

- Cut government spending—this means big cuts in healthcare, education and subsidies to farmers and the poor.
- Privatization—state-owned industries and services must be sold off to private corporations. Often foreign multinationals are the buyers. Many workers lose their jobs as government industries close down. Services like transportation and power become more expensive.
- Devalue the local currency—for example, in India the rupee should be worth less and less compared to the American dollar. The WB and IMF demand this so that what the country exports is cheaper in the international market. The WB and IMF say this will increase the country's exports so it can earn foreign dollars—and pay back the loans! But farmers and local industries get less for their goods. And the prices of imports go up!
- Export more—the country should export more to pay back loans. The agricultural sector should turn to commercial farming for the market and for export, rather than food production for local consumption.
- Open the door to foreign multinational companies.
- Reduce duties and tariffs on imports—in this way foreign multinationals can more easily sell their products in a country like India. Local industries find it hard to compete with cheaper imports.

National experiences show that the SAP has been detrimental to nation-states in every region. Yet the same prescriptions were applied later to nations such as India and the results have been predictable: rising prices, inflation, rising unemployment, change in cropping patterns, loss of food security, withdrawal of subsidies from public welfare services such as public health, education and the public distribution system. These have directly and selectively affected the already 'disadvantaged' in our country. Also, there is loss of sovereignty since our Parliament can no longer make policies favouring our people but at the behest of WB/IMF.

SAP-induced policies pushed countries to debt traps underwritten by large capitalist banks and multilateral lending institutions. The IMF forced further squeezes on the financing of social services. By the mid-1980s, the Third World was already a net exporter of money, i.e. debt servicing was higher than the total inflow of loans, bilateral and multilateral aid, and foreign direct investment. The results were felt most severely in the social sectors—health, education, food security, etc. In Tanzania, for example, debt service payments are nine times the expenditure on primary healthcare and four times the expenditure on education. In Peru, per capita food intake fell by 25% between 1975 and 1985. Somalia was ravaged by a famine that was entirely a result of IMF-dictated policies (and not civil war and drought as claimed by foreign 'experts').[3] Meanwhile, cheap wheat from the US and beef and dairy products from the European Union disrupted the country's agriculture which had been dependent on indigenously grown maize and sorghum and local livestock. It is possible to go on and on in the same vein. It has been estimated that at least six million children under five years of age have died each year since 1982 in Africa, Asia and Latin America, because of the SAPs. The magical words of globalization, privatization and liberalization have

[3] Evelyn Hong, 'Globalisation and the Impact on Health: A Third World view', Third World Network, for the Peoples Health Assembly, 2000.

led to absolute impoverishment of millions in the Third World.

WB and IMF-dictated policies also placed primacy on the necessity to be 'competitive' in the global market. In order to do so, poor countries were issued prescriptions to provide a 'safety net'—not comprehensive social security cover but a 'minimum' of facilities and services that could contain social unrest and political instability. Poverty figures in India, for example, indicate that rural poverty has increased in the 'reform' years while at the same time the government exults over benefits of reforms that have accrued to a small affluent section.[4] Clearly policy-making today targets this small section and ignores 80% of the population.

PUBLIC HEALTH—A CASUALTY

Public health is an obvious casualty of this process. There is a clear contradiction between the principal tenets of public health and the neoliberal economic theory that permeates policy-making today. The former posits that public health is a 'public good', i.e. its benefits cannot be individually appropriated or computed, but have to be seen in the context of benefits that accrue to the public. Thus, public health outcomes are shared, and their accumulation leads to better living conditions. Such goods never mechanically translate into visible economic determinants, viz. income levels or rates of economic growth. For example, per capita income in Kerala is not very high.[5] Many Indian states have per capita incomes higher than Kerala, but in terms of public health parameters it is way ahead of other Indian states. Its health achievements are comparable to developed countries. The infant mortality rate in Kerala is less than a third of any other large state in the country.

[4] Abhijit Sen, paper presented at the International Seminar on 'Understanding Socio-economic Changes through National Surveys', organized by the National Sample Survey Organisation, May 12–13, 2001, New Delhi.

[5] *Handbook of Statistics of Indian Economy 2003*, Reserve Bank of India, available online (https://www.rbi.org.in/Scripts/AnnualPublications.aspx?-head=Handbook+of+Statistics+on+Indian+Economy).

But neoliberal economic policies are loath to even acknowledge such benefits. The current economic policies would rather view health as a private good accessed via the market. SAP-induced economic policies had the following specific consequences for the health sector:

1. Cuts in welfare investment, leading to the gradual dismantling of public health services.
2. Introduction of service charges in public institutions, making their services inaccessible to the poor.
3. Handing over the responsibility of health service to the private sector and undermining the rationality of public health. The private sector on the other hand focused only on curative care.
4. The voluntary sector, which also stepped in to provide health services, is forced to concentrate on and prioritize only those areas where international aid is made available—like AIDS, population control, etc.

A heavily influential document in this context is the Bank's *World Development Report* 1993, titled 'Investing in Health'. This document represents the Bank's major foray into health policy formulation. Today, the Bank is the decisive voice in this regard, and organizations such as the WHO and UNICEF have been reduced to playing the role of 'drum beaters' of the Bank. As a Bank economist candidly reflected: 'Policy lending is where the bank really has power—I mean brute force. When countries really have their backs against the wall, they can be pushed into reforming things at a broad policy level (which) normally, in the context of projects, they can't. The health sector can be caught up in this issue of conditionality.'[6]

In almost every developing country, these prescriptions have been avidly lapped up. In the Philippines, health expenditure fell

[6] *World Development Report 1993.*

from 3.45% of GDP in 1985 to 2% in 1993; and in Mexico from 4.7% of GDP to 2.7% in the 1980s. Even developing countries with a strong tradition of providing comprehensive welfare benefits to their people were not spared (with the exception of Cuba). In China, health expenditure is reported to have fallen to 1% of GDP and 1.5 million TB cases are believed to have been left untreated since the country introduced mechanisms for cost recovery.[7] In Vietnam the number of villages with clinics and maternity centres fell from 93.1% to 75%.[8]

The WHO, long a silent spectator to the process whereby the Bank usurped its functions, attempted to make amends by setting up a Commission on Macroeconomics and Health. The Commission's Report was unveiled by Gro Brundlandt[9]—joined by other world-renowned figures—in December 2001.[10] Despite this, what we have before us, as a result of this exercise, is an unabashed attempt by the WHO to speak the language of the Bank. The ideological takeover of the WHO is, thus, complete. In its introduction the Report says, 'With globalization on trial as never before, the world must succeed in achieving its solemn commitments to reduce poverty and improve health.' In other words, poverty reduction and health improvement are goals that need to be achieved in order to rescue globalization from the dock! Clearly, the Report starts from the premise that healthcare can be broken down to a few 'magic bullets' appropriately delivered at a target. It is a premise that is the exact opposite of the essential tenets of public health.

The Report is also designed to set the ground rules for

[7] Hong, 'Globalisation and the Impact on Health'.

[8] Ibid.

[9] Three-term prime minister of Norway and director-general of the WHO from 1998 to 2003.

[10] *Macroeconomics and Health: Investing in Health for Economic Development*, Executive summary/report of the Commission on Macroeconomics and Health, World Health Organization, 2001.

developing countries wanting to access funds from donors (read rich developed countries). In an unabashed defence of donor-driven policies the Report says: 'Where countries are not willing to make a serious effort, though, or where funding is misused, prudence and credibility require that large-scale funding should not be provided. Even here, though, the record shows that donor assistance can do much to help, by building local capacity and through the involvement of civil society and NGOs.' The key message is clear: listen to donors, or else they will bypass sovereign governments and target NGOs and private institutions to drive their agenda through.

The Report's signature tune is best summed up by its comments on the pharmaceutical industry:

> The corporate principles that have spurred recent and highly laudable programmes of drug donations and price discounts need to be generalized ... Industry is ready, in our estimation, for such a commitment, enabling access of the poor to essential medicines, both through differential pricing and licensing their products to generics producers ... At the same time, it is vital to ensure that increased access for the poor does not undermine the stimulus to future innovation that derives from the system of intellectual property rights.

This reflects the particularly sympathetic attitude of the Commission on Macroeconomic Health towards the pharmaceutical industry, ignoring the mounting discontent against their inhuman denial of treatment to millions under the intellectual property system. Clearly, the Washington Consensus now extends to Geneva!

HEALTH-SECTOR REFORM IN INDIA

India embarked on its present path of economic liberalization relatively late, under instructions from the Bank and IMF. The infamous Manmohan Singh Budget of 1991 set the events in motion. The immediate fallout was a savage cut in budgetary support to the health sector. The cuts were severe in the first two years of the reform process, followed by some restoration in the following years. Between 1990–91 and 1993–94, there was a fall, in real terms, of expenditure on healthcare both for the Centre and the states, though it was much more pronounced in the case of the states. In this period there was a compression of total developmental expenditure of state governments.

Thus, in real terms, expenditure for state governments plummeted in 1991–92 and 1992–93, and just about touched the level of 1990–91 in 1993–94. The squeeze on the resources of states was distributed in a fairly secular fashion over expenditures incurred under all developmental heads. Healthcare was a major casualty, as the share of states constitutes a major portion of expenditure. A similar kind of squeeze in resource allocation was felt in all programmes, largely financed by the states, including water supply and sanitation. In contrast, even in the worst 'resource crunch' years, the almost exclusively centrally-funded family planning programme fared much better.

Expenditure patterns on healthcare are grossly skewed in favour of urban areas. Expenditure cuts further distort this picture with the axe on investment falling first on rural health services. As a result of this rollback of state support to healthcare, the first major casualty in infrastructure development has been the rural health sector. There has been a perceptible slowing down in infrastructure creation in rural areas.

Compression of funds available with states has had a number of far-reaching effects. Faced with limited funds, while salaries still require to be maintained at previous levels, the burden of cutbacks is increasingly placed on supplies and materials and reduced share of health in state budgets.[11] In reaction to this, desperate

[11] *National Health Policy 2002*, New Delhi: Ministry of Health and Family

Figure 3.2.1: Public expenditure on health as percentage of total health expenditure (selected countries)

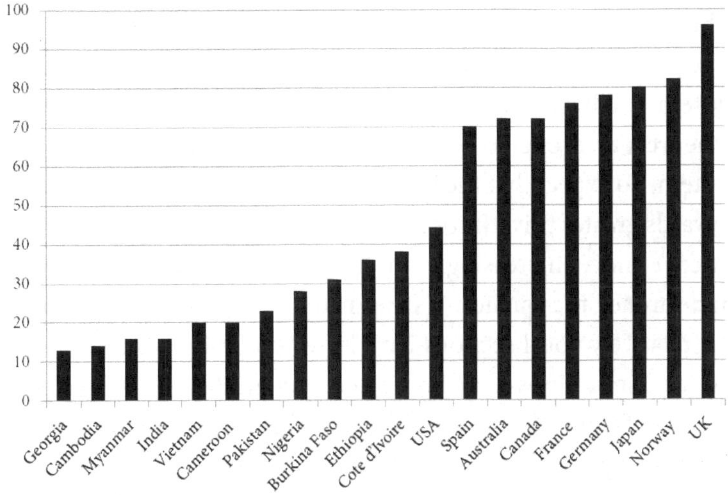

Source: WHO, 2000.

state governments are queuing up in front of the WB to receive Bank-aided projects. This is proving even more disastrous as these projects impose strict conditionalities like cost recovery.

COST RECOVERY AND HEALTH EXPENDITURE

Cost recovery is the lynchpin of Bank-sponsored policies in the country, in spite of irrefutable evidence that such schemes, without fail, result in the exclusion of the poorest. The case for user fees deploys the particularly seductive argument of equity. Seen in the abstract it appears to make sense that those who can pay should, and the benefits would be shared by those who cannot. Unfortunately, user fees do not work in this manner in the real world. The concept of user fees, rather, is used to legitimize the withdrawal of the state. Let us remember that the user fee argument is being forwarded in a situation where public funding of healthcare expenditure has fallen from 22% in the early 1990s to 16% in 2000.

Welfare, Government of India, 2002.

The concept of user fees works on the principle of cross subsidization—some pay more to subsidize expenditure for those who pay less or nothing. For the model to be successful there is an assumption that a majority of users are part of the public-funded system. Public facilities are utilized by those who do not have any other recourse, or a powerful elite who can milk the public-funded system. To expect that the latter will pay is unrealistic. As we move towards greater privatization, those who can pay (even to a limited extent) move increasingly to the private sector. This further undermines the quality of care in the public-funded system, as the relatively vocal sections have lesser stakes in its survival. Any mechanism of cross subsidy requires an arbiter who consciously works in favour of the poor. To believe that the present Indian state is going to play this role is to delude ourselves.

RESURGENCE OF COMMUNICABLE DISEASES

Globalization also leads to the transnationalization of risks to public health as evident in the global resurgence of communicable diseases. Every phase of human civilization that has seen a rapid expansion in exchange of populations across national borders has been characterized by a spread of communicable diseases. The early settlers in America, who came from Europe, carried with them small pox and measles that decimated the indigenous population of Native Americans. Plague travelled from the Orient to Europe in the Middle Ages, often killing more than a quarter of the population of cities in Europe (like the plague epidemic in London in the fifteenth century). This is a natural consequence of the exposure of local populations to exotic diseases, to which they have little or no natural immunity.

Today, what incubates in a tropical rainforest can emerge in a temperate suburb in affluent Europe, and likewise what festers in a metropolitan ghetto of the global North can re-emerge in a sleepy village in Asia—within weeks or days. However, the most badly affected are the poorest people in developing countries, because their immunity is compromised by under-nutrition and because they have little or no access to health facilities. In the case of AIDS the combination of global mobility and cuts in health facilities has been lethal for many developing countries—a whole generation has been ravaged by the disease in Africa, and now in Asia. AIDS emerged as an epidemic in the US, but it was Africa that felt the real force of its wrath. In the 1960s scientists were exulting over the possible conquest to be achieved over communicable diseases. Forty years later a whole new scenario is unfolding. AIDS is its most acute manifestation. We also have the resurgence of cholera, yellow fever and malaria in Sub-Saharan Africa, malaria and dengue in South America, multi-drug resistant TB, plague, dengue and malaria in India. We see the emergence of exotic viral diseases, like those caused by the Ebola and the Hanta virus.

ENVIRONMENTAL DEGRADATION AND UNHEALTHY LIFESTYLES

While unleashing new horrors in the form of disease, globalization has also compromised people's ability to combat them. The WTO agreement on patents (Trade-Related Intellectual Property Rights—TRIPS) has sanctified monopoly rent incomes for pharmaceutical MNCs, huge escalation of medicine prices and denial of equal access to medicines. Globalization has also set in motion a variety of unsafe and hazardous practices. The present global division of labour has led to the dumping of hazardous waste and the wholesale relocation of hazardous industries to developing countries.

The consumerist culture that is encouraged by corporate-led globalization has also put the long-term sustainability of the planet in jeopardy. Alongside this, corporates continue to pillage the biological resources of the globe, leading to the disappearance of a number of species of plants and animals. This has disrupted the ecology of the land and the sea. If the trend continues, the globe as we know it, may cease to exist a hundred years from now.

The same consumerist culture has led to unhealthy lifestyles—sedentary habits, preference for unhealthy 'junk foods', over-indulgence in addictions like tobacco and alcohol, etc. Globalization encourages trade in unhealthy products—alcohol, tobacco, baby foods. As a consequence people in the Third World are suffering from the ill effects of 'development' superimposed on the problems of underdevelopment.

REVERSING THE TREND: TOWARDS ALTERNATIVE POLICIES

Can these trends be reversed? I sincerely believe that they can. Primarily because of the contradiction that I talked about at the beginning of the paper. Precisely because we are in an age when communications and exchange is so much easier, the contradiction can be resolved only if we move towards true globalization. Globalization of ideas, knowledge and resources that are controlled by a majority, for the majority. Only this can counter what is being called globalization today, but is in essence its antithesis.

3. Global Governance of Health: A Minefield of Contradictions and Sectional Interests

AMIT SENGUPTA

Since its inception, the People's Health Movement has been the strongest voice in raising critical concerns about the role of multilateral, bilateral and private philanthropy in shaping the global health policy agenda. WHO Watch and Global Health Watch have grown to become powerful tools. As the editor of the last three volumes of the GHW, *Amit was at the forefront in developing a rigorous critique of international institutions, bringing out the conflicts of interest and contradictions in their functioning, scrutinizing their role in the diffusion of medical technology, as also their response to public health emergencies and in addressing the health concerns of billions of people in the global South. In this piece, Amit traces the changes globalization has brought to global health governance.*

The almost universal application of policies that promote integration of the globe through trade in goods and services and liberalized flow of finances—loosely termed 'globalization'—has also necessitated the development of fairly elaborate global structures of governance. In the health sector this manifests itself as global health governance, i.e. global structures that attempt to govern issues related to health that transcend national boundaries.

Coordination and cooperation between countries on matters

of global health (or international health, as it was then known) have existed since long in the past. Some of the earliest concerns had to do with those related to the spread of infectious diseases. Over a period, this led to the adoption of some of the first international regulations related to health, such as quarantine measures and mandatory norms on vaccination.

In earlier centuries, international regulations related to health were structured to protect the interests of the colonizing powers. When the era of colonization became history, international regulations were structured in a more egalitarian framework. In the health sector, this was reflected in 1948 with the birth of the WHO and its stewardship of global health policies. It was also reflected in the International Labour Organization (ILO), promoting global standards on occupational safety and health protection. The General Agreement on Tariffs and Trade (GATT), adopted in 1947, and the International Sanitary Regulations (adopted by the WHO in 1951 as the International Health Regulations) included provisions aimed at balancing the interests of health and trade. The WHO promoted global efforts to improve health in developing countries, through such strategies as promoting the right to health, Health for All, the Essential Drugs List, and the International Code on the Marketing of Breast Milk Substitutes.

In recent decades, issues under the purview of global health have moved far beyond the physical spread of diseases. Since the early 1980s, the global architecture of governance, trade and economics has come to be informed by globalization, and consequently national decision-making and national policies are often subject to global influences. This is true in the health sector as well,[1] and the advent of globalization marks a shift in institutions and structures that govern health at a global level.

The use of the term global instead of international, when

[1] D. Woodward, N. Drager, R. Beaglehole and D. Lipson, 'Globalization and Health: A framework for analysis and action', *Bulletin of the World Health Organization*, vol. 79, no. 9 (2001), pp. 875–81.

discussing issues of health that go beyond national boundaries, is in itself significant. International health held the connotation that national concerns and policies formed the bedrock of policies about supranational issues, while global health appears to start from the premise that global issues largely supersede national policies, concerns and priorities.

It is possible to identify four major developments in the last three decades that have had a profound impact on the structures and processes of global health governance. The first is the emergence of the World Bank as a major player in the arena of health governance in the 1980s, which has been discussed extensively in the previous chapter. Second, the growing importance of global trade in international relations, and its impact on health in different situations across countries, has led to a major role for the World Trade Organization (WTO) and regional and bilateral trade agreements in global health. Third, private foundations (such as the Bill and Melinda Gates Foundation) have entered through public-private partnerships and other avenues, to become big players in global health issues. The fourth development is the demise of the WHO as the premier organization in the area of global health governance. While all four are linked, each has arisen in specific contexts that are analysed below.

THE WTO STEPS IN

The WTO agreement in 1995 replaced the General Agreement on Tariffs and Trade (GATT). The much larger scope of the WTO can be understood from the fact that when GATT was established in 1947, there were twenty-three contracting parties, and its mandate was limited to trade in goods. Today, the WTO has 153 members[2] (who account for 97% of world trade), and includes trade in goods and services and the protection of intellectual property rights.

2 'Understanding the WTO: The Organization. Members and Observers', WTO website, July 23, 2008 [cited February 21, 2011] (http://www.wto.org/english/thewto_e/whatis_e/tif_e/org6_e.htm).

The earlier trade regime under GATT had marginal impact on the health sector, while the WTO, through the TRIPS agreement and the General Agreement on Trade in Services (GATS), directly affects health governance. In addition, the acceleration of trade liberalization after the signing of the WTO also has significant impact on the broader determinants of health—viz. the negative impact on food security and livelihoods in developing countries as a consequence of the effects of the Agreement on Agriculture, which forms part of the WTO agreement.[3]

Since 1995, the WTO has become the major international forum for debate and resolution of conflicts in the area of major health-related policies or policies that have an impact on health. The WTO's ability to intervene in global health issues is of a much higher order than that of the WHO, as the WTO agreement is a binding agreement with clear commitments made by contracting parties. The WTO imposes a 'rules-based system' and adherence to these rules is exercised through a dispute settlement mechanism. The dispute settlement mechanism allows member countries to use trade sanctions to enforce rulings against member states that fail to comply with its decisions. In contrast, the WHO does not have mechanisms that can force member countries to abide by its decisions. Thus, for example, health-specific legal agreements that have been endorsed by member countries in the WHO—such as the Framework Convention on Tobacco Control or the revised International Health Regulations 2005—do not contain compulsory dispute settlement and enforcement provisions.

The governance of global trade, and its impact on health governance, now go much beyond the WTO. The failure of the WTO to accommodate the interests of all countries, and the repeated and visible collapse of ministerial negotiations, has

[3] K. Watkins and P. Fowler, *Rigged Rules and Double Standards: Trade, globalization and the fight against poverty*, Washington, DC: Oxfam International, Practical Action Publishing, November 30, 2002, available online (http://en.oxfam.ru/upload/iblock/1ca/1ca3150c5e7d8c64ba45287978f0d4df.pdf).

prompted developed countries to look for other channels to promote global trade. Consequently, regional and bilateral trade agreements are an increasingly important part of trade and health governance. From 1990 to 2007, the number of such agreements notified to the WTO increased from twenty to 159. At present, over 250 regional and bilateral trade agreements govern more than 30% of world trade. An emerging concern related to such agreements is that they can include provisions that go beyond the WTO's provisions. In many cases, these agreements do not include the flexibilities and health safeguards available under the TRIPS agreement and can impose onerous terms in other areas as well.[4] A case in point is the Indo-EU trade agreement that is at present being negotiated,[5] where several provisions being demanded of India by the EU would impose regulations requiring stricter norms of intellectual property protection. These provisions also seek to liberalize areas such as government procurement (viz. for the public distribution system and for procurement of medicines for the public health system).

GLOBAL PUBLIC-PRIVATE PARTNERSHIPS

A new family of initiatives that have a major impact on global health governance are global public-private initiatives (GPPIs). In the past two decades several hundred such initiatives have been launched, with over 100 working in the health sector alone. The genesis of these GPPIs is fairly recent, dating back to the 1990s. GPPIs came to be developed based on an understanding

4 C.M. Correa, 'Implications of Bilateral Trade Agreements on Access to Medicines', *Bulletin of the World Health Organization*, vol. 84, no. 5 (2006), pp. 399–404.

5 The thirteenth round of negotiations between India and the European Free Trade Association took place in 2013. The negotiations remain incomplete today. See the following web page of the Ministry of Commerce and Industry, Government of India: https://commerce.gov.in/PageContent.aspx?Id=62; and the Wikipedia page for 'India–European Union relations' (https://en.wikipedia.org/wiki/India–European_Union_relations).

that multilateral co-operation in the present globalized world could no longer adhere to the older principle of multilateralism that primarily involved nation-states. Global partnerships were, thus, imbued with a new meaning, that involved not just nation-states, but also other entities, including, prominently, business organizations such as pharmaceutical companies that work through the medium of the market. These new partnerships were further promoted by philanthropic foundations, largely located in the United States, such as the Rockefeller Foundation and the Bill and Melinda Gates Foundation. Partnerships with the private sector and civil society are thus held up as the way to achieve what governments and the United Nations cannot manage alone.[6]

This new approach was reflected, for example, in the call issued at the World Health Assembly in 1993[7] to mobilize and encourage the support of all partners in health development, including non-governmental organizations and institutions in the private sector, to implement national strategies for health for all.

GPPIs need to be viewed in the context of an attempt to address the obvious failure of the market to deliver services and goods where most required, i.e. to the income- and resource-poor, while at the same time staying within the boundaries of neoliberal economic policies. They address what neoliberal economists describe as 'market failures', but at the same time do not question the fundamental faith in the ability of the market to regulate the global flow of goods and services.

While there has been no systematic evaluation of the impact and viability of GPPIs in the health sector, there have been several evaluations of specific GPPIs. Based on these evaluations some major concerns are beginning to emerge. The gross under-

[6] J. Martens, 'Multistakeholder Partnerships—Future models of multilateralism? Dialogue on globalization', Occasional Paper No. 29, Friedrich Ebert Stiftung, Berlin, 2007.

[7] K. Buse and A. Waxman, 'Public-Private Partnerships: A strategy for WHO', *Bulletin of the World Health Organization*, vol. 79, no. 8 (2001), pp. 748–54.

representation of the global South in the governance arrangements of GPPIs, coupled with secretariats often being located in the North, is reminiscent of imperial approaches to public health. GPPIs are seldom integrated with the health systems of the recipient countries. As a consequence, programmes are seldom sustainable particularly after a GPPI runs its course or withdraws support. GPPIs can allow transnational corporations to exert influence over agenda-setting and political decision-making by governments. Some partnerships can distort competition, because they provide the corporations involved with an image advantage, and also support those involved in opening up markets and help them gain access to governments.[8] It is problematic for the UN to collaborate with partners whose activities contravene the UN Charter and UN norms and standards or whose activities in a particular sector are seen as detrimental. Some such instances include collaboration between the United Nations Development Programme and Shell and Coca Cola; Nestlé's involvement in the Global Compact; partnerships between UNESCO and Microsoft; and UNICEF's partnership—in 2002—with McDonald's.[9] One can also add to this the various pharmaceutical transnational corporations who achieve legitimacy by working in GPPIs even as they cause countless deaths by denying access to their patented products at affordable prices.

THE WORLD HEALTH ORGANIZATION: TIME TO RECLAIM ITS MANDATED ROLE

Another disturbing feature is that the WHO's leadership in global governance issues has been seriously compromised with the usurpation of its mandate by multiple agencies—the World Bank, the WTO, GPPIs, etc. Increasingly, there is a tendency to

[8] K. Buse, 'Governing Public-Private Infectious Disease Partnerships', *Brown Journal of World Affairs*, vol. 10, no. 2 (2004), pp. 225–42.

[9] Martens, 'Multistakeholder Partnerships—Future models of multilateralism?'.

characterize the WHO as a 'technical' agency that should concern itself only with issues related to challenges of communicable disease control and the development of biomedical norms and standards.

The WHO faces three key challenges, related to its capacity, legitimacy and resources. Its legitimacy has been seriously compromised because of its inability to secure compliance with its own decisions—which are reflected in the various resolutions passed at the World Health Assembly. Developed countries which contribute the major share of finances to the functioning of the WHO have today a cynical disregard for the ability of the WHO to shape the global governance of health. They see the member state-driven process in the WHO (where each country has one vote) as a hindrance to their attempts to shape global health governance, and prefer to rely on institutions such as the World Bank and the WTO, where they can exercise their clout with greater ease.

As with many other UN organizations, the WHO's core funding has remained static because of a virtual freeze in the contributions of member states. Its budget amounts to a tiny fraction of the health spending of high-income member states.[10] In addition, a large proportion of the WHO's expenditure (about 80%) comes in the form of conditional, extra-budgetary funds that are earmarked for specific projects by contributing countries. For example, the Bill and Melinda Gates Foundation is today one of the largest single funders of the WHO, contributing more than most member countries. The executive board of the WHO (in January 2011) discussed a paper by the organization's secretariat that talked about the crisis in the WHO's finances.[11] Today, the

[10] 'Making WHO Work Better: An advocacy agenda for civil society', discussion document produced by *Global Health Watch*, August 2006, available online (https://www.ghwatch.org/sites/www.ghwatch.org/files/Making-WHOWorkBetter.pdf).

[11] 'The Future of Financing for WHO: Report of an informal consultation convened by the Director-General, Geneva, Switzerland', WHO, Geneva,

WHO is sustained through a financing system that undermines coherent planning and which forces WHO departments and divisions to compete with each other (and other organizations) for scarce funds. The consequence of this is that health priorities are distorted and even neglected to conform with the desires of donors and the requirement to demonstrate quick results to them. The WHO is in danger of being compromised because of conflict-of-interest issues that arise out of contradictions between the constitutional mandate of the WHO and the interests of individual donors.[12]

As a consequence of the above, the WHO is inadequately equipped to reclaim its leadership role in global health governance. At the global, regional and country level, WHO offices are weak and inadequately resourced, compared to the country-based offices of other international organizations and development agencies.

NEED TO RESTRUCTURE GLOBAL HEALTH GOVERNANCE

Clearly, the global governance of health is a minefield of contradictions. It is shaped by multiple agencies and by multiple interest groups. In a globalized world this is evidently a cause for concern. While tools designed to mitigate ill health and disease are now available as never before, access to such tools is a bigger problem than ever. A nation-state-driven process, premised on principles of equity, justice and sharing, is an urgent requirement if the global governance of health is to be restructured and this problem addressed. National governments, especially from the global South, need to take the lead in rescuing global health governance from the clutches of sectional interest groups.

January 12–13, 2010.

12 'Making WHO Work Better', *Global Health Watch*.

4. The Rise of Private Medicine in South Asia

AMIT SENGUPTA

Amit and his colleagues—Indranil Mukhopadhyay, Manuj C. Weerasinghe and Arjun Karki—argue that systematic neglect coupled with chronic cuts in public investment have led to the deterioration of public services in South Asia. Healthcare services in South Asia are characterized by low public investment, high dependence on the private sector for service provisioning, lack of financial protection and out-of-pocket expenses as the principal source of health financing. Only Sub-Saharan Africa has worse public health indicators than those seen in South Asia (with the exception of Sri Lanka), in terms of life expectancy, malnutrition, and infant and child mortality rates.[1] *South Asia is the only region in the world where health expenditure fell between 2000 and 2006.*[2] *This paper examines the evidence regarding the growth and characteristics of the private health sector in South Asia, the drivers of its sustenance and growth, and their implications for public health outcomes.*

The majority of people in South Asia depend on private

[1] *World Health Statistics 2015*, WHO, 2015, available online (www.who.int/gho/publications/world_health_statistics/EN_WHS2015_Part2.pdf?ua=1); and V. Haté and S. Gannon, 'Public Health in South Asia: A report of the CSIS Global Health Policy Center', Center for Strategic and International Studies, 2010 (https://www.csis.org/analysis/public-health-south-asia).

[2] Haté and Gannon, 'Public Health in South Asia'.

healthcare services, and this trend is accompanied by stagnant public investment in health (Table 3.4.1).[3] Government expenditure on health as a percentage of gross domestic product (GDP) in the region is just above 1% (with the exception of Nepal)—well below the average for low- and low-middle-income countries, and significantly under the global average (4.9%). There has been a small increase in government expenditure (as a percentage of GDP) in India, a definite increase in Nepal and Pakistan, but a sharp decline in Sri Lanka. Private health expenditure accounts for about two-thirds of total health expenditure in the region, similar to trends in low- and low-middle-income countries but much higher than the global average (42.4%) (Table 3.4.1). Economic growth in the region over the last decade is the highest for all regions.[4] The rapid rise in the GDP of countries in the region and the stagnant proportion of public expenditure on healthcare (only Nepal shows a notable increase) translates into an enormous increase in private expenditure.

Out-of-pocket spending, widely acknowledged as the most regressive form of financing, accounts for well over 80% of all private expenses, indicating very low penetration of financial protection mechanisms. As a consequence, in India, for example, fifty-five million people are pushed below the poverty line as a result of healthcare expenses.[5] In Nepal an estimated one million people fall below the poverty line for similar reasons,[6] while in

[3] *World Health Statistics 2015.*

[4] 'South Asia Remains World's Fastest Growing Region, But Should be Vigilant to Fading Tailwinds', World Bank website, 2016 (https://www.worldbank.org/en/news/press-release/2016/04/09/south-asia-fastest-growing-region-world-vigilant-fading-tailwinds).

[5] *National Health Policy 2015. Draft*, Ministry of Health and Family Welfare, Government of India, 2014, available online (https://www.nhp.gov.in/sites/default/files/pdf/draft_national_health_policy_2015.pdf).

[6] *Nepal Living Standard Survey 2010–11*, Central Bureau of Statistics, National Planning Commission, Government of Nepal (http://cbs.gov.np/nada/index.php/catalog/37).

Bangladesh 7% of households spend more than 25% of monthly non-food expenditure on healthcare.[7]

Table 3.4.1: Private health expenditure (PHE) in selected countries of South Asia: 2000–2012

Country	*Govt. expenditure as % of GDP 2012 (2000)*	*PHE as % of total health expenditure 2012 (2000)*	*Out-of-pocket expenditure as % of PHE 2012 (2000)*
Bangladesh	1.1 (1.1)	68.1 (59.3)	93.0 (97.4)
India	1.2 (1.2)	69.5 (73.0)	87.2 (91.8)
Sri Lanka	1.2 (1.8)	60.9 (51.6)	83.0 (80.8)
Nepal	2.2 (1.3)	60.5 (75.4)	81.4 (91.2)
Pakistan	1.0 (0.7)	63.1 (78.3)	86.8 (81.0)
Low income	1.5 (1.3)	61.2 (62.4)	77.6 (84.7)
Low middle income	1.5 (1.3)	63.6 (66.0)	86.7 (89.1)
Upper middle income	3.4 (2.8)	43.8 (46.7)	74.2 (80.4)
Global	4.9 (4.3)	42.4 (44.5)	52.6 (52.2)

Source: WHO, Global Health Expenditure database.

A significant driver of the growth of private expenditure is the private purchase of drugs. In Nepal, in the case of acute illnesses and injuries, around two-thirds of out-of-pocket expenses are on drugs, and this share goes up to more than four-fifths in the case of chronic illnesses.[8] In Bangladesh, nearly 62% of healthcare expenditure (a major portion of which is met by out-of-pocket

[7] R.P. Rannan-Eliya, G. Kasthuri, T. Begum, A. Rahman, N. Hossain and C. Anuranga, 'Impact of Maternal and Child Health Private Expenditure on Poverty and Inequity in Bangladesh', IDRC, 2012 (https://idl-bnc-idrc.dspacedirect.org/handle/10625/53840).

[8] *Overview of Public-Private Mix in Healthcare Service Delivery in Nepal*. Ministry of Health and Population, Government of Nepal, June 2010, available online (https://www.rti.org/sites/default/files/resources/42_nepal_overview-publicprivate.pdf).

expenses) is on purchasing drugs and medical consultations.[9] In India, 72% of medical expenses in rural areas and 68% in urban areas are accounted for by out-of-pocket spending on drugs.[10]

CURRENT TRENDS IN THE SIZE, STRUCTURE, AND GROWTH OF PRIVATE SECTOR

Private healthcare in South Asia encompasses large for-profit corporate entities, not-for-profit trusts (private and religious), general practitioners (both qualified and unqualified), chemists, and diagnostic laboratories. Table 2 gives an overview of the current size of the hospital-based infrastructure in the private sector for some of the countries in the region—with the exception of Afghanistan—that have data available.

Table 3.4.2: Private healthcare facilities in selected countries in South Asia for inpatient care

	India (2011–12)		*Nepal (2014)*		*Bangladesh (2013)*		*Pakistan (2012–13)*		*Sri Lanka (2011)*	
	Pvt	Pub	Pvt	Pub	Pvt	Pub	Pvt	Pub	Pvt	Pub
Hospitals	54,004[a]	20,306	350	97	2,983	559	692	1,142	155	592
Hospital beds	978,000[b]	675,779[c]	19,580	6,944	45,485	45,853	Around 20,000	128,998	5,205	70,000

Note: [a] Includes 352 charitable hospitals and 104 corporate hospitals; [b] Data for 2010; [c] Data for 2014.

In all countries in the region, a major proportion of primary care is accessed through private practitioners, often unqualified. The organized private sector, primarily the hospital sector, is

[9] N.M. Huq, A.Q. Al-Amin, S.R. Howlader and M.A. Kabir, 'Paying Out of Pocket for Healthcare in Bangladesh: A burden on poor?', *Iran Journal of Public Health*, vol. 44, 2015, pp. 1024–25.

[10] J. Singh, 'Medicine Costs Form Bulk of Out-of-Pocket Health Expenses: NSSO', Livemint, April 13, 2016 (https://www.livemint.com/Politics/30z-97MDZDMewkJHsfM5D6I/Medicine-costs-form-bulk-of-outofpock-et-health-expenses-N.html).

mostly located in large towns and cities as the paying clientele are concentrated in these areas. In Nepal, three-quarters of hospital beds are located in the Central Region where access is relatively good, compared with virtually no private hospitals in the Far Western Region.[11] An interesting trend is emerging in India where private facilities are expanding to smaller town and cities. Currently, 48% of all private hospitals and two-thirds of corporate hospitals are in the smaller cities.[12] In India, about 80% of outpatient services and 60% of inpatient services are provided by the private sector.[13] In Nepal, 55% of patients access private facilities for acute illnesses and 57% for chronic illnesses.[14] In Bangladesh, 13% of patients use government services, 27% access qualified practitioners in the private or non-governmental organization (NGO) sectors, and 60% access unqualified private practitioners.[15] In a survey conducted in Pakistan in 2010–11, 71% of people who had consulted a health provider in the past two weeks reported going to a private facility.[16] Sri Lanka provides a contrast with 66% reporting that they visited a public healthcare facility.[17]

Of the estimated 1.2 million private providers in India, four

[11] *Overview of Public-Private Mix in Healthcare Service Delivery in Nepal.*

[12] I. Mukhopadhyay, S. Selvaraj, S. Sharma and P. Datta, 'Changing Landscape of Private Healthcare Providers in India', Paper presented at International Public Policy Association Conference, Milan, July 2015.

[13] *National Health Policy 2015.*

[14] *Nepal Living Standard Survey 2010–11.*

[15] S.M. Ahmed, B.B. Alam, I. Anwar, T. Begum, R. Huque, J.A.M. Khan et al., *Bangladesh Health System Review*, vol. 5, no. 3, Manila: World Health Organization, Regional Office for the Western Pacific, 2015, available online (http://www.searo.who.int/entity/asia_pacific_observatory/publications/hits/hit_bangladesh/en/).

[16] S. Nishtar, T. Boerma, S. Amjad et al., 'Pakistan's Health System: Performance and prospects after the 18th constitutional amendment', *The Lancet*, vol. 381, no. 9884 (June 22, 2013), pp. 2193–206.

[17] M.C. Weerasinghe and D.N. Fernando, 'Access to Care in a Plural Health System', *Journal of the College of Community Physicians of Sri Lanka*, vol. 14, 2009.

out of five are run by a single person and half of them are located in rural areas.[18] This pattern is now changing: the share of sole-staffer enterprises declined from 96% to 90% between 1980 and 2004.[19] In Nepal, before 1991, there were only two private hospitals but the situation has since changed. The number of public and private hospitals in Nepal has grown: from 78 and 69, respectively, in 1995, to 97 and 350 in 2014.[20] In Bangladesh around 50% of doctors, 42% of nurses, and 65% of paramedics work exclusively in the private sector. Overall spending on hospital care in Bangladesh has increased from 17% to 27% of total healthcare expenditure, driven by increasing expenditure at private hospitals.[21] In Sri Lanka, private hospital provision increased by more than 120% between 1990 and 2011, accompanied by a shift in the private sector from smaller to larger (100+ bed) facilities.[22]

There is a growing trend towards private-sector participation in medical education in the region, accompanied by high costs. In India, the share of seats in private medical colleges grew from 1.4% in 1950 to 52.1% in 2014.[23] In Nepal, nineteen out of twenty-three

[18] *National Sample Survey. 67th Round*, National Sample Survey Organisation, February 2013, available online (http://mospi.nic.in/sites/default/files/publication_reports/Revised_ReportNo549.pdf).

[19] *Report of the National Commission of Macroeconomics and Health, 2005*, Ministry of Health and Family Welfare, Government of India, August 2005, available online (http://www.rfhha.org/images/pdf/rare_collection/Report_of_the_National_Commission.pdf).

[20] *A Report on Market Data for Private Sector Investments in Nepal Healthcare Sector*, Dolma Development Fund, 2014, available online (http://www.dolmaimpact.com/pdf/DIF%20I-%20Healthcare%20Market%20Report_Final_1-10-2014.pdf).

[21] *Health Bulletin, 2013*, Ministry of Health and Family Welfare, Government of the People's Republic of Bangladesh, Dhaka, available online (https://dghs.gov.bd/images/docs/Other_Publication/HB%202013%20final%20-%20Full%20version%201March14.pdf).

[22] *Private Health Sector Review, 2012*, IHP Technical Reports Series, No. 2, Institute for Health Policy, August 2015, available online (www.ihp.lk/publications/docs/PHSR2012.pdf).

[23] P.K. Choudhury, 'Role of Private Sector in Medical Education and Hu-

medical colleges are in the private sector and a large proportion of hospital beds in private facilities are located in private medical colleges. In Bangladesh there were no medical colleges in the private sector in 1996, but by 2011 there were forty-four private medical colleges.[24]

PROVISION OF CARE BY PRIVATE NOT-FOR-PROFIT PROVIDERS

While for-profit private facilities are currently the major providers of healthcare in the region, faith-based groups and NGOs provide a large proportion of care in some parts of the region. Historically, Christian missionary hospitals played a prominent role in the Indian subcontinent and in 1920 Christian institutions ran nearly half of all hospitals. In 1947, there were around 900 of these hospitals in the region. The number has now dwindled to around 200.[25] Mission hospitals still play a role in providing healthcare in India, especially in underserved areas. Currently, Christian healthcare networks manage over 3,731 healthcare facilities and around 80,895 beds.[26] However, they also face challenges—such as dwindling donor support from external missions and difficulty attracting personnel—that threaten their survival. In Pakistan, local NGOs providing healthcare are funded by philanthropic contributions and the Islamic *zakat* (charity tax) from citizens and private companies.[27] In Bangladesh, healthcare provided by NGOs plays a significant role. An estimated 4,000

man Resource Development for Health in India', Working Paper No. 169, Institute for Studies in Industrial Development, New Delhi, October 2014, available online (http://isid.org.in/pdf/WP169.pdf).

[24] *Health Bulletin, 2013*, Government of the People's Republic of Bangladesh.

[25] Oommen C. Kurian, *Free Medical Care for the Poor: The Case of State-aided Charitable Hospitals in Mumbai*, Mumbai: CEHAT, 2003.

[26] Ibid.

[27] 'Primary care systems profiles and performance. Pakistan Case Study', Alliance for Health Policy and Systems Research, 2016, available online (https://www.who.int/alliance-hpsr/projects/AHPSR-Pakistan-061016.pdf).

NGOs, including international and large national organizations, provide healthcare services.[28] In India, the Public Charitable Trust Act 1950 was enacted to enable private entities to set up charities and the act includes a waiver for income tax. While, historically, many philanthropists invested in setting up charitable hospitals (also called trust hospitals), the act is now being misused widely by commercial hospitals, and some of the biggest private hospitals in Mumbai operate as trust hospitals.[29]

GOVERNMENT POLICIES THAT DRIVE EXPANSION OF PRIVATE HEALTHCARE

A number of public policies foster the growth of the private sector—several forms of input subsidies in land, electricity, import of capital goods, and technologies are available; while a wide range of clinical and non-clinical services in public facilities are being outsourced.[30] In India, since the liberalization of foreign direct investment (FDI) norms in the hospital sector in 2000 (100% FDI permitted under the automatic route), FDI inflow to the sector increased from $6.93 million (£5.52 million; €6.39 million) in 2001–02 to $684.58 million in 2013–14.[31] The promotion of medical tourism, particularly in India, is also a driver in the growth of large corporate hospitals. Since 2006, the government has issued medical visas to patients (and spouse). In

[28] *Bangladesh Health Facility Survey, 2014*, National Institute of Population Research and Training (NIPORT), Ministry of Health and Family Welfare, Dhaka, p. 6, available online (https://dhsprogram.com/pubs/pdf/SPA23/SPA23.pdf).

[29] R. Duggal, 'The Uncharitable Trust Hospitals', *Economic and Political Weekly*, vol. 47, no. 25 (June 2012), pp. 23–24.

[30] K. Sen, 'Health Reforms and Developing Countries: A critique', in *Public Health and Poverty of Reforms: A South Asian Perspective*, eds. I. Qadeer, K. Sen and K.R. Nayar, Sage, 2011.

[31] S.K. Hooda, 'Foreign Investment In Hospital Sector in India: Trends, Patterns and Issues', ISID Working Paper No. 181, Institute for Studies in Industrial Development, New Delhi, April 2015, available online (http://isid.org.in/pdf/WP181.pdf).

2009, the ministry of tourism extended its market development assistance scheme to cover hospitals certified by Joint Commission International, an international organization that accredits healthcare facilities.[32] Tax-funded health insurance schemes have become a recent mechanism for transferring public funds to strengthen private facilities. India introduced several public-funded insurance schemes about ten years ago but coverage and benefits are weak.[33] In 2014, only 13% of rural and 12% of urban households were covered. Coverage extends only to pre-selected packages for hospital-based care and an assessment of the Rajiv Aarogyasri scheme of Andhra Pradesh, one of the oldest public-funded schemes, shows that 25% of the state's health budget dedicated to the scheme addressed only 2% of the burden of disease.[34] These schemes involve outsourcing a major proportion of care to private facilities.[35] There have been several reports of unscrupulous private facilities milking these insurance schemes by conducting unnecessary procedures. Horrific incidents have been reported, for example, of unnecessary hysterectomies performed on young women.[36] Despite such reports, other countries in the

[32] Amit Sengupta, 'Medical Tourism: Reverse subsidy for the elite', *Signs* (Chic), vol. 36, no. 2 (2012), pp. 312–19.

[33] S. Selvaraj, A. Karan and I. Mukhopadhyay, 'Publicly-Financed Health Insurance Schemes in India: How effective are they in providing Financial Risk Protection?', in *India: Social Development Report 2014: Challenges of Public Health*, Council for Social Development, 2014.

[34] Disease burden is a multi-dimensional term that not only captures the number of people suffering from disease or its fatality, but also its impact on people, in terms of disability and the alteration of life.

[35] N. Purendra Prasad and P. Raghavendra, 'Healthcare Models in the Era of Medical Neo-liberalism: A study of Aarogyasri in Andhra Pradesh', Economic and Political Weekly, vol. 47, no. 43 (October 27, 2012).

[36] M. Rao, 'Bihar Women Who Lost Their Wombs to Needless Surgeries Suffer While Doctors Thrive', *Scroll*, September 19, 2016 (https://scroll.in/pulse/816202/ bihar-women-who-lost-their-wombs-to-needlesssurgeries-suffer-while-doctors-thrive); also see A. Jaiswal, 'Uterus Scam: Chhattisgarh doctors get away with one year suspension', *The Times of India*, June 24, 2013 (https://timesofindia.indiatimes.com/city/raipur/Uterus-scam-Chhat-

region are starting to follow suit. In 2015, the government of Nepal signalled the initiation of social health insurance involving public funding and mixed provision of care, with the first phase of the scheme to be piloted in three districts.[37] In Pakistan, under the Prime Minister's National Health Insurance Programme, which covers families earning less than PKR 200 (£1.5; €1.76; $1.9) per day, soft loans of PKR 5–10 million will be provided to empanelled private hospitals.[38]

Unethical behaviour by providers is a known risk, given the increasing private-sector involvement in public-funded insurance schemes and the absence of effective measures to regulate private facilities. The Indian parliament adopted the Clinical Establishments Act in 2010. It was designed to regulate standards of care in all facilities but its implementation has virtually stalled in parts of the country because of lobbying by private physicians. Recently, the government of Maharashtra was admonished by the state's high court for non-implementation of the Act.[39] Pakistan, Bangladesh, and Nepal report that existing regulations are ineffective.[40] In Sri Lanka, the Private Medical Institutions (Registration) Act was adopted in 2006 but the implementation of its provisions remains weak.[41] Private practice by doctors

tisgarh-doctors-get-away-with-one-year-suspension/articleshow/20748235.cms).

37 M. Fernando, 'Patients Die Despite Stringent Laws', *Sunday Observer*, February 24, 2013 (http://archives.sundayobserver.lk/2013/02/24/fea11.asp).

38 S.R. Mishra et al., 'National Health Insurance Policy in Nepal: Challenges for implementation', *Global Health Action*, vol. 8, no. 1 (2015) (doi:10.3402/gha.v8.28763).

39 *Human Rights Report. Pakistan 2015*, Human Rights Commission of Pakistan, available online (https://photos.state.gov/libraries/pakistan/231771/PDFs/pakistan-2015-hr-report.pdf).

40 M. Plumber, 'Bombay High Court Asks Maharashtra for Steps Taken to Curb Illegal Abortion', *DNA*, March 10, 2017 (https://www.dnaindia.com/health/report-bombay-high-court-asks-maharashtra-for-steps-taken-to-curb-illegal-abortion-2348263).

41 Ahmed et al., *Bangladesh Health System Review*, vol. 5, no. 3.

employed in public services is rampant in the region and acts as a conduit for the transfer of patients to private facilities. In Pakistan, even though publicly-employed doctors receive non-practising allowances, a significant number use their work in the public sector to boost their private practice.[42] In Bangladesh, a substantial number of government doctors practise privately after office hours.[43] In Sri Lanka, the number of government doctors working part-time in private hospitals is reported as 2,100.[44] In India, rules regarding private practice by government doctors vary—some states have completely banned such practices while others allow private practice during 'off-duty hours'.

RECOMMENDATIONS

The growth of private medicine in the region is a function of both active and passive measures instituted by governments. Poor public funding has led to the vacuum being filled by a large and unregulated private sector. The growth is also driven by concessions and subsidies provided to set up private facilities, public-funded insurance where care is largely outsourced, and weak efforts to regulate private providers. The absence of a robust public sector also acts as a barrier to regulation, as private facilities do not have to compete with a well-functioning public system. The end result is the segmentation of healthcare services into a poorly resourced public system for the poor, and a growing private system for the rich. The rich, while opting out of the public system, also draw resources, political clout, and accountability away from

[42] 'Pakistan's Health Sector: Does corruption lurk?', Transparency International-Government of NWFP-Pakistan's Health Policy Forum-Heartfile, 2007, available online (http://www.heartfile.org/pdf/health-sector-corruption-pakistan.pdf).

[43] *Human Rights Report. Pakistan 2015.*

[44] 'Health Statistics Census of Private, Co-operative and Estate Hospitals, 2013', Institute of Policy Studies of Sri Lanka, available online (http://www.ips.lk/health-statistics-census-of-private-co-operative-and-estate-hospitals-2013/).

it. Given that for-profit commercial enterprises target the hospital sector, resources—both financial and human—have a tendency to shift towards tertiary care at the expense of primary care. Several characteristics of private provision have a negative impact on the quality of care. For example, unnecessary interventions reduce the quality, efficiency, and accessibility of care, and increase out-of-pocket expenditure.[45]

The private sector, furthermore, absorbs a disproportionate share of the health workforce, and is inaccessible to most of the population. Two other points merit attention. Private procurement of drugs is the single largest component of high out-of-pocket healthcare expenses, signifying poor access to public facilities. Secondly, the rapid commercialization of medical education draws young professionals into the private commercial sector, as they seek to recover the high cost of private medical education. Goal 3 of the Sustainable Development Goals[46] is a call to 'Ensure healthy lives and promote well-being for all at all ages'. More specifically, Goal 3.8 calls upon countries to 'Achieve universal health coverage, including financial risk protection, access to quality essential healthcare services, and access to safe, effective, quality, and affordable essential medicines and vaccines for all'. It is unlikely that the unregulated and rapid growth of private medicine in South Asia will provide an enabling environment to meet these goals. South Asian countries need to take action if they are to achieve universal health coverage that includes financial risk protection.

If the growth of the private sector continues unregulated, the outcomes will include healthcare funded through out-of-pocket

[45] R. Morgan, T. Ensor and H. Waters, 'Performance of Private Sector Health Care: Implications for universal health coverage', *The Lancet*, vol. 388, no. 10044 (August 6, 2016), pp. 606–12.

[46] Seventeen SDGs were adopted by the UN in 2015, as part of its '2030 Agenda for Sustainable Development'. See the following link for more information: https://sustainabledevelopment.un.org/sdgs.

expenses in the absence of effective financial protection measures, uneven and poor-quality care in the absence of the regulation of private facilities, and lack of access to healthcare services for a large proportion of the population.

5. Universal Health Coverage: Beyond Rhetoric

AMIT SENGUPTA

Amit exposes the politics behind the rhetoric of universal health coverage (UHC). Interrogating its ideological foundations, he argues that the international agencies are pursuing a particular agenda under the guise of UHC, whereby the government's role is confined to that of a financing source and 'strategic purchaser' of care organized on market principles. Amit points out that in the experience of developing countries, health insurance and private provisioning have been ineffective in improving financial protection, quality of care, equity or efficiency. He argues that such strategies have disastrous consequences for people's health, while destroying the institutional scaffolding of public and collective health. With systematic analysis of the theoretical arguments and a review of empirical evidence from various countries, he exposes the perils of market-based healthcare models and brings out the advantages of public systems in terms of equity, efficiency, rational care and cost containment. Amit goes into the history of capitalist countries to bring home the point that UHC models in countries like Germany emerged as an incremental response to the demands of the labour movement in these countries, not from a coherent outlook on healthcare.

In less than a decade the discourse on universal health coverage has come to dominate most international discussions on healthcare access. UHC is now seen as the solution to pressing healthcare needs in low- and middle-income countries (LMICs), making it all the more important to understand what it actually promises.

On the international stage, one of the earliest mentions of UHC was at the Fifty-eighth World Health Assembly in 2005, in a resolution calling on member states to: 'ensure that health-financing systems include a method for prepayment of financial contributions for healthcare, with a view to sharing risk among the population and avoiding catastrophic healthcare expenditure and impoverishment of individuals as a result of seeking care'.[1] Thus, the conceptual underpinning of UHC lay in 'sustainable health financing' and not in the mechanisms of healthcare delivery or nature of health systems. Soon, UHC as a vehicle to secure sustainable financing for health systems began to be conflated with health-systems design, promoting the systematic participation of the private sector in the provision of health services.[2] The use of the term 'coverage' rather than 'care' symbolizes the move away from concerns of health-systems design and towards financing.

International agencies rallied behind UHC as a response to the precipitous rise in catastrophic out-of-pocket expenditure on healthcare,[3] in the backdrop of crumbling public health systems. The latter was a consequence of a prolonged period of neglect of public healthcare and the privatization of health systems, as

[1] 'Sustainable Health Financing, Universal Coverage and Social Health Insurance', World Health Assembly Resolution 58.33, Geneva.

[2] While most LMICs already had a significant presence of the private sector in healthcare delivery, the UHC model provided a framework for the incorporation of private providers in a planned manner.

[3] Catastrophic expenditure on healthcare is defined as expenditure of a household on healthcare that exceeds 10% of its total expenditure. Out-of-pocket expenses are the expenditure on healthcare borne by households at the point of care delivery. This is generally an indicator that care delivery is not free, or the costs are not covered by a reimbursement scheme—such as insurance of some kind, which may be publicly funded, co-funded by individual and social contributions, or entirely privately funded.

prescribed by global financial institutions' infamous structural adjustment programmes in the 1980s.[4]

In its 1993 *World Development Report*, the World Bank published a ranking of common healthcare interventions according to their cost-effectiveness and used it to propose a minimum package of public healthcare services for low- and middle-income countries as part of their reforms programme. Some common ailments like emergency treatment of moderately severe injuries and the treatment of chronic conditions including diabetes, cataract, hypertension, mental illness and cervical cancer were duly withdrawn from public provisioning by developing countries, leading to a high burden of out-of-pocket expenses.[5]

Health-sector reforms had disastrous consequences for the health of the people. The budget cuts led to a crumbling public health system, with poor infrastructure, falling morale among health workers and diminishing resources. In this process, the private sector expanded to fill the vacuum created by the retreat of public services. This was especially true in the case of secondary and tertiary care services, where profit opportunities for the commercial sector were greater. In consequence, there was a rise in catastrophic health expenditures by households, a large proportion of which was 'out of pocket'.

To remedy the situation, there could have been efforts to prioritize the rebuilding and strengthening of public systems. Instead, the emphasis shifted from using public resources for the provisioning of services to financing under the rubric of UHC. The underlying belief appeared to be that if the finances were secured,

4 B. McPake and A. Mills, 'What Can We Learn from International Comparisons of Health Systems and Health System Reform?', *Bulletin of the World Health Organization*, vol. 78, no. 6 (2000), pp. 811–20 (http://www. who.int/bulletin/archives/78(6)811.

5 M. Segall, 'District Health Systems in a Neoliberal World: A review of five key policy areas', *International Journal of Health Planning and Management*, vol. 18, 2003, pp. S5–S26.

the provisioning of health services could be taken care of by a mix of private and public sector. Such an assumption completely misses the point that a health system is not a mere aggregate of dispersed facilities and service providers, but an integrated network of facilities and services that are appropriately situated at primary, secondary and tertiary levels.

The contours of UHC that began to take shape were based on some early initiatives in the late 1990s and early 2000s—especially in Latin America where reforms were based on universal insurance schemes. Mechanisms adopted in Chile, Colombia and Mexico, for example, shared certain key features: increases in national healthcare expenditure, both public and private; and a market logic centred on 'individual care' conceived as a 'private' good. At the end of the day, there was no regional consensus on the success of the reforms, and some reviews of the Chile and Colombia experiences suggest that they did not improve the quality of care, equity or efficiency; yet transnational corporations and consultancy firms accrued significant benefits.[6] Worse, the market logic destroyed the institutional scaffolding of public and collective health. The result was the re-emergence of previously controlled diseases and the reduction of preventive interventions.[7] However, the powerful global institutions behind these reforms were able to put a positive spin on their impact.[8] Notably, the World Bank played a key role in building consensus around reforms that were to become

[6] N. Homedes and A. Ugalde, 'Why Neoliberal Health Reforms have Failed in Latin America', *Health Policy*, vol. 71, no. 1 (2005), pp. 83–96.

[7] A.C. Laurell, 'Can Insurance Guarantee Universal Access to Health Services?', *Social Medicine*, vol. 5, no. 3 (2010), pp. 137–38.

[8] For example, an article in *The Lancet* in 2009, argues: 'The entire Latin American continent is on track to achieve universal health coverage within the next decade. The achievement of Latin America offers hope to Africa, the Middle East, and Asia—but success looms only because of years of hard work and innovation across the continent.' See L. Garrett, A.M.R. Chouwdhury and A. Pablos-Méndez, 'All for universal health coverage', *The Lancet*, vol. 374, no. 9697 (2009), p. 1297.

precursors to UHC. This was much before the WHO formally adopted UHC as part of its policy plank.[9]

THE IDEOLOGICAL FOUNDATIONS OF UHC

The 2010 *World Health Report* illustrated the concept of UHC with a diagram, reproduced in Figure 3.5.1.

UHC is conceived as a system that would progressively move towards: (a) the coverage of the entire population by a package of services; (b) an increasing range of services; and (c) a rising share of pooled funds as the main source of funding for healthcare, and thereby a decrease in co-payments by those accessing healthcare services. It is argued that such a system requires a split between the provider and purchaser of health services, with issues of financing and management being entirely divorced from provisioning. Among the main proponents of the concept, Julio Frenk, the architect of the Mexican health insurance system, suggests that stewardship (including deployment of equitable policies) and fair financing are essential public responsibilities, whereas the delivery of services is best served through a pluralistic mix that includes the private sector and civil society.[10]

A purchaser-provider split puts a price on services; that is, it commodifies them, which is the precondition for their transaction in the marketplace.[11] Advocates of UHC emphasize the role played by governments in strategically 'purchasing' care to improve 'efficiency'. The *WHO Bulletin* argues: 'Countries cannot simply spend their way to UHC. To sustain progress, efficiency and accountability must be ensured. The main health financing instrument for promoting efficiency in the use of funds

[9] J. Kutzin, 'Towards Universal Health Care Coverage: Health, nutrition and population', Discussion Paper, Washington, DC: World Bank, July 2000.

[10] J. Frenk and D. de Ferranti, 'Universal Health Coverage: Good health, good economics', *The Lancet*, vol. 380, no. 9845 (2012), pp. 862–64.

[11] A.C. Laurell, 'Health System Reform in Mexico: A critical review', *International Journal of Health Services*, vol. 37, no. 3 (2012), pp. 515–35.

is purchasing and more specifically, strategic purchasing.'[12]

The role of the state is defined by the 2010 *World Health Report* in the following manner: 'Governments have a responsibility to ensure that all providers, public and private, operate appropriately and attend to patients' needs cost-effectively and efficiently.'[13] In other words, UHC does not discriminate between public and private services, its only concerns are 'cost effectiveness' and 'efficiency'. In practice, this impartial role of the state can be interpreted in many ways and largely depends on the functioning of public health services in any given country. With most public health systems in disarray, it is an appealing option for states to choose not to rebuild public systems but to rely increasingly on private providers. The logic is that the catastrophic impact of out-of-pocket expenditures needs an immediate remedy, and as the public system is too weak to respond, it seems better strategy to turn to the private sector. The UHC model, thus, provides the opportunity to choose to open up a country's health system to private providers rather than considering public provision of services as the mainstay of the system.

The retreat of the state as a provider of public services[14] has been accompanied by a clear reform push in public services often referred to as 'new public management'.[15] The UHC proposal is no stranger to this trend. The strategy has been to introduce private-sector management, organization and labour market ethos and practices into the public sector with the expectation that public services can be made to deliver with the 'efficiency' that the private

[12] J. Kutzin, 'Anything Goes on the Path to Universal Health Coverage?', *Bulletin of the World Health Organization*, vol. 90, no. 11 (November 1, 2012), pp. 867–68.

[13] *Health Systems Financing: The path to universal coverage*, World Health Report 2010, Geneva: WHO.

[14] By public services we mean services both publicly financed and provisioned.

[15] M. Vabø, 'New Public Management: The neoliberal way of governance', Working Paper No. 4., National and University Library of Iceland, Reykjavik, 2009.

sector (and its competitive environment) has supposedly realized. More specifically, there has been an aspiration to introduce 'internal markets' within the domain of public provision. As part of these reforms, public funding has been retained but steps have been taken to isolate purchasers from providers. The intention is that individual 'units' should compete for consumers. The purchaser of these services (patients or their surrogates) should be able to choose between providers with relative ease. This reorganization along the lines of new public management appears crucial for a subsequent privatization of public services.[16]

This UHC approach is in sharp contrast to the vision of PHC envisaged in the Alma-Ata Declaration of 1978, which called for the building of health systems that would provide comprehensive care, would be integrated, organized to promote equity, and driven by community needs.[17] Instead, UHC envisages healthcare as bits and pieces of a jigsaw puzzle, connected only by a common financing pool and by the regulation of an array of private and public providers.

In fact, universal health 'coverage' is only one aspect of universal healthcare. Coverage as a strategy focuses primarily on the achievement of a wide network of health providers and health institutions extending access to health services to the vast majority of the population. The components that are 'sufficient' to be considered adequate coverage remain highly contested, however.[18]

16 Privatization of public services in sectors as varied as electricity, water, telecom services, railways, have all followed a pattern. The first step has been to disaggregate various roles that the state traditionally played. In the electricity sector, for example, it involved the 'unbundling' of different functions (generation, transmission and distribution); see also P. Pierson, *The New Politics of the Welfare State*, Oxford: Oxford University Press, 2001.

17 PHM, Global Equity Gauge Alliance, Medact and University of South Africa, 2005. See 'Health Care Systems and Approaches to Health', *Global Health Watch*, vol. 1.

18 D. Stuckler, A.B. Feigl, S. Basu and M. McKee, 'The Political Economy of Universal Health Coverage', Background paper for the Global Symposium

UHC is essentially designed to universalize 'coverage' rather than 'care'.

Nonetheless, UHC is a step forward to the extent that it represents an explicit recognition of two important aspects of public health. First, by prescribing a central role to the state in securing funding for healthcare and in regulating the quality and range of services, UHC recognizes that 'market failures' are a feature of private healthcare detrimental to the interests of patients. Second, UHC also recognizes that health is a 'public good' with externalities, and the state has a responsibility to ensure access to health services. Thus, UHC provides for a possible exercise of choice, and progressive governments can try to privilege public systems and examine funding mechanisms that promote equity. Financial pooling through UHC makes it easier to develop comprehensive public systems, but whether that happens is a matter of political choice.

THE AMBIGUITIES OF UHC

There are two levels of ambiguity embedded in the present concept of UHC. First, while it proposes that funding for health should be pooled, it does not propose the same for the provision of services; that is, it does not propose a unified system of public provision. Second, by not defining the 'depth' of coverage it allows for a minimalist interpretation of coverage—a very basic package—akin to the World Bank's health prescriptions of the previous decades. This latter point is captured by the UHC proposition that the exact mechanisms for pooling will depend on social processes and political action to establish the parameters for an acceptable public role in healthcare.

The UHC concept provides choices in a particular political and economic environment that is not neutral. The dominant

on Health Systems Research, November 16–19, 2010, Montreux, Switzerland.

neoliberal environment can exploit the ambiguities inherent in the conceptualization of UHC and promote a model that is market-driven. Such a model becomes a convenient way for private capital to extract profits using public resources, through a combination of pooled funds and private provision. With the state intervening to pool healthcare funds in one basket (the locus of collection may range from primarily tax-based to a combination of employee, employer and government contributions), new avenues for profit-making are opened up through the medium of insurance companies and health management organizations.

Pooling of funds provides an effective demand (i.e. purchasing power) for the healthcare industry in settings where most people live in extreme poverty. It also opens up a new and lucrative private market: the administration of health insurance funds. Further, in an insurance-based UHC model, although more public funds are earmarked for health, this is done through demand subsidization (putting money in the hands of users) rather than subsidizing supply by increasing the budget of public institutions. As a result, a new layer of competition is added to the system. Not only do public and private service providers compete, we also see competition between public and private insurance plans. Furthermore, private companies are offered a series of advantages in order to break the 'monopoly' of public institutions.[19]

WHERE IS THE EVIDENCE?

Finding evidence to assess the impact of newly implemented UHC schemes is particularly challenging[20] and methodologies designed to collect good evidence are singularly lacking. Many

[19] Laurell, 'Can Insurance Guarantee Universal Access to Health Services?'.

[20] U. Giedion, E.A. Alfonso and Y. Díaz, *The Impact of Universal Coverage Schemes in the Developing World: A review of the existing evidence*, Washington, DC: World Bank, 2013, available online (http://documents.worldbank.org/curated/en/349621468158382497/The-impact-of-universal-coverage-schemes-in-the-developing-world-a-review-of-the-existing-evidence).

evaluations of UHC schemes end up measuring the impact on out-of-pocket expenses incurred[21] but do not measure the quality and depth of the services on offer. As a consequence, proof of UHC's positive impact on health outcomes remains extremely thin and faces huge methodological challenges to compile. For example, some evaluations of the much-acclaimed Seguro Popular scheme in Mexico reported no effect on self-reported health indicators and did not report change in general patterns of service use.[22]

The most basic argument for pooled financing and insurance—the hallmark of UHC—is that it reduces financial risk. However, insurance also opens up new opportunities for consuming expensive high-technology care, permitting health improvements that are valued by the patient, especially because the private provider is able to exploit its informational advantage; it is an open question, however, whether insurance (of any form) will in practice reduce financial risk. A large 2005 study of China's health insurance schemes indicates that it may, to the contrary, be associated with increased risk of large out-of-pocket payments.[23]

There is little evidence available about what strategies within the UHC approach are more promising. And there is virtually no data comparing the relative merits of approaches that are premised on a predominantly public delivery of services, versus those that follow a private-public mix with a predominant private-sector delivery of services.

PUBLIC SYSTEM EFFICIENCIES

There are, however, clear structural reasons why market-driven

[21] Ibid.

[22] R. Moreno-Serra and P.C. Smith, 'Towards an index of health coverage', Discussion Paper 2012/11, Imperial Business School and Centre for Health Policy, 2011.

[23] A. Wagstaff and M. Lindelow, 'Can Insurance Increase Financial Risk?: The curious case of health insurance in China', *Journal of Health Economics*, vol. 27, no. 4 (2005), pp. 990–1005 (https://repository.upenn.edu/cgi/viewcontent.cgi?article=1019&context=gansu_papers).

healthcare and competition do not in fact promote efficiency[24] or quality.[25] Commercialized healthcare systems often have very high transaction costs, which are necessary to manage or regulate the market. A study of long-term care facilities in the US estimated that in 1999, as much as $294.3 billion was used for administrative costs, representing 31% of healthcare expenditures in the country. Transaction costs tend to be much lower in more public systems; for example, the transaction costs in the National Health System in the mid-1970s, before it began to convert into a market, were estimated at 5–6% of total expenditure.[26]

Public systems are more efficient because they ensure economies of scale in the purchasing, supply and distribution of drugs and equipment.[27] In the Indian state of Tamil Nadu, for example, pooled purchasing of medicines through a public-sector entity has driven down medicine costs significantly and other states are engaged in replicating the model.[28] Public systems are best placed to avoid wasteful capital investment, duplication of equipment and services, and the emphasis on frills that are endemic to hospitals in a competitive market environment.[29]

[24] Here we use the term 'efficiency' not in the way it would be used in a market environment, but as regards the returns achieved through investment in a public good.

[25] T. Rice, 'Can Markets Give Us the Health System We Want?', *Journal of Health Politics, Policy and Law*, vol. 22, 1997, pp. 383–426.

[26] C. Leys and S. Player, *The Plot Against the NHS*, Wales: Merlin Press, 2011.

[27] M. Robinson and G. White, 'The Role of Civic Organizations in the Provision of Social Services: Towards synergy', in *Social Provision in Low-Income Countries—New patterns and emerging trends*, eds. G. Mwabu, C. Ugaz and G. White, chap. 4. Oxford: OUP, 2001.

[28] P.V. Singh, A. Tatambhotla, R. Kalvakuntla and M. Chokshi, 'Understanding Public Drug Procurement in India: A comparative qualitative study of five Indian states', *BMJ Open*, vol. 3, no. 2 (2013), pp. 1–11 (https://bmjopen.bmj.com/content/3/2/e001987).

[29] M. Ramesh, W. Xun and M. Howlett, 'Second Best Governance? Governments and governance in the imperfect world of health care delivery in China, India and Thailand', Paper presented at the International Conference on Public Policy, June 26–28, 2013, Grenoble, France, available online (https://

Figure 3.5.1: Three dimensions to consider when moving towards universal coverage

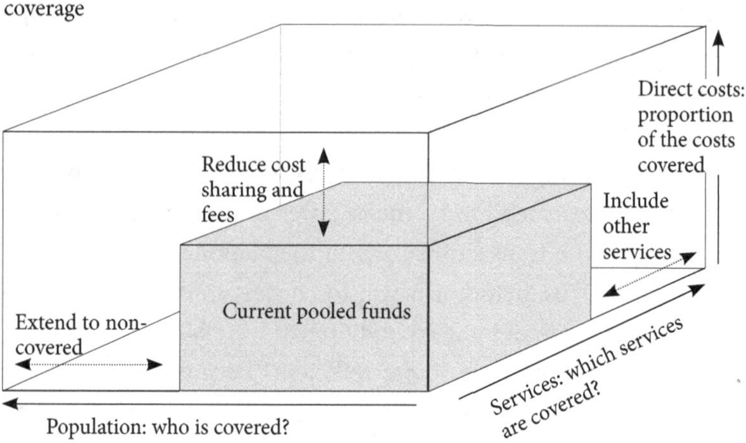

Public systems also perform tasks that are not directly linked to providing curative services. These include maintaining disease surveillance systems, providing immunization to the entire population, vector control measures, health promotion activities such as ante-natal and school health check-ups, and so on. It can be argued that an array of private providers could offer these services if mandated to do so by robust regulatory mechanisms. In practice, however, public goods such as mass coverage, public awareness, community outreach and emergency services are more effectively provided through public programmes rather than the sum of regulated private programmes.[30]

If health systems are to provide universal care, there are significant marginal costs involved in delivery to the most inaccessible or the most disadvantaged sections of the population. Health services for those with pre-existing chronic conditions are often relatively more expensive, as is the treatment of rare diseases.[31]

www.tandfonline.com/doi/abs/10.1080/13876988.2014.889903).

30 J.D. Sachs, 'Achieving Universal Health Coverage in Low-Income Settings', *The Lancet*, vol. 380, no. 9845 (2012), pp. 944–47.

31 P. Allotey, S. Yasin, S. Tang, S.L. Chong, J.C. Ho Cheah and D.D. Reidpath, 'Universal Coverage in an Era of Privatisation: Can we guarantee health for

In rapidly-aging societies a very high proportion of healthcare needs are concentrated in the last few months or years of life. Public systems can absorb these marginal costs and spread them across an entire population. Private systems, on the other hand, would find such costs unacceptable and would avoid care provision to people who live in underserved areas, who are disadvantaged, or those who suffer from conditions that require expensive care or long-term care. Public systems, thus, promote equity while even the best-designed private systems risk undermining equity concerns.

The argument that health systems in LMICs should leverage the already dominant private sector for wider and better care is clearly misplaced. The large out-of-pocket expenditures and the importance of private provision in low-income countries is mainly a reflection of inadequate public services, forcing the middle and upper classes to go directly to private providers while the poor are left without reliable basic services. This reality is unfortunate, but it is not a convincing case for private provision; rather it should serve as a call to action to bolster the deeply under-financed public sector.[32]

UHC IN ADVANCED CAPITALIST COUNTRIES

Variants of today's UHC model have existed in parts of the globe for over 130 years, starting with Germany under Bismarck in the second half of the nineteenth century. Such models inform the design of health systems in most developed countries to this day (with the notable exception of the US).

While trying to project the future trajectory of UHC in LMICs it is important to learn from these historical experiences for two reasons. First, because models of UHC being promoted in LMICs today are justified on the basis of evidence from models in developed countries, yet they are blind to the fact that these

all?', *BMC Public Health*, vol. 12, suppl. 1 (2012), p. S1.

32 Sachs, 'Achieving Universal Health Coverage in Low-Income Settings'.

models are imperfect, born out of a long history of social struggle and compromise in capitalist states. Second, many of these systems are now under strain and face the prospect of reforms, which are largely designed to open up opportunities for the private sector—as is happening in the global South.

HEALTH AND THE NEGOTIATING POWER OF LABOUR

The introduction of UHC schemes in Europe and elsewhere has its roots in attempts to quell rising discontent among the working class. Initially, they were designed as welfare payments during sickness and later integrated into entitlements for healthcare. European countries introduced compulsory sickness insurance for workers, beginning with Germany in 1883; other countries, including Austria, Britain, Hungary, the Netherlands, Norway and Russia, followed by 1912. Other European countries, including Sweden in 1891, Denmark in 1892, France in 1910, and Switzerland in 1912, opted to subsidize the mutual benefit societies formed by workers. The primary reason for the emergence of these programmes in Europe was income stabilization and protection against the wage loss of sickness, rather than payment for medical expenses, which came later. Programmes were originally conceived as a means to maintain incomes and buy the political allegiance of workers.[33]

The impetus for UHC came from a need to offer concessions to the working poor, and not from a coherent view of how health services were to be organized. All developed capitalist countries shied away from adopting an entirely public system, though there was enormous variation in the public-private mix that was

[33] K.S. Palmer, 'A Brief History: Universal health care efforts in the US', transcribed from a talk given at the Spring 1999 Physicians for a National Health Program (PNHP) meeting, San Francisco, United States (http://www.pnhp.org/facts/a-brief-history-universal-health-care-efforts-in-the-us).

implemented. The fact that universal systems in Western Europe are still largely functioning is not a comment on their viability and efficiency. Rather, it reveals some nimble footwork from the ruling classes—when forced to respond to popular mobilization against poor healthcare access—and their ultimate success in warding off the introduction of entirely public-funded care under a single, publicly-run system.

INTERNAL CONTRADICTIONS

The current strains on universal health systems in the global North—in the form of rising costs and the inability of systems to keep pace with the health needs of the population—are a function of the reluctance to build truly comprehensive public systems for the delivery of healthcare. Such challenges have led to health-system reforms in many of these countries. Paradoxically, almost without fail, the prescription offered is to introduce more pronounced market mechanisms.

The European experience is important to our discussion because health systems on the continent were generally built around the notion of social solidarity. Irrespective of the forces that led to their inception, this principle of social solidarity is inherent to the two principal models in Europe: the so-called Bismarck model that exists in large parts of continental Europe, and the Beveridge model in the UK, which emerged after the Second World War. A third, the Semashko model, that was prevalent in the erstwhile socialist states of the Soviet Union and Eastern Europe,[34] has virtually disappeared.

[34] The 'Bismarck' model is so termed as it was introduced in Germany during the reign of Chancellor Otto von Bismarck, beginning with the introduction in 1883 of a health insurance bill to mandatorily cover all workers. The Semashko system was named after the first minister of health of the USSR. The Beveridge system, introduced (in the form of the National Health System) by the UK government after the Second World War, was based on the Report of the Inter-Departmental Committee on Social Insurance and Allied Services (chaired by the British economist William Beveridge).

The Bismarck model, typically known as social health insurance, pooled health funds contributed by the state, employers and employees in a common fund, while healthcare was provided by a mix of public and private facilities. The organization of care delivery differed by country, but where private facilities were involved they were tightly controlled. Across the English Channel, the financing of the Beveridge model was tax-based. Primary care was provided by a network of general practitioners, and secondary and tertiary services by public institutions. The general practitioners, while not technically government employees, were tightly bound to the system through contracts with the National Health System. The Semashko system, which existed in the Soviet Union and Eastern Europe, was state-funded and care provision was the sole prerogative of state-run facilities.

Both the Bismarck and the Beveridge models explicitly recognized the role of social solidarity, while devising different ways to fund healthcare. They were, however, built around fundamental contradictions. The first contradiction was between the solidarity character of the financing and the private appropriation of collectively-generated funds by care providers, including industries such as pharmaceutical enterprises and producers of medical equipment. Secondly, individuals and society as a whole had an interest in safe, efficient and cheap healthcare, which contradicted the private providers and producers' interest in selling ever more products, performing ever more operations, etc.[35] This resulted, for example, in European patients contributing to the super-profits of pharmaceutical manufacturers through solidarity funding (either through tax contributions or contributions to health funds).

THE DEMISE OF SOLIDARITY-BASED SYSTEMS

Cost containment and efficiency are driving a re-

[35] T. Pato, 'Health systems in Europe: changes and resistance', Opening report to health workers' conference, July 4, 2011 (internationalviewpoint.org/spip.php?article2180).

commodification of healthcare in Europe even if no convincing evidence has been offered to support the idea that private markets accomplish these goals. To the contrary, there is evidence globally that non-profit-oriented systems score better on both counts. Across the Atlantic, a review of 132 studies comparing for-profit and not-for-profit hospitals and other healthcare institutions in the US, between 1980 and 2000, showed that non-profits were often superior in terms of cost-efficiency and quality.[36]

The private sector never ceased to exist in Western Europe, in spite of solidarity-based health systems being introduced, and it re-emerged in Eastern Europe after the 1980s. This private healthcare sector has made new inroads into the public sector,[37] especially in the last two decades. While there are several factors at play in the transformation of solidarity-based health systems into market-based ones, a major enabling factor has been the weakened bargaining power of labour after the 1970s. This weakness of labour has become an opportunity for capital to strike back and reclaim health services for profit-making.

A combination of tax cuts and budget austerity heralded the European health-system reforms of the 1980s. This not only concerned the tax-based systems but also countries with social health insurance. In the latter case, hospital infrastructure was typically funded by local government funds, which came under strain. Social insurance was also affected because of the difficulty in raising premiums paid by workers already suffering from stagnation in wages.[38]

The National Health System (NHS) in the UK has been progressively dismantled and privatized by successive governments

[36] C. Leys, 'Health, health care and capitalism', in *Morbid Symptoms: Health under Capitalism*, eds. L. Panitch and C. Leys, Pontypool: Merlin Press, 2009, p. 17.

[37] Ibid., p. 20.

[38] C. Hermann, 'The Marketisation of Healthcare in Europe', in *Morbid Symptoms: Health under Capitalism*, pp. 125–44.

over the past quarter-century. This process and its consequences have been profoundly anti-democratic and opaque. Catchphrases such as 'public-private partnerships', 'modernization', 'value for money', and 'local ownership' conceal the extent and real nature of what has happened, and the complexity of healthcare allows the reality of its transformation to be buried under a thousand half-truths.[39] But the NHS represented what was anathema to capital, a well-functioning tax-funded and predominantly public health system in a developed capitalist economy.[40]

UHC IN LOW- AND MIDDLE-INCOME COUNTRIES

Low- and middle-income countries face a series of challenges that high-income countries did not confront when they began to develop UHC systems. The demands on healthcare systems were fewer in the early twentieth century because the available medical technologies were also less developed. Epidemiological challenges facing LMICs today might also be more serious because they have faster growing populations, a higher prevalence of infectious diseases, and a growing burden of non-communicable illnesses compared with countries that attained UHC in the past century.[41]

We have, in earlier sections, briefly discussed the trajectory of UHC reforms in some Latin American countries such as Mexico and Colombia in the 1980s and 1990s. We will now turn to two countries—Brazil and India—to highlight current challenges faced by LMICs while trying to secure universal healthcare.

39 A.M. Pollock, ed., *NHS plc: The Privatisation of Our Health Care*, London: Verso, 2009.

40 The story of the privatization of the NHS has been told in detail by Leys and Player (*The Plot Against the NHS*, 2011). The book recounts how global (mainly US-based) health management organizations, managed care providers, insurance companies and consultancy firms plotted in tandem with the British political class to bring down the edifice that was the NHS.

41 W.D. Savedoff, D. de Ferranti, A.L. Smith and V. Fan, 'Political and Economic Aspects of the Transition to Universal Health Coverage', *The Lancet*, vol. 380, no. 9845 (2012), pp. 924–32.

Before we proceed, however, it is important to mention that beyond the confines of 'coverage', there are several alternative examples of how quality care has been, or is being, provided by public systems in the global South, such as in Costa Rica, Cuba, Malaysia, Sri Lanka, and in Rwanda and Venezuela much more recently. A complete or partial rejuvenation of public systems in many of these countries is noteworthy.[42] The following section analyses the cases of Brazil and India to understand how UHC is being projected in LMICs today, in contrast with such models of comprehensive, integrated healthcare systems, and how the approach is imbued with a neoliberal ethos.

Brazil: Comprehensive Primary Care, Private Hospital Care

Brazil went against the neoliberal trend in vogue in the rest of Latin America by creating the tax-funded Sistema Único de Salud (SUS, the Unified Health System) in 1986 and by proclaiming in its 1988 constitution the government's duty to provide free healthcare for all, despite strong opposition from a powerful and mobilized private health sector. This progressive stance was the culmination of decades of mobilization in favour of better healthcare that was part of the struggle to restore democracy in Brazil.

The creation of the SUS resulted in the roll-out of an impressive primary care scheme, which now covers almost the entire country.[43] Paradoxically, in June 2013, when millions came out to demonstrate on the streets of several Brazilian towns, one of the key concerns expressed was lack of access to healthcare.[44] The problem

[42] For a brief discussion on trends in Malaysia and Sri Lanka see, for example, Amit Sengupta, 'Creating, reclaiming, defending: non-commercialized alternatives in the health sector in Asia', in *Alternatives to Privatization*, eds. D.A. McDonald and G. Ruiters, New York: Routledge, 2012. This essay has been reproduced here in Chapter 6 of this section.

[43] J. Paim, C. Travassos, C. Almeida, L. Bahia and J. Macinko, 'The Brazilian Health System: History, advances, and challenges', *The Lancet*, vol. 377, 2011, pp. 1778–97.

[44] G. Gupta and O. Crellin, 'Brazil Protests Run Gamut from Health Care to

is that while most PHC is provided by a vast network of public providers and facilities, hospital care is largely provided by private facilities. Based on an arrangement typical of the UHC approach,[45] the state purchases a bulk of secondary and tertiary care from the private sector and only a small percentage of such care is provided by public facilities. An important part of healthcare services is contracted out to the private sector by the SUS, especially in the case of high-cost, tertiary care procedures. Primary care clinics and emergency units remain largely public, whereas hospitals, outpatient clinics as well as diagnostic and therapeutic services are in private hands.[46] A renewed public-private segmentation of health services has been created since the launch of the 1988 reforms, whereby the public sector is responsible for high-volume basic health services as well as some high-cost services, while the private sector covers the more profitable services.[47]

India: Poor Public Care, Ineffective Health Insurance

UHC as implemented in India exemplifies an entirely different set of issues and challenges, which have accompanied the introduction of social health insurance programmes elsewhere. Historically, government intervention in healthcare has largely taken the form of direct provision of services, through a network of public hospitals, primary healthcare centres and dispensaries. This was supplemented by relatively small social health insurance schemes—the Central Government Health Scheme (CGHS) and

World Cup', *USA Today*, June 23, 2013 (http://www.usatoday.com/story/news/world/2013/06/23/brazil-protests/2449079/).

45 It should be noted that the Brazilian reforms started before UHC was developed as a model, and the Brazilian system has not been designated as modelled on the concept of UHC. However, nomenclature notwithstanding, Brazil's problems are very similar to those being faced by UHC models elsewhere.

46 Paim et al., 'The Brazilian Health System: History, advances, and challenges'.

47 P.E.M. Elias and A. Cohn, 'Health Reform in Brazil: Lessons to consider', *American Journal of Public Health*, vol. 93, no. 1 (2003), pp. 44–48.

the Employees State Insurance Scheme (ESIS) for workers in larger industrial units.

However, the public sector is in a state of neglect and has traditionally been poorly funded. Public expenditure on health stood at around 1.04% of GDP in 2012, one of the lowest in the world.[48] Consequently, large sections of the population depend on a poorly regulated private sector, increasingly dominated by networked corporate hospital chains, which have an infamous track record of unethical practices. With private healthcare accounting for 80% of outpatient and 60% of inpatient care, India is also one of the most privatized systems in the world.[49] The programme initiated in 2005 to strengthen the public health system, the National Rural Health Mission, has made some inroads but positive changes are still uneven and inadequate.[50]

Out-of-pocket expenditure on healthcare (approximately 70% of household healthcare expenses) contributes to widespread poverty in India.[51] In an attempt to protect patients from catastrophic health expenses, publicly-funded social health insurance schemes have been rolled out in recent years (starting with the Rajiv Aarogyasri scheme in the state of Andhra Pradesh in 2007). The scaling-up of government-funded health insurance schemes has been impressive: by the end of 2010 an estimated 247 million people—a quarter of the population—were covered by

[48] *Twelfth Five-Year Plan (2012–2017): Social Sectors*, vol. 3, New Delhi: Planning Commission, Government of India, 2013.

[49] *Morbidity, Health Care and the Condition of the Aged. Report No. 507, NSS 60th Round (January–June 2004)*, New Delhi: National Sample Survey Organisation (NSSO), Ministry of Statistics and Programme Implementation, Government of India, 2006 (http://mospi.nic.in/sites/default/files/publication_reports/507_final.pdf).

[50] For a detailed discussion of the Indian situation, see Sengupta, 'Creating, reclaiming, defending: non-commercialized alternatives in the health sector in Asia.'

[51] *High Level Expert Group (HLEG) Report on Universal Health Coverage (UHC) for India*. New Delhi: Planning Commission of India, 2011, available online (https://www.ncbi.nlm.nih.gov/pmc/articles/PMC3354908/).

one or more of these schemes, and coverage has since expanded.[52]

The government-funded health insurance schemes only cover for hospital-based care for a specific list of procedures. Patients are provided a choice of accredited institutions where they can receive treatment and be reimbursed for costs not surpassing a set ceiling. A large majority of accredited institutions are in the private sector. For example, in the case of the Aarogyasri scheme in Andhra Pradesh, the total payments to facilities accredited under the scheme from 2007 to 2013 amounted to Rs 47.23 billion, of which Rs 10.71 billion was paid to public facilities and Rs 36.52 billion went to private facilities.[53]

Beneficiaries are insured against a set of ailments that require hospitalization, but almost all infectious diseases that are treated in outpatient settings—such as tuberculosis which requires prolonged treatment, along with most chronic diseases (diabetes, hypertension and heart diseases) and cancer treatments that do not call for hospitalization—are excluded from coverage. In the case of Aarogyasri, for example, the scheme draws 25% of the state's health budget while covering only 2% of the burden of disease.[54]

The net impact of the publicly-funded and largely-public-funded health insurance schemes has been to further distort the entire structure of the country's health system. Public money is now being employed to strengthen an already dominant private sector. The schemes are also distorting the flow of resources to the hospital-based tertiary care sector (largely private) and away from primary care services. In 2009–10, direct government expenditure on tertiary care was slightly over 20% of total health expenditure

[52] 'Dysfunctional Health Systems: Case studies from China, India and the US', in *Global Health Watch*, vol. 3.

[53] J. Yellaiah, 'Health Insurance in India: Rajiv Aarogyasri health insurance scheme in Andhra Pradesh', *IOSR Journal of Humanities and Social Science*, vol. 8, no. 1 (2013), pp. 7–14.

[54] Purendra Prasad and Raghavendra, 'Healthcare Models in the Era of Medical Neo-liberalism'.

but if one adds spending on the insurance schemes that focus entirely on hospital-based care, the total public expenditure on tertiary care would be closer to 37%.[55]

A COMMON TREND

Brazil and India present some interesting commonalities when it comes to their UHC approach. While the settings are diverse, they show a similar persistence with private-sector participation in the provision of care, despite the fact that both are tax-funded health systems. In both cases, public funding does not match needs and this opens space for the progressive creep of the private sector into the larger health system. Consequently, both countries have a powerful private sector that influences the functioning of the system as a whole, jeopardizing the integrity of the public sector and drawing away resources, both financial and human, from resource-starved public facilities. In spite of strong policies in favour of universal public healthcare (in the case of Brazil and Thailand at least), the neoliberal ethos appears too strong to shake off. In other words, the three countries typify the kind of challenges that LMICs face while attempting to construct universal systems that borrow from the internal logic of UHC.

CONCLUSIONS

We have discussed the genesis of UHC and how it builds on the notion of health systems as promoted by the World Bank and other global institutions: segmented parallel private and public systems, in which the poor are provided only 'basic services' by under-funded public facilities, while the rich migrate to a burgeoning private system. The logic for UHC is driven by the need to secure pooled funds for health systems that are organized on market principles. The role of the state is increasingly that of a

[55] Selvaraj and Karan, 'Why Publicly-Financed Health Insurance Schemes are Ineffective in Providing Financial Risk Protection'.

'steward', not a provider of healthcare services. New management techniques are being introduced in order to accomplish this, based on the notion of a 'purchaser-provider' split. The state, in such a system, harnesses public funds and then as a purchaser of services makes these funds available for private capital to extract profits. At a global level, we are now seeing a convergence of health systems in the developed and the developing countries whereby health becomes a marketable commodity. In the global North and South, countries are reforming existing systems and moving away from solidarity-based healthcare to market-based provision of health services.

We have briefly looked at early (Chile, Colombia, Mexico) and more recent evidence (Brazil, India) that shows how systems built in the name of UHC, usually as an insurance-based model of fund-pooling and increasing private provision, end up decreasing equity and efficiency in health systems. Our discussions lead us to conclude that the dominant UHC approach being promoted worldwide—based on 'universal' insurance—offers no proven advantage and indeed presents many disadvantages against a single public health system, funded by tax revenue, and offering universal and free access to healthcare. The latter continues to promise more equitable health outcomes, and it is more affordable for LMICs as it keeps investments and social control in public hands and limits administrative expenses.[56]

If health outcomes are to be improved the central question that needs to be asked is not how public systems are to be privatized but how existing public systems can be made truly universal. Public systems need to be reclaimed by citizens, reformed in the interest of the people and made accountable. People's movements and organizations have much to lose from the present drift legitimized by the UHC discourse. Historically, healthcare systems worldwide have been shaped by labour's fight for better conditions

[56] Laurell, 'Can Insurance Guarantee Universal Access to Health Services?'.

of living—either by transforming the capitalist system itself or by extracting better terms from the ruling classes. The fight for a just and equitable health system has to be part of the broader struggle for comprehensive rights and entitlements. To take this struggle forward, the dominant interpretation of UHC today—one of weakening public systems and the pursuit of private profit—needs to be understood and questioned.

6. Creating, Reclaiming, Defending Non-Commercialized Alternatives in the Health Sector in Asia

AMIT SENGUPTA

Asian countries have followed broadly similar trajectories of neoliberal health-sector reforms—withdrawal of welfare provisions, contraction in public expenditure on health, gradual depletion of publicly provided health services, commercialization of healthcare and increasing inequity in access. Amit maps out some important experiments that are sustainable and promote health equity, as alternatives to the rapidly commercialized healthcare across Asia. They include large national initiatives as well as experiments conducted by NGOs in the areas of comprehensive primary care, secondary care via hospitalization, and specific aspects of service delivery. The examples discussed in the paper, led by community-based organizations or NGOs, have great potential to be integrated into public systems. However, there appears to be a trade-off between the ability (and intent) to scale up the implementation, and engagement with issues of solidarity and ideological commitment to a public ethos. While calling to strengthen the public system as an alternative to profit-oriented market-based healthcare delivery, Amit demands that the public system be re-imagined as one which attempts to provide the best services possible to all, while addressing the special needs of those most vulnerable. Such a system can only be built, he argues, by keeping popular needs at the centre, and with people's participation in planning and implementation: a system accountable to the people.

The health sector encompasses a very large canvas, including not just healthcare services but also allied services that contribute to health, such as water supply and sanitation, as well as determinants of health such as food security, secure employment, gender equity, education, housing, and a clean environment. However, for the purposes of this chapter, we limit ourselves to healthcare services in order to focus the analysis on the ownership and management systems that operate them and the extent to which these systems can be considered alternatives to privatization. Like other parts of the world, the neoliberal framework of public policy formulation has permeated Asia over the past three decades. A typical feature of neoliberal policies has been the progressive abolition of welfare rights related to economic security, health services, and education, materialized through cuts in welfare programmes, such as anti-poverty initiatives, food and agricultural subsidies, and free or subsidized public-sector services.[1] In the health sector, it is ironic that this shift in public policy was set in motion before the ink was dry on the resolution on primary healthcare (PHC) adopted in Alma-Ata in 1978.[2]

There is no single 'Asian reality', given that Asia is home to 60% of humanity and includes countries with very diverse histories,

[1] M.S. Haque, 'Global Rise of Neoliberal State and its Impact on Citizenship: Experiences in developing nations', *Asian Journal of Social Science*, vol. 36, 2008, pp. 11–34.

[2] *Inter alia*, the Alma-Ata Declaration, issued at the conclusion of the International Conference on PHC, Alma-Ata, USSR, September 6–12, 1978, stated: 'Governments have a responsibility for the health of their people which can be fulfilled only by the provision of adequate health and social measures. A main social target of governments, international organizations and the whole world community in the coming decades should be the attainment by all peoples of the world by the year 2000 of a level of health that will permit them to lead a socially and economically productive life' (Article V).

political systems, and social conditions. Nonetheless, in the last three decades, virtually the entire continent has adopted a neoliberal framework while 'reforming' the healthcare sector. Such reforms are evident, for example, in the two most populous countries of the world—China and India. China's Gini coefficient (a standard measure of income inequality) was a low 0.29 in 1981 but reached 0.41 in 1995, similar to the US. The rural-urban divide increased, regional disparities widened, and access to opportunities became less equal during the 1990s. Only the incomes of the richest quintile of the Chinese population grew faster than the national average—again remarkably similar to the US. The government's share of health expenditures fell by over half between 1980 and 1998, almost tripling the portion paid by families.[3] In India, while elements of neoliberal policies were introduced in the 1980s, formal structural adjustment measures for the economy were introduced relatively late, in 1991. The immediate fallout was savage cuts in budgetary support to the health sector, particularly in the first two years of the reform process. Indonesia, Thailand, and the Philippines were forced to undergo neoliberal reforms to access IMF loans in the midst of the Asian economic crisis in the 1990s. Cambodia, Laos, and Vietnam turned to the IMF/WB for funding and advice in the 1980s, while attempting to build their war-ravaged economies.[4] In Vietnam, in the process of economic restructuring in the 1980s, more than a million workers and over 20,000 public employees (of whom the majority were health workers and teachers) were laid off. The agreement signed with the IMF prohibited the state from providing budget support either to the state-owned economy or to an incipient private sector.

SEEKING ALTERNATIVES

A key feature of health service provisioning in the region is

[3] *Global Health Watch*, vol. 1.

[4] A. McGregor, *Southeast Asian Development*, New York: Routledge, 2008.

the overwhelming dominance of the private sector. In the period 2000–06, although per capita public health expenditure increased in all the relevant countries, in Malaysia and Sri Lanka private expenditure expanded faster than public expenditure, even though historically they had better performing public systems.

At the same time there exist important *alternative* forms of service delivery in both government and non-government sectors, which do not involve the participation of the private, for-profit sector. Essential information regarding these various initiatives is consolidated below and analysed based on a range of predefined 'criteria for success'. This mapping exercise is seen as a step towards identifying healthcare practices in the Asian context that may be used to suggest alternative strategies for health systems in the public domain, strategies which are sustainable and advance health equity.

The research was carried out by first identifying possible initiatives that needed to be documented, predominantly through literature reviews. The process was augmented by sending out requests to contacts in different parts of the region to provide information about interesting initiatives that fit the criteria of 'alternatives to privatization'. Additional information was also obtained from the available documentation of the Health Systems Knowledge Network of the Commission on Social Determinants of Health.[5] Based on the above, examples of 'alternatives to privatization' were shortlisted for more detailed analysis. These initiatives were researched further, using information received from respondents in different countries, published reports and papers, and material available on the Internet.

[5] L. Gilson, J. Doherty, R. Loewenson and V. Francis, *Challenging inequity through health systems: Final Report, Knowledge Network on Health Systems*, WHO Commission on Social Determinants of Health, 2007, available online (https://www.who.int/social_determinants/resources/csdh_media/hskn_final_2007_en.pdf).

TYPOLOGIES OF 'ALTERNATIVES'

The word 'alternatives' is intentionally placed in quotation marks. Some of the cases identified and discussed do not fit an ideal notion of alternative (as distinct from the present trend towards privatization and commercialization of healthcare and delivery mechanisms). However, as the short narratives provided below attempt to make clear, many of these initiatives are important because they do bring out the tension between the neoliberal ethos and the purported intent of addressing issues of inequity related to health and access to healthcare. While none of the cases discussed has an overt agenda to promote privatization, an ideological mindset is evident in many of the cases we have identified. This mindset is unable to visualize a system of healthcare delivery that is entirely publicly owned and financed. Below, we discuss some of the important features of the identified alternatives within different typologies. There is a degree of overlap, and we have, for example, grouped together NGO and government programmes which address a specific aspect of access to health services. The initiatives we have mapped can be classified as follows:

- Large national initiatives by governments that aim to provide comprehensive access to health services;
- Primary care initiatives by not-for-profit non-governmental organizations, which have a large span of coverage;
- Primary care initiatives, which have a limited span of coverage but are useful models to take note of;
- Initiatives that address a specific aspect of access to health services, such as access to medicines, HIV treatment, etc.

LARGE NATIONAL INITIATIVES BY GOVERNMENTS

China: New Rural Cooperative Medical Scheme (NCMS)

The NCMS was introduced in China in July 2003. It is a consequence of the Chinese government's stated effort to restructure health services, with a larger focus on improvement of equity in health and healthcare.[6] The scheme is the result of a large consultative process and aims to remedy the visible decline in access to healthcare services in China since the economic reforms initiated in the 1970s. The de-collectivization of agriculture resulted in a decrease of support for the collective welfare system, of which healthcare was part. In 1984, surveys showed that only 40–45% of the rural population was covered by an organized cooperative medical system, as compared with 80–90% in 1979. Specifically, the NCMS aims to reverse this situation and target the problems related to catastrophic out-of-pocket expenditures incurred by people to take care of medical expenses. The scheme started operating in 2003, and by 2008 over 800 million people in China's rural areas were covered by it. The premium under the NCMS is paid by three sources: Chinese national and local authorities as well as individuals. By the end of 2009, 80% of the total premium came from the central and local governments, and individuals paid 20%.[7]

Reviewing the programme shows that the scheme has led to some increase in access to inpatient care for vulnerable populations, but out-of-pocket expenses continue to be a major issue. Reimbursement of expenses for inpatient care is still low (if expanding), at approximately 30% of total costs.[8] The scheme envisages that by 2020, it will help achieve its goal of 'safe, effective, convenient, and low-cost' medical care for the entire population. Higher-end treatment will continue to be available, although

[6] Q. Meng, *Developing and implementing equity-promoting health care policies in China*, Health Systems Knowledge Network of the Commission on Social Determinants of Health, 2007, available online (https://www.who.int/social_determinants/resources/csdh_media/equity_health_china_2007_en.pdf).

[7] S. Wang, 'China's Double Movement in Health Care', in *Morbid Symptoms: Health under Capitalism*, eds. L. Panitch and C. Leys, New Delhi: LeftWord Books, 2009, pp. 240–61.

[8] J. Parry and C. Weiyuan, 'Making Health Care Affordable in China', *Bulletin of the World Health Organization*, vol. 86, no. 11 (2008), pp. 822–25 (https://www.who.int/bulletin/volumes/86/11/08-011108/en/).

funded only through private insurance schemes. A more detailed implementation plan for the three years until 2011 is being developed and is expected to receive 850 billion yuan (US$124 billion) for the reform in three years. This is the largest and most sustained initiative in post-liberalization China to reverse the trend of privatization and inequity in healthcare and access.[9] The programme is designed to provide comprehensive coverage by 2020, and its importance is immense as it seeks to reverse a three-decade trend of rolling back public support for health services. Over the last five years, there has been significant expansion, and there seems to be a political will to sustain the momentum.[10]

Iran: PHC through 'Health Houses'

The Iranian health houses, conceived and introduced during the 1980–88 war with Iraq, lie at the core of the PHC system in Iran. The system relies on the following components: (a) establishing health houses in remote and sparsely populated villages; (b) staffing health houses with health workers, known as *behvarzan* (meaning 'good skills' in Farsi), recruited from local communities; (c) developing a simple but well-integrated health information system; and (d) a referral system linking with rural and urban health centres and hospitals.[11] The health house is the most basic unit of the Iranian PHC network. Located in individual villages, it is designed to cover

9 The NCMS is a voluntary insurance scheme designed mainly for rural residents. Financed with the cooperation of individual, local, and central governments, it has a risk-pooling unit in one rural county. By the end of 2014, 98.9% rural residents (approximately 736 million) in China had joined the NCMS. It plays a very important role in Chinese rural residents' healthcare and it has raised concerns for health service quality and drug-use safety in rural China. See D. Gu et al., 'Innovating New Rural Cooperative Medical Scheme (NCMS) for Better Patient Satisfaction in Rural China', *International Journal of Environmental Research and Public Health*, vol. 15, no. 9 (2007).

10 Wang, 'China's Double Movement in Health Care'.

11 B. Sadrizadeh, 'Primary Health Care Experience in Iran', *Medical Journal of the Iranian Red Crescent*, vol. 7, no. 1 (2004), pp. 79–90.

a target population of about 1,500. The distance between the village in which the health house is located and the satellite villages served by it is typically no more than a one-hour walk.

The health houses refer patients to rural health centres, which cover about 6,000 to 10,000 people, and have up to two physicians and several health technicians. These centres are responsible for elective and emergency case management, supporting the health houses, and supervising both the health technicians and the *behvarzan*, or community health workers.[12] One male and one or more female health workers run each rural health house. The health workers are chosen from among local people familiar with the households in the village. Training occurs at the district level; students receive free training and financial support throughout the two-year training period. In return, they are formally obliged to remain and serve at the village health house for a minimum of four years after completing their study. The system is funded entirely by the national government. The challenges before it now include sustaining financial support in the face of the sanctions imposed on Iran, the need to strengthen the referral system, the need to better address non-communicable diseases and the need to strengthen secondary and tertiary levels of care.[13] The system is perhaps the most comprehensive of the alternatives discussed here—both in terms of service coverage and the range of services offered. The primary-care elements are better organized than secondary and tertiary care, but overall, its sustenance and expansion appear to be an integral part of public policy.

[12] M.S. Abbas, 'A Case Study on Intersectoral Action for Health in I.R. of Iran: Community-based initiatives experience', WHO, Tehran, 2007, available online (www.who.int/social_determinants/resources/isa_community_initiatives_irn.pdf).

[13] M. Tavassoli, 'Iranian Health Houses Open the Door to Primary Care', *Bulletin of the World Health Oorganization*, vol. 86, no. 8 (2008), pp. 577–656 (www.who.int/bulletin/volumes/86/8/en/).

Malaysia: PHC System

PHC is seen as the thrust and foundation of the public health system in Malaysia. It is a two-tier system comprised of health clinics, which cater to a population of 15,000–20,000, and community clinics that cater to 2,000–4,000 people. It is a nationwide programme funded by the country's national budget. Health clinics provide eight identified essential services, as well as dental and mental healthcare. Community clinics provide maternal and child health services and outpatient care for minor ailments. The system comprises about 900 health clinics and 2,000 community clinics across the country. The health clinics are linked to public hospitals by a referral system.[14] The system caters to the bulk of the population (about 65%) but is served by just 45% of all registered doctors, and even fewer specialists (25–30%). Patients pay only nominal fees for access to outpatient and hospitalization services. Medical and surgical emergencies are also adequately provided for, with a government-managed fleet of ambulances, including airlift capacities for more remote sites. Doctors, nurses, pharmacists, dentists, and other allied healthcare workers are appointed by the ministry of health to various healthcare centres: from rural clinics to district hospitals to tertiary, specialist hospitals throughout the country. The distribution of these resources is based on the size, need and population of the various districts and states. However, in rural and more mountainous or remote regions, the deployment of facilities as well as manpower is uneven, and there remains great disparity and inequitable distribution of healthcare personnel, especially doctors.

There appears to be a covert—if unannounced—shift to thinking that an eventual corporatization of the public-sector facilities and services should be allowed to unfold in Malaysia, where market forces dictate the price, extent and quality of the

14 N. Awin, 'A Review of Primary Health Care in Malaysia', WHO, Western Pacific Region, Manila, 2007.

services offered. However, public dissent has ensured that over the past twenty (or so) years there have been only sporadic and partially successful attempts to privatize or corporatize various components of the public health sector—e.g. the government's drug procurement and distribution centre, and the divestment of its support services (cleaning, linen, laundry, clinical waste management, biomedical engineering maintenance). Nevertheless, commercialization remains a concern, with a shortage of trained personnel and some speciality services being purchased by the public system from the for-profit private sector.[15]

Thailand: Universal Healthcare Coverage Scheme

Thailand's National Health Insurance Bill was enacted in 2002, creating the Universal Healthcare Coverage Scheme (or UC, formerly known as the 'thirty baht scheme', in reference to the Thai currency). The UC scheme shifted away from a means-tested healthcare coverage insurance programme for low-income patients, to a comprehensive healthcare plan that provides universal coverage. Originally, participants in the UC scheme were charged a co-payment of thirty baht (approximately US$1 in 2002), but this co-payment was later abolished. The UC scheme focuses on providing PHC services to Thais who were left out of the healthcare system prior to 2002. Thais joining the UC scheme receive a 'gold card', which allows them to access services in their health district and be referred to a specialist if necessary. The scheme is administered by the Thai National Health Security Office and is primarily funded by the government, based on a budget calculated at a per capita rate. At present the scheme covers an estimated 46.95 million Thais (out of a total population of 62 million).[16] One of the key elements

15 C. Chee Khoon, 'Re-inventing the Welfarist State? The Malaysian health system in transition', *Journal of Contemporary Asia*, vol. 40, no. 3 (2010), pp. 444–65.

16 V. Tangcharoensathien, P. Prakongsai, S. Limwattananon, W. Patcharanarumol and P. Jongudomsuk, 'Achieving Universal Coverage in Thailand: What

of the programme is that reimbursement of expenses to public hospitals by the government is based on enrolled populations in the hospitals' service areas. The system is geographically structured, and hospitals have fixed revenues based on the local population. Their financial viability depends on an ability to control costs.[17]

Before the UC scheme was introduced, public health insurance covered only 9% of the population. There has been progressive strengthening of the system in recent years, in spite of overall economic liberalization programmes pursued by the government. Among all the alternatives that we analyse here, the Thai UC scheme appears to have had the fastest trajectory in transforming a largely private healthcare system into a robust publicly funded system.[18]

Sri Lanka: Public Health System

The public health system in Sri Lanka, unlike other countries in the South Asian region, dates back to its pre-independence period, before 1948, with free healthcare subsequently introduced in 1953. In spite of political changes, the public system has survived and expanded, comprising a network of medical institutions (larger, intermediate, and smaller peripheral institutions) and health units. As of 2008, there were 258 health unit areas with populations

lessons do we learn?', Health Systems Knowledge Network, WHO Commission on Social Determinants of Health, Thailand, 2007.

17 S. Wibulpolprasert and S. Thaiprayoon, 'Thailand: Good Practice in Expanding Health Coverage—Lessons from the Thai health care reforms', in *Good Practice in Health Financing: Lessons from reforms in low- and middle-income countries*, eds. P. Gottret, G. Schieber, and H. Waters, Washington, DC: World Bank, 2008, pp. 355–83.

18 By the year 2011, the UCS covered 98% of the Thai population. Share of out-of-pocket expenditure declined as coverage of the scheme expanded. The number of people falling below poverty line went down from 2.7% population to 0.5% in 2009. The UCS is entirely funded by the government of Thailand, mostly through revenue from general taxes. See: http://millionssaved.cgdev.org/case-studies/thailands-universal-coverage-scheme.

ranging from 40,000 to 60,000.[19] The health unit area is a clearly defined region congruent with the administrative divisions of the country. Health units are managed by medical officers supported by a team of public health personnel comprising one or two public health nursing sisters, four to six public health inspectors, one or two supervising public health midwives, and twenty to twenty-five public health midwives. Each health unit area is subdivided into public health midwife areas, which constitute the smallest working units in the public system. Each public health midwife has a well-defined area consisting of a population ranging from 2,000 to 4,000.[20] Of the total ambulatory care market, 50% is serviced by the private sector, although 95% of inpatient care is still provided by the public sector. Although all Sri Lankans have this entitlement, those who can afford private-sector services may choose them.

The private health sector only began to develop in earnest during the 1960s. It focuses particularly on ambulatory care in the form of general practitioners. Although there are some full-time private general practitioners, most private provision takes the form of dual practice by doctors who are employed in the public health sector and have a limited private practice outside of official working hours.[21] Problems with this system include a lower utilization of peripheral facilities and overcrowding in secondary and tertiary facilities. New challenges to the system are emerging in the form of policies related to the overall neoliberal thrust of the economy, although the health system is still relatively secure.

[19] R.P. Rannan-Eliya and L. Sikurajapathy, 'Good Practice in Expanding Health Care Coverage in Sri Lanka', in *Good Practice in Health Financing: Lessons from reforms in low- and middle-income countries*, pp. 311–54.

[20] M. Perera, 'Intersectoral Action for Health in Sri Lanka', Health Systems Knowledge Network, WHO's Commission on Social Determinants of Health, 2006, available online (http://www.who.int/social_determinants/resources/csdh_media/intersectoral_action_sri_lanka_2007_en.pdf).

[21] Rannan-Eliya and Sikurajapathy, 'Good Practice in Expanding Health Care Coverage in Sri Lanka'.

Another challenge is the entry of the corporate private sector (often imported from India). The Sri Lankan system is often discussed as one of the 'success stories' of a public system. There is considerable merit in these arguments given that the country has consistently performed in a situation where other South Asian neighbours have floundered. There are several historical reasons why this is so.

The trajectory of development followed by Sri Lanka has been described as 'support-led security', in which public provision and funding of health and other social services has promoted social progress. Even before independence in 1948, there was a rapid expansion of public investment in education and health facilities in the 1930s and 1940s. Free education was introduced in 1947 and free healthcare in 1953. Along with strong support for publicly funded social services, the commitment to social justice, with particular emphasis on addressing the needs of the worst off, was a key feature of state policy. Despite low income-levels and only gradual economic growth, as well as relatively low levels of spending on health (with public healthcare expenditure only being equivalent to 2% of GDP), Sri Lanka has achieved remarkably good health status and a high literacy rate. These achievements are testimony to the effectiveness of sustained public spending on social services and a consistent commitment to equity and social justice, which is also borne out by the relatively equitable distribution of income (with a Gini index of only 33).[22] Similar to the Malaysian situation, Sri Lanka's system faces the threat of reforms that seek to align it with the neoliberal ethos of commercialization. The

[22] D. McIntyre, *Country Case Study: Universal tax funded health system in Sri Lanka*, Cape Town: Health Economics Unit, University of Cape Town, 2006; see also by the same author, 'Sri Lanka Tax and insurance funding for health systems' (http://bezak.umms.med.umich.edu/CIRHT/Content/Other%20Health%20Open%20Educational%20Resources/Epidemiology/Interactive%20Module-Promoting%20Equitable%20Access%20to%20Health%20Care%20for%20Households-UCT-CC%20BY%20NC%20SA//sri_lanka.html).

attempted reforms have been less sustained than in Malaysia but do pose a threat. The unfolding of the dynamics would be useful to study in detail, especially given that public investment in social infrastructure in Sri Lanka has enjoyed such a large consensus across the political spectrum for decades.

India: National Rural Health Mission

The National Rural Health Mission (NRHM) was launched in April 2005, as a response to a large body of criticism regarding the performance of the public health system in India. The NRHM is designed to strengthen the existing public health system, which is a three-tiered system offering primary care linked to a network of secondary and tertiary public health facilities.[23] In large parts of the country the primary healthcare network barely functions, as a consequence of poor resourcing and maintenance. Shortage of personnel and material resources plague the system.[24] The focus of the NRHM has been on family planning and maternal-child health services, in line with the Millennium Development Goals (MDGs) of reducing infant and maternal mortality. NRHM uses five approaches to its mission, which include: (a) Communitization, (b) Improved Management through Capacity, (c) Flexible Financing, (d) Innovation in Human Resource Management, and (e) Monitoring Progress against Standards. A major reformative character of this programme has been its focus on rebuilding rural health infrastructure, in line with the needs of primary healthcare.

The achievements of the NRHM have been modest so far. There

[23] The primary care system is an extensive network comprising sub-centres (covering population areas of between 3,000–5,000), primary health centres (covering 20,000–30,000 people), and community health centres (covering a population of 100,000). Across the country, as of 2007, there were a total of 145,272 sub-centres, 22,370 primary health centres, and 4,045 community health centres.

[24] M. Rao, 'Health for All and Neoliberal Globalization: An Indian rope trick', in *Morbid Symptoms: Health under Capitalism*, 2009, pp. 262–78.

has been a perceptible advance towards some strengthening of the public system, but the impact is still fragmented and inadequate to prevent a high dependence of patients on the private for-profit sector. The flagship programme of the mission is the training and deployment of accredited social health activists (ASHAs). While a massive drive towards this has been initiated, the impact is still limited. This is due, in part, to the fact that the ASHA is not conceived as a full-fledged and fully remunerated health worker but rather as a health 'assistant' who is remunerated for services delivered. However, some states are moving towards providing a fixed honorarium for ASHAs. Introduction of the NRHM could bring about some sort of reversal in decline on public spending on health and improved access to maternal and child health services.[25] However, the contractualization of healthcare personnel and their limited mandate have halted the process of strengthening public systems.

In ways similar to China, the 'alternative' being discussed here is the first cogent response of the government in India to growing health inequities in the neoliberal era. India, of course, differs from China in that it has always had a flourishing private sector in health and a relatively weak public sector. The imbalance has worsened since the early 1990s. Given this background the NRHM merits a close look as it unfolds. Parts of it continue to be informed by the neoliberal ethos (e.g. its stated intent to promote public-private partnerships in the secondary and tertiary sectors, some attempts to promote user fees, and so on). However, the initiative is important because it is an attempt to go against the overall trend of neoliberal reforms in other sectors.

[25] As per WHO-NHA data from 2015, public spending on health crawled up to 1.2% of GDP by 2009 starting from less than a percent during 2004. The latest NSSO report (71st round) shows dramatic increase in institutional deliveries—from 36% a decade ago to 80% now.

PRIMARY CARE INITIATIVES WITH LARGE SPAN OF COVERAGE

Bangladesh: Integrated Rural Healthcare (Gonoshasthaya Kendra)

At the time of the Liberation War of Bangladesh in 1971, a group of Bengali expatriate doctors working in London organized the Bangladesh Medical Association. Two of the doctors, Dr Zafrullah Chowdhury and Dr M.A. Mobin, visited the frontlines of the war and began treating wounded soldiers who were fighting a guerrilla war against the Pakistan army. With the help of the Bangladesh government in exile in Calcutta, they established a 480-bed makeshift hospital on the eastern border of Bangladesh. After the independence of Bangladesh in December 1971, some of the volunteers of the Bangladesh Field Hospital formed an NGO called Gonoshasthaya Kendra (GK; 'People's Health Centre') to provide healthcare to rural communities as part of the national effort to rebuild the war-torn country.[26] The GK has come a long way since this time, both in terms of programme coverage and achievements. During the last three-and-a-half decades, it has increased its basic healthcare coverage, including reproductive and child healthcare, from serving about 50,000 people in fifty villages in 1972, to over 1.2 million people in 592 villages geographically spread across the country in thirty-one unions of seventeen *upazilas* in fifteen districts. The GK provides an integrated package of health services, through its village/community-based health workers and secondary- and tertiary-level care and with strong referral linkages that run through the GK system and up to government hospitals. The GK also offers a locally organized

[26] N. Upham, 'Making Health Care Work for the poor: Review of the NGO experiences in selected Asian countries', Background document, WHO Asian Civil Society Conference on Macroeconomics and Health, April 27–28, 2004, Colombo, Sri Lanka, p. 16 (http://www.who.int/macrohealth/action/en/ngo_paper_sri_lanka.pdf).

Gonoshasthaya Bima, a community-based cooperative health insurance scheme, and runs a training programme for traditional birth attendants (TBAs) to upgrade their skills and become trained TBAs. GK health workers link with the TBAs to ensure an effective referral system. The GK is known for its advocacy role on many issues and its innovations to promote gender equity.[27]

The GK is explicit in stating that it is not in competition with the government of Bangladesh, arguing that its role is to supplement the public health system. Its primary focus has been to work with the state so that its innovative schemes, if found productive, can be adopted by the public sector. Many activities are self-supporting (e.g. the hospitals, pharmaceutical unit, medical college), but a large annual subsidy (20–30% of the overall budget, sourced primarily from donor agencies such as the French Support Committee to GK-Savar, Medicos, Germany, etc.) is still necessary to continue the programme.[28] Major challenges being faced include problems in retaining trained personnel, who are lured away by the growing private sector (as well as better-funded NGOs), the need to constantly seek donor funding, and the paucity of a robust second-line leadership. The hospital in Dhaka also faces difficulty in competing with the private hospitals that have emerged in the city. The GK alternative is an important initiative that has attracted attention in the South Asian region, partly because of its early association with the country's liberation struggle. The organization also played host to the first People's Health Assembly in 2000, out of which developed the global People's Health Movement.[29] An

[27] C.R. Huda and Z. Chowdhury, 'Maternal Mortality in Rural Bangladesh: Lessons learned from Gonoshasthaya Kendra programme villages', *Asia-Pacific Population Journal*, vol. 23, 2008, pp. 55–78.

[28] Based on personal communications between the author and Dr Zafrullah Chowdhury, one of the founders of GK, a face-to-face meeting on August 26, 2009, and several visits by the author to the GK before 2007.

[29] For more information on the People's Health Movement, see www.phmovement.org.

important aspect of this 'alternative' is that it has forged purposive links with the programme and political campaigns on access to health and medicines. Also of importance is the strong focus on gender issues and gender empowerment.

Bangladesh: Essential Healthcare by BRAC

The Bangladesh Rural Advancement Committee (BRAC) started its activities in 1972 in the district of Sylhet, as a relief and rehabilitation project to help returning refugees after the Liberation War of 1971. BRAC has also diversified its activities outside Bangladesh and operates different programmes, such as those in microfinance and education in nine countries across Asia and Africa. The organization is 80% self-funded through a number of commercial enterprises that include a dairy and food project and a chain of retail handicraft stores called Aarong.[30] In 1979, BRAC began working on health issues through the nationwide Oral Therapy Extension Programme, a campaign to combat diarrhoea, the leading cause of the high child mortality rate in Bangladesh. Over a ten-year period, 1,200 BRAC workers went door-to-door to teach twelve million mothers the preparation of homemade oral rehydration solution (ORS). Since 2002, all of BRAC's health interventions have been incorporated under the BRAC Health Programme.

Until 2006, the programme provided health support to members of BRAC's village organizations. In 2007, there was a shift in operations towards a more community-centred approach, meaning that everyone in the community was offered BRAC's essential healthcare services. Perhaps no discussion of NGO initiatives is complete without a discussion of some aspects of BRAC's work in Bangladesh, if for no other reason than that it operates the world's largest NGO programme and is the second-largest employer in Bangladesh after the state! The health

[30] BRAC website: www.brac.net.

programme has been scaled up to the extent that it is an alternate structure to the government's public health system. To be fair, the two often collaborate and work together, though their governance systems remain fairly distinct. The growth of such large NGO-led programmes is also related to large donors putting their faith in NGOs rather than national governments, as the former are often perceived as more honest, more responsive to community needs, and more efficient.[31] What is also interesting is to contrast the trajectory of the GK health programme with BRAC's. While the former is also large, BRAC has scaled up much faster and is by far the larger programme. This has occurred in a situation in which BRAC has focused more on expanding its operational activities and has not been as upfront about linkages to ideological movements and its own positions regarding inequity and access. It may be argued that this has made it easier for integration and collaboration with public systems. Another important aspect of BRAC's work is its practice of cross-subsidizing its developmental work through incomes from its commercial activities, raising questions about just how non-commercial its health initiatives really are.

PRIMARY CARE INITIATIVES WITH LIMITED SPAN OF COVERAGE

Laos: Comprehensive PHC Project in Sayaboury Province

In partnership with the ministry of public health and with funding support from AusAID, a comprehensive PHC project began in 1992 in Sayaboury Province in Laos with Save the Children Australia (SCA) and the Sayaboury Department of Health. The programme has been carried out in four phases, each phase spanning three years and building on its predecessor's successes.[32]

[31] A. Green and A. Matthias, 'NGOs—A policy panacea for the next millennium?', *Journal of International Development*, vol. 7, no. 3 (1995), pp. 565–73.

[32] C.T. Perks, J. Michael and K. Phouthonsy, 'District Health Programmes and

The first phase focused on strengthening the management and training skills of the provincial management team, which conducted in-service training for district teams and dispensary staff. During the second phase, the programme expanded into four additional districts and was geared towards integrating PHC activities at all levels. The third phase expanded into four newly created districts in the north that were quite remote. The International Fund for Agricultural Development (IFAD) constructed dispensaries, augmenting the construction programme instituted by SCA and expanding access to first-line health services. The fourth phase aimed to strengthen the skills of health workers, with an emphasis on those in the northern districts. The integrated management of childhood illness (IMCI) strategy was adopted in all districts.

The Sayaboury programme has shown significant successes, at the very affordable cost of only US$1 per person each year, which means a total project cost of US$4 million over a twelve-year period. The project is seen as a model for the country and efforts are under way to upscale the programme in other provinces.[33] Laos has very poor health indicators and a high incidence of private expenditure on health. In such a situation the present initiative to extend primary health coverage in one province is important to examine, especially given that the initiative is now being scaled up in other provinces of the country.

India: 'Public-Private Partnership'[34] for PHC (Karuna Trust)

Karuna Trust, a leading NGO in India working to provide PHC services, was tasked with the responsibility of managing the

Health-Sector Reform: Case study in the Lao People's Democratic Republic', *Bulletin of the World Health Organization*, vol. 84, no. 2 (2006), pp. 132–38.

33 See the SCA website: https://www.savethechildren.net/news-stories.

34 We describe a partnership between a not-for-profit NGO and government as a public-private partnership, as this is the nomenclature used by the Indian government regarding initiatives in which individual PHC centres are given out to NGOs to administer and provide services.

Gumballi PHC Centre, in the state of Karnataka, in 1996. This was part of an experiment by the government of Karnataka to outsource the running of some Primary Health Centres to non-government entities. While Primary Health Centres are the hub of the primary care system, a large majority of them function sub-optimally. In a majority of cases, inpatient services are not available, and in a significant number the centre is reduced to a dispensary that functions for just two to three hours a day. This is the context in which the Karnataka government chose to outsource the running of the primary health centre to an NGO (Karuna Trust[35]). The Karuna Trust integrated the activities of all national health programmes, including reproductive and child health, into the activities of the centre. It ensured that, under its management, it would provide round-the-clock emergency and casualty services, outpatient facilities six days a week, a ten-bed inpatient department, and 24-hour labour and essential obstetric facilities. Additionally, the Karuna Trust has introduced innovations such as integration of mental health services, eye care, and specialist services at primary-care level.

In the area covered by the Gumballi primary health centre there have been significant improvements as regards a number of indicators, in comparison to indicators in the state of Karnataka. The success of the Gumballi primary health centre and its impact as a 'model' have strengthened the idea of public-private partnerships as a viable model among policy makers. Its success led the Karnataka government to issue a formal policy on public-private partnerships in 2000. The initiative has been a subject of considerable debate within the country. The Trust sees itself as building 'models', and does not see the initiative as an alternative to the state taking the responsibility in managing and maintaining the public healthcare system. Its experience in managing the primary health centres indicates that success is variable and depends crucially on strong

[35] Karuna Trust website: www.karunatrust.com.

support from the local public health department. India's public health system, especially at the primary level of care, has been perennially plagued with problems, including its inability to attract human resources, inefficiency, poor infrastructure, and corruption. A way out is sought in outsourcing primary care facilities to private entities, especially in resource-poor areas. The Karuna Trust alternative represents one of the largest such ventures involving a not-for-profit trust that has been promoting primary care through its own programmes. While the outsourcing of public facilities is an issue that is a cause for a larger debate, the apparent initial success of the initiative merits further investigation.[36]

India: Comprehensive Rural Health Project (CRHP) in Jamkhed, Maharashtra

The Comprehensive Rural Health Project (CHRP), Jamkhed, was founded in 1970. The extremely poor and drought-prone area of Jamkhed was plagued by high rates of malnutrition, infectious diseases, maternal deaths, and occupational injuries. Social injustices such as the low status of women and caste-based prejudices contributed significantly to this chronic state of ill health. Initially covering eight villages with a combined population of 10,000, the project rapidly expanded in its early years, reaching out to a larger number of village communities. By 1980, the CRHP expanded to cover a total of seventy villages with a combined population of 100,000. By 1985, a total of 250,000 people in 250 villages in Karjat and Jamkhed *talukas* were working with the CRHP. Eventually over 300 villages with a combined population of 500,000 were participating in the CRHP through the selection, training, and support of village health workers (VHWs) and through the formation of community-based organizations (CBOs)

36 B. Ghanshyam, 'Can Public-Private Partnerships Improve Health in India?', *The Lancet*, vol. 372, no. 9642 (2008), pp. 878–79 (https://www.thelancet.com/journals/lancet/article/PIIS0140-6736(08)61380-X/fulltext).

such as farmers' clubs, women's clubs (*mahila vikas mandals*), and self-help groups (SHGs).[37]

The trained VHW acts as the local agent of positive health and social change. She is selected by her community and receives training in health, community development and organization, communication skills, and personal development from the CRHP. Her primary role is to freely share the knowledge she obtains with everyone in the community, to organize community groups, and to facilitate action, especially among women, the poor, and the marginalized. At the outset, many of these VHWs were often illiterate women from the 'untouchable' (Dalit) caste. The VHWs, working entirely as volunteers, became empowered by learning skills with which to earn a living through microenterprise. The impact of the programme is visible. Unlike many other NGO-led programmes in the region, the Jamkhed project has resolutely resisted the temptation to scale up. However, scaling up can be seen in a different way—small programmes all over the world, from Nepal to Brazil, use Jamkhed's principles. The Indian government also sends its own officials for orientation and training to Jamkhed. The project is financed (the annual budget is about US$500,000) through fees (which are very reasonable and sought only from those who can pay) earned by a small hospital in Jamkhed and individual donations from people across the world. The Jamkhed project has been held up, globally, as a true example of a community-based and community-owned primary care programme, and one that has been in existence for over four decades. Also interesting to learn from are the community mobilization and health worker training methodologies used in the programme.[38]

[37] Jamkhed website: www.jamkhed.org.

[38] T. Rosenberg, 'Necessary Angels', *National Geographic Magazine*, no. 214 (2008), pp. 66–85.

INITIATIVE ADDRESSING A SPECIFIC ASPECT OF ACCESS TO HEALTH SERVICES

India: Home-based Neonatal Care in Gadchiroli, Maharashtra

This programme was initiated by the Society for Education Action and Research in Community Health (SEARCH), a non-profit NGO set up by a husband-and-wife team of doctors in 1986. They identified the main causes of infant mortality in the region and devised a strategy of home-based neonatal care to address them. The programme hinges on trained community health workers (CHWs), or *arogyadu*, who are at the centre of efforts to reduce neonatal and infant morbidity and mortality. SEARCH recruited village women with a minimum of four years' schooling and trained them to provide care for women during pregnancy and for their babies after birth.

The CHWs visit pregnant women to provide information on caring for themselves during pregnancy, and the recognition of signs which may indicate that there are complications. Their work is complementary to that of the traditional birth attendants, except that the latter focus on newborns, and the roles are kept distinct. After the birth, they visit the mother and baby at home eight times during the first month (or twelve times if the baby is at high risk). Among the types of preventive care they can offer are examining the baby, checking weight, temperature, and respiratory rate, and administering vitamin K. The CHWs also advise mothers on caring for the newborn, including breastfeeding, prevention of hypothermia, and recognizing danger signs. They can diagnose asphyxia, sepsis, low birth weight, and breastfeeding problems, using simple, standardized criteria. Simple treatment is carried out on sick newborns at home by following standard practices learned during training. Many innovations have been introduced to provide support to the programme. One such innovation is the design and local fabrication of 'breath counters' that are used by CHWs in place of stethoscopes.

The programme operates in forty-two villages, and around eighty village health workers and 120 traditional midwives have learned to diagnose and treat major killers such as neonatal sepsis and infant pneumonia. An evaluation of the work of CHWs showed that there was a 62% reduction in the neonatal mortality rate, 71% reduction in the perinatal mortality rate, and 49% reduction in incidence of neonatal illnesses. In addition, the fatality rate in cases of sepsis/pneumonia fell from 16.6% to 2.8%, and the fatality rate among premature newborns and/or newborns with low birth weight went down by 60%.[39] The incidence of post-partum maternal illness was reduced by 51%. The positive findings from the Gadchiroli project have resulted in trials to upscale the programme, including some by the government's health department in its National Rural Health Mission. Although this is not an alternative to commercialization that covers the entire spectrum of health services, the programme nonetheless dovetails with primary care systems. Of interest are moves to scale up the programme through its adoption in the country's public system. Innovations used in training and training materials are useful to note, especially in the context of fairly high success rates reported in controlling childhood mortality and morbidity.

India: Sonagachi HIV/AIDS International Project (SHIP)

In 1992, the All India Institute of Hygiene and Public Health (AIIHPH) initiated a conventional sexually transmitted infections treatment and prevention programme in Sonagachi, the principal 'red-light' district of Kolkata, home to over 7,000 sex workers. The Sonagachi HIV/AIDS International Project (SHIP)

[39] A.T. Bang, R.A. Bang, S. Baitule, M. Deshmukh, H.M. Reddy, 'Burden of morbidities and the unmet need for health care in rural neonates—a prospective observational study in Gadchiroli, India', *Indian Pediatrics*, vol. 38, 2001, pp. 952–65.

was implemented through an inter-sectoral partnership of the WHO, AIIHPH, the British Council, and a number of ministries and local NGOs. The project quickly moved beyond traditional treatment and education to focus on the empowerment of the sex workers. Key interventions during the first five years included vaccination and treatment services for the sex workers' children, literacy classes for the women, political activism and advocacy, microcredit schemes, and cultural programmes.[40] The sex workers created their own membership organization, the Durbar Mahila Samanwaya Committee (DMSC), which successfully negotiated for better treatment by controllers ('madams'), landlords, and local authorities.

In 1999, the DMSC took over the management of SHIP, and has since expanded it to include forty 'red-light' districts across West Bengal, including a community of around 65,000 female, transgender and male sex workers based in brothels, streets, and hotels. The DMSC's work includes struggle against extortion and harassment by local hooligans and police, fighting against the eviction of individual sex workers from their homes, running an HIV helpline, and action against forcible HIV/AIDS surveillance. The DMSC's efforts have resulted in the creation of a self-regulatory board that, whenever a new girl/woman arrives in Sonagachi, scans legal issues such as her age and whether she is willingly entering this sector of work. The initiative receives support from the Ford Foundation, the United Nations Development Programme (UNDP), Action Aid, and the National Aids Control Organisation (NACO) of the government of India.[41]

Efforts to empower people with knowledge and tools for health are at the centre of this programme. Peer educators provide

[40] S. Jana and S. Singh, 'Beyond medical model of STD intervention—lessons from Sonagachi', *Indian Journal of Public Health*, vol. 39, no. 3 (1995), pp. 125–31.

[41] J. Smarajit, 'The Sonagachi Project: A sustainable community intervention program', *AIDS Education and Prevention*, vol. 16, no. 5 (2004), pp. 405–14.

sexual health and HIV education to sex workers and madams and distribute condoms. To support non-formal education efforts, twenty-nine educational centres have been set up in and around Sonagachi. To foster economic security, sex workers seeking financial credit are encouraged to become members of a community-lending cooperative that provides affordable loans. As part of its empowerment strategy, the Sonagachi Project also promotes the self-expression of sex workers through a cultural wing—the Komal Gandhar.

In addition, an anti-trafficking unit, controlled by self-regulatory boards, works across West Bengal to protect children; two homes are also in operation to provide a safe shelter to children in distress. Evidence suggests that the project has had a major impact. In 1992, the rate of consistent condom use with clients in the previous two months was a mere 1%. By 2001, that figure had increased to 65%. Prevalence of syphilis dropped during that period from 25% to 8.76%. The programme has attracted substantial attention as an example of a health-sector intervention that is premised on community involvement and organization. Of particular importance is the fact that the community of sex workers is one of the most marginalized. Within such a context, it is useful to examine the success of the alternative to provide a political voice to the community and to combine it with programmes that address several determinants of good health in the sex-worker community. The expansion of the initiative and its proposed adoption within the public health system are also areas that merit further scrutiny.

Nepal: Community-based Management of Childhood Pneumonia

Pneumonia is a leading cause of mortality among children aged under five in Nepal. Female community health volunteers (FCHV) were selected to manage childhood pneumonia at the community level, using oral antibiotics. A technical working group composed of government officials, local experts, and donor partners embarked on a process to develop a strategy to pilot the approach and expand it nationally. Community-based management of pneumonia doubled the total number of cases treated, compared to districts with facility-based treatment only. Over half of the cases were treated by the FCHVs. The programme was phased over fourteen years and 69% of Nepal's under-five population gained access to pneumonia treatment.[42] The FCHVs were selected by the communities and trained by the ministry of health. The WHO, UNICEF, and United States Agency for International Development (USAID) supported the development of technical guidelines for programme implementation. UNICEF conducted a focused ethnographic study to understand community-perceived danger signs of pneumonia and care-seeking practices. Training and behaviour-change communications materials were developed by members of the technical working group.

To address the low literacy level of some FCHVs, extensive effort was put into developing pictorial training manuals, educational materials, and reporting booklets. This preparation phase took place in 1993–94. Training began in June 1995 involving role-play and practical skills development. FCHV supervisors were included in training to strengthen their links with the FCHVs for future follow-up and field monitoring. Four districts were selected for the pilot intervention—two in 'treatment' and two 'referral'—with a total of 1,497 FCHVs and 525 health facility staff trained. In all four districts, health facility staff were trained in both pneumonia and programme management to ensure that FCHVs received the necessary supportive supervision, feedback, and replenishment of supplies. District health office staff were trained in monitoring and supervision for follow-up and documentation. Mothers' groups and village leader orientations were held in all villages to

[42] P. Dawson, Y.V. Pradhan, R. Houston, S. Karki, D. Poudel S Hodgins, 'From Research to National Expansion: 20 years' experience of community-based management of childhood pneumonia in Nepal', *Bulletin of the World Health Organization*, vol. 86, no. 5 (2008), pp. 339–43.

encourage prompt care-seeking and local support.

In 1997, the two 'referral' districts were converted to 'treatment' and the programme gradually expanded. By 2007, forty-two of Nepal's seventy-five districts were included, where 69% of the population of children aged less than five years resides. The quality of care provided by the FCHVs is regularly monitored by district and partner staff, and remains high. Standardized checklists are used and immediate feedback is given. Community-based pneumonia treatment data are part of the government's routine Health Monitoring Information System. An estimated 6,000 lives are currently saved each year through this intervention in Nepal.[43]

Nepal is one of the poorest countries in Asia and has suffered the consequences of political turmoil and devastation through natural disasters in recent decades. What has gone largely unnoticed, however, is some remarkable progress in Nepal in recent years in terms of reduction in mortality and morbidity indicators. Some commentators have ascribed this to the success of focused, donor agency-supported programmes that have been successful in harvesting the 'low-hanging fruits' of PHC. While this analysis has some merit, it would be interesting to examine programmes such as the one described above. The FCHV initiative is also interesting to follow as it addresses pneumonia, one of the key downstream causes of childhood mortality.

India: Affordable Drugs for Everyone (Locost)

Low Cost Standard Therapeutics, or Locost, was set up to enable all Indians, even the poor in remote areas, to access quality medicines at affordable prices. Locost was founded in 1983 as a non-profit charitable trust registered in Baroda, Gujarat. Locost's medicine prices are significantly lower than those of other manufacturers. For example, atenolol, a drug used to treat high blood pressure and available at retail stores for Rs 20–25 a strip, is

[43] Ibid.

sold by Locost at Rs 3 per strip. A strip of paracetamol from Locost costs Rs 2, while proprietary brands cost Rs 9 per strip (one rupee is approximately US$0.02).[44] Locost's small-scale manufacturing unit makes over sixty essential medicines in eighty formulations (liquid, capsule, tablet). Locost buys the active pharmaceutical ingredient from bulk drug manufacturers and then manufactures its own formulations. Locost also pays its workers more than the regular wages; its wage scales are, in fact, the highest among the small-scale industries.

Despite all the expenses that go into maintaining a high standard, Locost is able to sell its drugs at one-fourth to one-tenth of the price of drugs being sold in the retail market. With such competitive prices, Locost makes a profit of about 10% on annual sales, which it ploughs back into production to scale up volumes.[45]

Locost has been supplying drugs to over 100 civil society and charitable organizations. The idea of making the Locost drugs available at various retail outlets is, however, a relatively new concept. Besides its manufacturing unit in Baroda, Locost has a retail store in Vadodara, a depot in Karnataka (Bangalore) and the Northeast (Guwahati), and small retail outlets in various parts of Maharashtra.

Locost also has an education cell that focuses on issues related to education and training for rational use of medicines. It brings out a Gujarati language monthly, *Apnu Swasthya*, and other publications for the general public, the latest being the Gujarati version of the famous classic *Where There Is No Doctor*; as well as *A Lay Person's Guide to Medicine*, a guide on the use and political economy of medicines. Locost is also active in pharmaceutical policy advocacy at regional and national levels. Its partnership, as respondent, in an ongoing case in the Supreme Court has resulted in the elimination of several categories of harmful and irrational

[44] Locost website: www.locostindia.com.

[45] Information based on personal communication of the author with founder and director of Locost, S. Srinivasan, July 2009.

drugs. India's generic pharmaceutical industry has been called the 'pharmacy of the South' because of its ability to supply low-cost medicines to a large number of poor countries across the globe. However, within India, access to medicines is still a big issue, and the major constraint continues to be the price of medicines. An estimated 50–80% of people in India do not have access to essential medicines. The 'alternative' presented here addresses this issue by making available medicines at low prices to community health programmes. It is an alternative to commercial pharmaceutical production and distribution that has the potential for replication in many resource-poor settings.

EVALUATION OF ALTERNATIVES

It would be inappropriate to suggest overly specific trends or make broad generalizations based on the limited evidence of alternatives to commercialization presented here. There are, however, some general developments that can be commented upon, divided into two areas: those relating to the public sector and those related to the private not-for-profit sector.

Public Sector

There is an interest and some urgency among governments that have followed neoliberal reforms and dismantled public systems (e.g. China, India, Laos) to attempt to remedy the negative impact of these reforms through some strengthening of public systems. Unfortunately, most public initiatives continue to be informed by, and located in, an understanding that public strengthening must go hand in hand with partnerships with the private sector.

- Neoliberal ideologies permeate the thinking on health systems even in countries where public systems are acknowledged to have produced laudable results (e.g. Sri Lanka and Malaysia). However, the 'reform' towards commercialization faces popular opposition and has not proceeded at the pace projected by the neoliberal lobby.

- The presence of a growing private sector impacts on the ability of the public system to thrive and expand, by drawing away technical and human resources.
- Generally, 'reform' ideology is prominent in the secondary and tertiary healthcare sectors, for the good reason that the for-profit private sector is not interested in the primary level of care. This is creating a move towards the bifurcation of health systems, where the primary sector is seen as the domain of public systems and the secondary/tertiary sectors are opened up to the private sector.

Not-for-profit Sector

- Several alternatives are being developed and implemented by the not-for-profit sector, which have the potential for adoption within public systems. A systematic analysis of these can inform many public initiatives.
- Community-based organizations implementing alternatives find it difficult to scale up when they need to reach out to regions that are outside their immediate geographical area of work.
- There appears to be a trade-off between scaling up, versus loosening bonds of community solidarity and commitments to a larger public ethos.
- The role of donor agencies in supporting programmes by not-for-profit organizations, in preference to government programmes, needs to be analysed.
- The dividing line between a 'contractor' of services for the government and a community mobilizer is often blurred. Some criteria need to be developed to examine programmes that involve partnerships between government and not-for-profit organizations.

WAYS FORWARD

The 'public' has virtually disappeared from healthcare systems in many parts of the world. It is therefore necessary to address wrong perceptions and blatant untruths about the public sector, particularly given the systematic attempts to portray the private sector as more 'efficient' and to argue that market-based competition and incentives lead to better care and more choices. Such arguments turn a blind eye to the fact that the public sector has played the major role in almost all situations in which health outcomes have improved significantly. Health systems that have depended on the public sector have been the norm, rather than the exception, even in wealthy countries. The success stories of health system development in the global South (e.g. Sri Lanka, Costa Rica, and Cuba) are those of public-sector health systems. But the success of the public sector is not limited to healthcare systems. Publicly funded research in national institutes of science and universities has laid the foundations for many, if not most, developments in the medical sciences. Public systems are desirable because they promote equity. This is perhaps the most important reason why the public sector needs to play a leading role in healthcare systems—no matter which part of the world we are talking about. People have a right to healthcare in an equitable manner, independent of their ability to pay. Governments, not markets, can ensure that health systems address the needs of the poorest and the most marginalized. There also need to be conscious elements within public systems that promote equity. The mere fact that a system is funded through public funds does not mean that it necessarily promotes equity. There are various elements that come into play, including, for example, how such a system targets those who need health services the most. This does not mean that public health services are 'poor services for poor people'. They should be seen as attempts to provide the best services possible to all, while addressing the special needs of those most vulnerable. An equitable and efficient healthcare system requires planning that is based on local conditions. It is impossible for a profit-driven, fragmented system with multiple (often contradictory) objectives to do so. For such a system to work optimally, it needs to connect regularly with people's needs and priorities. This is best achieved when popular participation ensures that the public is not just a recipient of public healthcare but is also involved in its planning and execution. It is only through the operation of an adequately financed public service that the link between the income of healthcare providers and the delivery of healthcare can be broken. Unethical behaviour of healthcare providers is directly linked with the fact that if care is linked to profit, more ill health means more profit!

Public Initiatives that Need to be Reclaimed

The alternatives discussed above indicate some ways of moving forward and suggest that there is a genuine concern in many countries of the region that the marginalization of the public sector needs to be reversed. Some of this interest may be more practical than ideological, however, which suggests continuing tension between the neoliberal ethos of 'new public management' and the practical evidence that commercialized healthcare systems are failing to deliver. Many neoliberal economists now admit this and have even resorted to coining the phrase 'market failure' to explain away the fundamental bias in neoliberal economics against welfare programmes.[46] However, especially in the Indian case, there is still hesitation to go 'all the way', and methods are being sought to still find a significant role for the private sector. Within the public systems discussed here, that of Thailand merits special mention. For countries in the region, there is a strong case to study the Thai system and to draw appropriate lessons for emulation.

Public Initiatives that Need to be Defended

We have consciously chosen also to discuss public systems that

[46] *Global Health Watch*, vol. 1.

exhibit tendencies towards undermining the public ethos, e.g. the cases of Malaysia and Sri Lanka. Of importance in these cases is the fact that while public policy in some sectors has shown a faster trajectory towards liberalization, public scrutiny and resistance have slowed down intended reforms in the healthcare sector. This indicates a strong case for promoting civil society scrutiny and mobilization around the issue of public provision of health services.

Innovations and Alternatives: Models for Adoption

The alternatives in the not-for-profit sector raise a distinct set of issues to inform future directions. It would be incorrect to dub any of these as alternatives that can transform the entire healthcare system. However, these programmes carry innovations that public systems can nurture and scale up. Importantly, these alternatives often keep alive the notions of public provisioning, community participation, comprehensive care, etc.—notions that were at the core of the Alma-Ata Declaration in 1978 but which governments worldwide have failed to take forward. Finally, notwithstanding short-term and intermediate-term tactics, public systems can survive and grow only at the expense of the private sector. This is a central message that we need to take forward. An analysis of many of the alternatives in the health sector in Asia shows that the private sector is a pernicious influence that erodes public systems. The future battle, where public systems are being resurrected, is to ensure that they are built at the expense of the private sector and not to complement it.

7. Forty Years of Alma-Ata Declaration: 'Health for All' Still a Far Cry

AMIT SENGUPTA

In one of his last pieces, marking forty years of the Alma-Ata Declaration (2018), Amit once more points out the dangers of the neoliberal policies pursued since the 1980s, and their impact on social and gender justice, climate change, biodiversity, and a range of other areas of concern. He reiterates the need for restructuring the global economic order to address inequalities and focus on the social determinants of health to achieve Health for All in a more just society.

> Primary healthcare is essential healthcare based on practical, scientifically sound and socially acceptable methods and technology made universally accessible to individuals and families in the community through their full participation and at a cost that the community and country can afford to maintain at every stage of their development in the spirit of self-reliance and self-determination.
>
> —Declaration of Alma-Ata[1]

The primary healthcare (PHC) principles affirm health as a human right based on equity and social justice, implemented

[1] 'Declaration of Alma-Ata', International Conference on Primary Health Care, Alma-Ata, USSR, September 6–12, 1978, available online (https://www.who.int/publications/almaata_declaration_en.pdf).

through community engagement, health promotion, the appropriate use of resources, and inter-sectoral action based on a 'new international economic order'. The declaration enunciated the vision of 'Health for All' by the year 2000.

The Alma-Ata Declaration, which completes forty years in 2018, came at a time of major global economic changes, including the economic slowdown of the 1970s, the debt crisis and structural adjustments. Shortly after Alma-Ata, UNICEF and the Rockefeller Foundation declared a commitment to 'selective PHC' instead of 'comprehensive PHC', which under structural adjustments became the dominant paradigm and model of PHC.[2] Structural adjustment programmes led to a reduction of staff, narrow benefit packages and a lack of resources in the public sector. They weakened already weak health systems.

In 2010, the WHO introduced the concept of universal health coverage (UHC), which was defined as access to health services without financial hardship.[3] While, in general, the notion of UHC seems consistent with the concept of Health for All, a key issue that remains unresolved is the primacy accorded to public or not-for-profit services under PHC, and, conversely, the larger role envisioned for private, for-profit providers while implementing UHC. Private providers are replacing public services in many countries. Of special concern is the increase of corporate chains of providers, mainly supported by private insurance.

While impressive medical and technological advances have taken place around the world, improvements in the health status of

[2] S. Rifkin and G. Walt, 'Why Health Improves: Defining the issues concerning "comprehensive primary health care" and "selective primary health care"', *Social Science and Medicine*, vol. 23, 1986, pp. 559–66; J.P. Unger and J. Killingsworth, 'Selective Primary Health Care: A Critical Review of Methods and Results', *Social Science and Medicine*, vol. 10, 1986, pp. 1001–02; M. Cueto, 'The Origins of Primary Health Care and Selective Primary Health Care: 1864–1874', *American Journal of Public Health*, vol. 94, no. 11 (November 2004).

[3] *World Health Report 2010.*

people have been moderate and inconsistent between and within countries. The biomedical and technical approach to health has its limitations in generating real improvements in health, especially among marginalized and poor populations, and has contributed to the neglect of other determinants of health.

Health systems must be built on the principles of comprehensive primary healthcare, which includes community engagement, adequate healthcare infrastructure, a skilled, supported and motivated health workforce, access to essential drugs of good quality that are rationally used, in addition to new advancements and technologies that must be accessible to all.

COMMUNITIES AS OWNERS AND PARTNERS

> The people have the right and duty to participate individually and collectively in the planning and implementation of their healthcare.
>
> —Declaration of Alma-Ata

Communities are at the heart of PHC and must be owners and partners in making Health for All a reality. They must not be reduced to mere consumers of health services. Health systems must be accountable to the people and communities they serve. Strong people's organizations and movements are fundamental to more democratic, transparent and accountable decision-making in health.

Community health workers are an important link between communities and the formal health system. They play an essential role in order to strengthen local health services and make them accessible to all. Therefore, community health workers must be recognized in their specific role, supported, trained and remunerated accordingly.

Community health workers must become part of a skilled and motivated health workforce. In the light of changing global demographics, the global health worker migration and the lack of a trained health workforce in developing countries, health systems must ensure an environment that will enable and retain skilled and motivated health workers at all levels.

> JUSTICE, COOPERATION AND SOLIDARITY
> The existing gross inequality in the health status of the people particularly between developed and developing countries as well as within countries is politically, socially and economically unacceptable and is, therefore, of common concern to all countries.
>
> —Declaration of Alma-Ata

Health is not only a matter of human rights, but also of justice. Governments who are not making provision for decent healthcare are denying justice to their people.

The Alma-Ata Declaration recognized the need to restructure the global economic order to address inequalities and enable countries to generate resources for decent healthcare and tackle the root causes of poor health. This still remains a critically important task today.

In contrast to the New International Economic Order referred to in the Declaration, the dominant contemporary paradigm of export-led development has contributed to a loss of tax receipts at the national level because of the competition for investment which drives reduced tax rates and the constant pressure to reduce the cost of production or extraction. These have led to a deterioration of people's living circumstances and contributed to ill health, instability, even war.

It is vital that we build solidarity within and across nations and regions. The existing system of international aid and the associated charity narrative legitimize an unfair economic framework which prevents national self-determination and weakens the building of strong and resilient local health systems. Health for all requires the redistribution of wealth nationally and globally.

Public financing is essential to secure health for all. This requires tax justice that will clamp down on tax avoidance and control tax competition between countries. The regulation of transnational corporations through appropriate agreements is essential.

ADDRESSING ROOT CAUSES OF HEALTH INEQUITY

> The attainment of the highest possible level of health is a most important worldwide social goal whose realization requires the action of many other social and economic sectors in addition to the health sector.
>
> —Declaration of Alma-Ata

The WHO's Commission on Social Determinants of Health in 2008 demonstrated that poor health is not randomly distributed, but rather follows a predictable pattern with systematic differences among social groups (i.e. of gender, class, race/ethnicity) caused by unequal exposure to, and distribution of, the social determinants of health.[4] Social justice is a matter of life and death. Addressing the root causes of health inequity and investing in society is the only way that health for all and sustainable development can be achieved.

The broader context, shaped since the late 1980s by neoliberal economic globalization, has profoundly influenced our health situation today. This can be seen in the impact of globalization on social justice, the effect of climate change on livelihoods; the loss of biodiversity, the detrimental effects of agribusiness on peasant farmers and small-holder farmers, who provide most of the world's food; the impact of land grabs and the grabbing of water bodies by big business; the influence of patriarchy on society; tax evasion leading to the lack of public funds; the unbridled growth

4 'Closing the Gap in a Generation: health equity through action on the social determinants of health', Final Report of the Commission on Social Determinants of Health, World Health Organization, Geneva, 2008.

of the arms trade; and the effects of migration, to name only a few. All these issues require collaboration across sectors and policies that will address the root causes of illness and the determinants of health inequity.

As in the Alma-Ata Declaration, a new global economic order is needed to facilitate a safe and just space for humanity. We call upon governments and people from across the globe to take forward the principles of PHC that are so clearly articulated in the Alma-Ata Declaration.

Section 4

REMEMBERING

AMIT SENGUPTA

THE HEALTH ACTIVIST

1. The 1986 Drug Seminar: Bringing Together Various Movements

J.S. MAJUMDAR

J.S. Majumdar writes of the gap between the Alma-Ata Declaration of Health for All and the restrictive patents regime pushed by developed countries and their pharmaceutical manufacturers. He also traces the coming together of diverse people and groups to work towards a drug industry which increases access to rational, affordable medicines. A number of papers presented at the Delhi Science Forum's 1986 seminar—on different aspects of the industry, on medicines and their relation to the people—were later edited by Amit and published as a book. Drug Industry and Indian People *(1986) remains a useful reference for the range of issues it deals with and its in-depth studies of the sector. Comrade Amit Sengupta was one of the key organizers of the seminar, and the main person behind the editing and publication of the book.*

In 1986, a seminar on the 'Drug Industry and the Indian People' became a turning point for health movements. In the process of organizing this seminar, I came in contact with the leading activists of the DSF who were already involved in the people's science movement. They include Prabir Purkayastha, D. Raghunandan, Dinesh Abrol, Amit and others. The seminar, jointly organized by the Federation of Medical and Sales Representatives Associations of India (FMRAI) and the Delhi Science Forum (DSF), was held at the Constitution Club in New Delhi. It was inaugurated by Justice (retired) V.R. Krishna Iyer.

Much of what happened in the 1980s and later can be traced back to that seminar. It brought together different kinds of movements and activists; as well as doctors, legal experts and research scholars. Together they addressed the following issues, particularly relevant given the background of the Alma-Ata Declaration 'Health for All by the Year 2000' of the World Health Assembly, 1978:

1. What are rational and irrational drug combinations?
2. How can an indigenous drug industry develop?
3. Generics versus brand names; and
4. How do the Indian people fight drug multinationals, who still have a stranglehold over the market?

Already a group of activists had got together under the umbrella of the All India Drug Action Network (AIDAN), of which the Delhi Science Forum (DSF) was a part. Two trade unions—the All India Chemical and Pharmaceutical Employees Federation (AICAPEF), and the Federation of Medical and Sales Representatives Association of India—were also part of the struggle against drug companies.[1] The policy-related issues we wanted to address emerged from a class perspective, making use of the experience of the working class in their struggle for wages, better working conditions, and legal coverage. We also wanted to highlight the victimization of workers in pharmaceutical factories—of the MNCs, mostly—in the 1960s and 1970s. We realized that the class issues in our struggle against the MNCs—who then controlled the sector—could not be advanced independent of the health needs of the people.

These two strands came together to form the genesis of the

[1] J.S. Majumdar was the general secretary of AICAPEF and later of FMRAI.

1986 seminar. The seminar built a much larger community of activists and intellectuals focused on specific aspects of the drug industry, and also connected the workers of the industry with the larger people's interest. The key, we concluded, was a strong indigenous manufacturing capacity—free of the shackles of intellectual property rights, the use of money power by the MNCs, and consequent high drug prices. The issues raised at the seminar were not an academic exercise. Rather, discussion of these policy-related, public-interest issues would provide a framework for future struggle, to develop progressive policies on people's health. The issues included:

1. defending the Indian Patents Act, 1970, from US pressure, with their Super 301 and Special 301 Acts;
2. self-reliance in drug production;
3. a leading role for the public sector under the Major General S.S. Sokhey[2] Plan;[3]
4. availability of medicines at affordable prices; and
5. medicine pricing and drug prices control. (Some of these were in the Hathi Committee Report of 1975.)

In the 1970s, the supply of medicines in India stood at an 80:20 ratio between MNCs and Indian companies. This was to change

[2] Major General Sokhey was the first Indian director of the Haffkine Institute, India's premier research institute on microbiology and vaccines. He helped set up the public-sector drug manufacturing companies, Hindustan Antibiotics, and Indian Drugs and Pharmaceuticals Limited (IDPL). He was president of the Association of Scientific Workers of India; vice president, All-India Peace Council, and the Pharmaceutical and Drugs Committee of the Council for Scientific and Industrial Research (CSIR).

[3] Major General Sokhey chaired the National Planning Committee's sub-committee on national health set up by the Indian National Congress in 1938, under the chairmanship of Jawaharlal Nehru. (The Report was submitted only in 1948.) Independent India's position on patents is derived from the Sokhey Committee Report.

dramatically. The policies that began with India's innovative Patents Act, 1971, and the Hathi Committee Report for drug price controls, made it possible for Indian companies to secure a major share of the Indian market. Within a decade, the ratio of MNCs and Indian companies reversed. Today, India is one of the biggest exporters of generic medicines, including to the US and Europe.

One of the main reasons for this change is that India did not surrender to the patents blackmail of drug MNCs. Even after India's ruling class accepted the highly restrictive regime of the agreement on Trade-Related Aspects of Intellectual Property Rights (TRIPS), the Left and others could ensure certain safeguards that allowed for a relatively less restrictive patents regime. Dr Amit Sengupta's contributions were significant in this fight.

The Patents Act, 1970, did not recognize the 'product patent' of medicines, only a 'process patent'. Any country had the legal right to develop its own patents regime. Only processes could be patented, not the final chemical entity. So Indian companies began to produce generic versions of medicinal products via independent chemical processes distinct from those of the product patent holders. These medicines could be produced at much lower costs than those of the MNCs, and sold at much lower prices in the Indian and world markets.

The MNCs called this 'patent piracy'. They brought patents within the General Agreement on Tariffs and Trade (GATT), calling them trade-related intellectual property rights, and hence within the purview of trade discussions. This is the genesis of the World Trade Organization (WTO), and its TRIPS agreement. The union commerce minister then, Pranab Mukherjee, was India's representative. He accepted the 'product patent' on medicines at the Marrakesh conference that concluded the Uruguay Round of the GATT negotiations and constituted the WTO in 1994. India had a ten-year grace period, after which its patents law had to be amended to conform to the TRIPS agreement of the WTO.

This was the battle the Left fought. Helped by the National

Working Group on Patents Law, the fight was about the kind of law India could produce that would, at least partially, protect the Indian people. The exercise addressed the question of how to use the flexibilities within TRIPS that India and other developing countries had fought for and introduced. How could they be used to dilute the product patent regime that would replace the process patent one?

Comrade Amit Sengupta played a significant role in this process of ensuring that the amendment to the Patents Act, 1970, was carefully drafted to reduce the impact of evergreening of patents; not allowing new use or new dosage to be patented; and introducing other safeguards. Section 3(d)[4] in the Patents Act is most important in this respect. This was adopted by Parliament in 2005. The Section says that *the mere discovery of a new form of a known substance which does not result in the enhancement of the known efficacy of that substance is not an invention within the meaning of the Act.* It is this clause that led to the denial of patents in India for a range of drugs, which denial was later upheld by the Supreme Court.

The drug seminar of 1986 also triggered off other activities. Several organizations in the people's science movement had already been working in different states. After the drug seminar, the FMRAI and existing people's science organizations helped reactivate older science organizations and create new ones in other places. These organizations then came together at the all-India level for activities related to health, literacy and the development of scientific temper. The DSF became an important coordinating body, with Comrade Amit as one of its key functionaries, especially in the area of health.

These all-India coordination activities helped launch five

[4] The Left parties had originally put forward the clause that only a new chemical substance would qualify for a patent, but later accepted the 3(d) formulation of the Indian Drug Manufacturers Association, which was similar in intent.

Bharat Jan Vigyan Jathas (BJVJ) in 1987, culminating in Bhopal, site of the gas tragedy. The *jathas* had two main components: conveying the message of a scientific approach through performing arts, and exposing the fake 'magic powers' of the alleged '*babas*' (many of whom are now behind bars). The BJVJ laid the foundation of the All India Peoples Science Network (AIPSN) the following year in Kerala. Comrade Amit remained one of the anchors of the AIPSN.

Comrade Amit is no longer with us to defend the struggles for drug and health policies as designed in the 1986 seminar. But the need for this struggle persists. Amit's memory is now inspiration for us to carry forward the struggle.

2. From GATT and WTO to the Patents Act, 2005: The Long Arc of Resistance

S.P. SHUKLA

The Trade-Related Intellectual Property Rights (TRIPS) Agreement was a cornerstone of the World Trade Organization's architecture. All the patents laws of member countries of the WTO had to conform to the provisions of the TRIPS Agreement. Where they did not, the countries would be liable to various penal provisions of the WTO, including retaliations in other areas. In order to understand how the TRIPS Agreement carried implications for the Indian Patents Act, it is necessary first to delve into the history of negotiations for the General Agreement on Tariffs and Trade (GATT) during the Uruguay Round, before we turn to the amended Indian Patents Act, 2005, in which Amit played such an important role.

Between GATT, signed in 1947, and the founding of the WTO in 1995, there took place a paradigm shift. The US, the European Economic Community and Japan wanted to use trade negotiations to bring about *structural changes within countries*, changes conducive to big capital or multinational corporations. This is the real essence of the shift from GATT to the WTO regime. It is how patents, copyrights, and other such provisions became part of what is now called the TRIPS Agreement. But TRIPS was not the only means by which these countries sought to change the internal laws of developing countries. There were also others, such as the General Agreement on Trade in Services.

GATT was originally about trade in goods—rules meant to govern the cross-border flow of goods, without arbitrary restrictions or a discriminatory regime between trading partners. The entire structure of GATT was built around this understanding. By a sleight of hand, the word 'trade' came to be attached to each of the issues—patents, services, investments, trademark and copyright; the intent was to use the Uruguay Round of GATT negotiations to change the fundamental character of GATT itself.

One of the articles in GATT was Article 20D. It talked about trademarks and patents, but said that each contracting party has a *sovereign right to have its own regime* regarding such issues, as long as its rules do not impose unreasonable restrictions on trade or discriminate between countries in the name of protecting trademarks or patents. This was also the approach GATT took on many related issues such as state subsidy, domestic support to industries, etc. The main objective was to avoid creating arbitrary restrictions and discriminatory regimes with respect to trade.

During the 1970s and 1980s, in the Tokyo Round of GATT negotiations, European countries and the US complained about trade in counterfeit goods. This was addressed by a limited proposal that countries may safeguard their national interest by promoting fair trade, but not in counterfeits. The US, the European Economic Community[1] and Japan sought to extend this plank to pharmaceuticals, chemicals and informatics. The independent legislation that many developing countries had introduced to promote local industries now began to be called 'patent piracy'. The attempt was to recast the whole history of patents and trademarks initiatives of countries such as India, Brazil, South Korea, and Argentina, as the trade of counterfeit goods. These countries had

[1] After the formation of the European Union, it was incorporated and renamed as the European Community, and finally absorbed into the EU.

changed their national laws in order to break the monopoly and profiteering of multinational drug companies, and to produce medicines and agricultural chemicals cheaply for their people.

One of the major triggers to the change in the Indian Patents Act were the US Senate Committee hearings in 1959–60, led by Senator Estes Kefauver. They went into the issue of drug prices. The Committee's report said that US drug companies were fleecing the American poor. There was a small paragraph adding that these drug companies were not only fleecing the American public, but also *charging the highest prices for the most essential drugs* in one of the poorest countries of the world, namely India.

In April 1957, the Indian government had set up a single-member committee under Justice N. Rajagopala Ayyangar. The Ayyangar Committee submitted a detailed report[2] in September 1959, which formed the basis of India's Patents Act passed in 1970. While Senator Kefauver was able to pass Amendments to the Federal Food, Drug, and Cosmetic Act in 1962[3]—after pharmaceutical companies came under attack with the thalidomide[4] scandal—India took considerably longer to put together a law of its own.

The Indian Patents Act, 1970, abolished product patents in pharmaceutical products, food and chemicals, permitting only process patents in these areas. This is what allowed India to build up a strong, indigenous pharmaceutical industry, with the support of the Council of Scientific and Industrial Research (CSIR) and its laboratories.

[2] *Report on the Revision of the Patents Law*, Shri Justice N. Rajagopala Ayyangar, September 1959, available online (https://spicyip.com/wp-content/uploads/2013/10/ayyangar_committee_report.pdf).

[3] 'Reform, Regulation, and Pharmaceuticals—The Kefauver–Harris Amendments at 50', *New England Journal of Medicine*, vol. 367, no. 16 (October 18, 2012), pp. 1481–83.

[4] Bara Fintel, Athena T. Samaras, Edson Carias, 'The Thalidomide Tragedy: Lessons for Drug Safety and Regulations', *Helix*, July 28, 2009 (https://helix.northwestern.edu/article/thalidomide-tragedy-lessons-drug-safety-and-regulation).

In the 1970s and 1980s, the US industries—particularly manufacturing, steel, chemical, rubber, automobiles—were losing ground. The country still had an edge in the drugs and pharmaceutical industry, owing to its strong research capabilities and dominance in the global market. The US now attempted to capture the market in countries that had developed indigenous industries after decolonization and were producing cheap medicines. To recapture their markets, there was a need to destroy the patents laws of these countries.

The other attempt by the US-EEC-Japan block was to focus on services within other countries as prospective markets, not simply as cross-border services. This meant allowing companies to enter the domestic markets of other countries with banking, audio-visual services, informatics, civil aviation. Getting these countries to allow foreign investment was the third major new issue in the Uruguay Round of negotiations that started at Punta del Este, in 1986.

The problem for developing countries was that they needed access to the markets of developed countries for the export of fabrics and textiles. However, they did not want this need to be used against them, prising open their markets to banking, insurance and other services. Thus, they opposed tooth and nail the inclusion of services in GATT. When developed countries raised the other two issues—of investments and intellectual property rights—their major emphasis was on services.

The parties arrived at a compromise: they would negotiate on services but not as a part of GATT. GATT would remain a body to formulate rules about trade in goods. If services were to be discussed, such negotiations should respect *national* policy objectives.[5] We, the developing countries, restricted negotiations on services within this boundary. We also insisted that services not

[5] For example, bank nationalization in India was a part of our sovereign banking policies.

be a part of GATT, so that trade in goods could not be leveraged to force open developing countries as service markets. It was resolved that there would be a separate track of negotiations for this, not to be combined with the trade in goods.

On the two other issues, of investments and intellectual property, our answer was that we were ready to discuss them, provided there were articles relating to these issues in GATT's founding document of 1947. Just as there is a reference to trademarks and patents in Article 20D, there are references to investments in other articles. Our stand was that we could discuss these issues only within the parameters of those articles. Ultimately, they agreed that negotiations with regard to intellectual property would take place within the parameters of Article 20D. On the need for strengthening the patents regime, our stand was that this was a substantive issue, not to be mixed with the *objective* of the ongoing negotiations. In the event, a compromise was reached—strengthening the patents regime could be taken into account while formulating the rules. The issue of patents became a kind of subsidiary addendum to be considered, not determining the subject matter of the negotiations. The US and other developed countries accepted our stand, albeit grudgingly.

While I was in Geneva, sometime around 1985–86, and we were in the thick of negotiations that ultimately led to the Punta del Este mandate, I got a letter from B.K. Keayla, informing me that he was trying to organize a national working group on patents.[6] Since I was the government negotiator, representing India's position on the patents aspect of several issues, he asked whether I could help the working group when they wanted information on the negotiations. I wrote back immediately, saying that theirs was indeed a welcome initiative as we were in negotiations that had a

[6] The Working Group on Patents Law was formed at the initiative of B.K. Keayla in 1988. Obviously, it was already in Keayla's mind before its official formation. See Amit Sengupta's article on B.K. Keayla in Section 1 of this volume.

great bearing on India's future. This was important not only for the drug industry, but also the Indian people. Our negotiating stand, based on a pro-people and a pro-self-reliance position, would be greatly helped by such an initiative coming from the drug industry, research scholars, scientists and the health movement. I welcomed it and offered my full cooperation. That's how my association with the working group started.

For two to three years after Punta del Este, we succeeded in checking the developed countries' attempts to widen the ambit of the Uruguay Round discussions. India, Brazil, Argentina, Cuba, Egypt, Nicaragua, Nigeria, Peru, Tanzania and Yugoslavia formed a group. Ambassador Paolo Batista, Brazil's ambassador to GATT, and I as India's ambassador, worked together in these negotiations with other developing countries.

Within months of the understanding reached in Punta del Este, the US began pushing back against it and wanted to raise investment and intellectual property as substantive issues in the Uruguay Round negotiations. This tussle went on for some two or three years. In December 1988, in Montreal, there were two key drafts—one from our side and one from the developed countries. They wanted to bring back to the main negotiations the same issues we had opposed earlier, while we maintained that these fell outside the ambit of GATT. The Montreal mid-term ministerial meetings—between some ninety ministers of trade, the economy, industry and agriculture—failed to reach an agreement on the issues of intellectual property rights, services, safeguards, textiles, etc., and the stalemate continued. We had added the issue of safeguards as a bargaining measure in the negotiations, as under this clause GATT allowed special protections to our list of concerns.

In December 1988, India and Brazil were leading this battle. The Big Pharma lobby—Pfizer, Roche and others—was putting pressure on us, as were financial sector companies such as CITI Bank, and the informatics industry, who were all part of the US delegation. However, they were foiled by a few negotiators from the developing countries, particularly the ambassadors to GATT from Brazil and India.

Enormous bilateral pressure was put on India and Brazil. In early 1989, the internal political situation in both countries was fragile. The Brazilian president was assassinated, causing political instability there. In India, V.P. Singh, finance minister in the Rajiv Gandhi government, had resigned in 1988, over the Bofors corruption case. Although Rajiv Gandhi had a huge majority in Parliament, V.P. Singh's campaign bruised the government's image and there was political uncertainty back home. The US was also stepping up the bilateral pressure by threatening the use of Section 301[7] against India. The net result was that the Brazilian ambassador Batista was transferred, he was sent to New York as a permanent representative to the UN. I was brought back to Delhi, to my new appointment as special secretary, family welfare—far away from the economic ministries: finance or commerce.

Meanwhile, in Geneva, there was a vacuum. No ambassador was posted there, there was no senior officer—only a first secretary was in charge of the GATT negotiations. The joint secretary from the ministry of commerce, N.S. Sodha, who was looking after these matters from Delhi, and A.N. Verma, who was the commerce secretary, were not in sync with my views on our stand in the GATT negotiations. At the time, despite all weaknesses, autonomous policy-making was valued. Planning, and having objectives in consonance with people's requirements were acknowledged. Market fundamentalism had not made the tremendous dent in the thinking and policy-making of the government that it was later to do. Although there were elements in the government, such as

[7] Sections 301 through 310 of the Trade Act of 1974, as amended, are commonly referred to as 'Section 301'. It is one of the principal statutory means by which the United States pursues its interests under trade agreements and addresses 'unfair' foreign barriers to US exports. See the following Congressional Research Service document, 'Enforcing U.S. Trade Laws: Section 301 and China', available online (https://fas.org/sgp/crs/row/IF10708.pdf).

Montek Singh Ahluwalia and others, who were toeing the pro-US and neoliberal line, they were still on the margins.

A.N. Verma is no more, but I have to say that he was easily influenced by the US. He went to the GATT negotiations in Geneva, which the director general Arthur Dunkel had called in April 1989, and virtually surrendered all the positions for which we had fought so hard. If you see the April 1989 agreement, India yielded on all the four contentious issues—safeguards, textile, agriculture and intellectual property. In agriculture there wasn't a comparable fallout, as the European Economic Commission was still in doubt regarding an agreement on agriculture.

Brazil and India had led the developing countries in their opposition to bringing intellectual property into trade negotiations. Both were neutralized. The new Brazilian ambassador did try to oppose the April 1989 Agreement, and was very unhappy that India had thrown in the towel. Under pressure, he also surrendered. The net result was that the mandate agreed to was practically everything the US had wanted. The substantive issues of norms and standards of intellectual property—i.e. changing the patents laws of various countries to conform to some 'common international standards'—which we had held in check for years, became the subject matter of the negotiations. This is how the process patents in the Indian Patents Act came under attack in the subsequent negotiations; they had to be changed in 2004 to conform to the TRIPS Agreement. Some verbiage was added, to the effect that the concerns of the developing countries had been taken on board. There were also some pieties about taking public policy objectives into consideration while working out norms and standards, but this was simple window dressing devoid of any real meaning.

The whole history of the Patents Act and the reason the 1970 Patents Act was amended, the way the drug industry was set up and the generic sector developed, the emergence of India as the world's pharmacy, all this was endangered by the surrender to

US pressure. There was nothing left of our earlier stand starting from Punta del Este. We now agreed to substantive negotiations on patents, made it an integral part of the trade negotiations in goods, and allowed the champions of 'intellectual property' to use their trade leverage against us to amend our Patents Act. We had walked into their trap.

After the April 1989 surrender, there was a change of government in India and V.P. Singh's government came to power in December that year. From December 1989 to December 1990, I was the commerce secretary. V.P. Singh removed A.N. Verma and placed me in that position. He said, 'So many things have been lost, and now I want you to go back. Do what you like, but bring back as much as you can, and you have the full authority to do so.' Our ambassador at the time was B.K. Zutshi. Together, he and I fought a rearguard battle to preserve India's long-standing position.

When I became the commerce secretary, I called up Keayla and told him there were issues we were trying to revive again after suffering big losses. It was important that there be public awareness on these issues, and pressure on the government, including me. I also promised him that I would give the National Working Group on Patent Law support for international and national meetings and seminars, to build a larger awareness on these issues. This would help us in our negotiations, both externally and internally. That is how my work with the Group started.

A major development we should have arrested but did not (and by this time I was out of the government altogether, having quit in September 1991) was that the block of developed nations surreptitiously introduced, without negotiations, the idea of a multilateral trade organization. This would become the World Trade Organization. The idea was to bring in an overarching agreement under which all other agreements could be subsumed, linking them, making one agreement conditional on another, so that the big powers gained a significant cross-retaliation ability against other countries. Their coup was executed in the name of a multinational trade organization. The proposal was put forward as a draft, not the negotiated draft of any of the contracting parties who participated in the Uruguay Round of negotiations, but by certain 'experts'. Arthur Dunkel, the director general of the WTO during the Uruguay Round, 'sold' the idea to the developed countries, who obviously liked it. The famous (or infamous) Dunkel Draft was then put to the entire community of the contracting parties in GATT. This happened in 1994, at Marrakesh, where the Uruguay Round came to a close and the WTO was hatched.

The idea of consensus, through which GATT had worked, was turned on its head to reach the Marrakesh Agreement. The option given to countries was that if they wanted any amendment to this draft, it would be accepted only if supported by a consensus among all the contracting parties. If no such consensus could be produced, the draft would go through. This is putting the cart before the horse: you have prepared a draft which favours developed countries; you have not consulted the vast majority of contracting parties, the developing countries; then you tell those who have objections that they must first get the developed countries to agree with their objections, secure a consensus in their favour, and only then will the draft be changed. This impossible condition was imposed on the developing countries, and India's representative accepted it meekly, as did the Brazilians, and other developing countries. It was a total surrender.

The Marrakesh Agreement[8] that established the World Trade Organization (WTO Agreement) expanded the scope of the WTO far beyond GATT. It contained the following agreements as annexes and made them binding on all the contracting parties:

- General Agreement on Trade in Services (GATS) (Annexe 1B)

[8] A detailed account of the GATT negotiations is in S.P. Shukla's 'From GATT to WTO and Beyond', Working Paper No. 195, UNU World Institute for Development Economics Research, 2002, available online (https://www.wider.unu.edu/publication/gatt-wto-and-beyond).

- Agreement on Trade-Related Aspects of Intellectual Property Rights (TRIPS) (Annexe 1C);
- Understanding on Rules and Procedures Governing the Settlement of Disputes (DSU) (Annexe 2); and
- Trade Policy Review Mechanism (Annexe 3).

This short and apparently simple provision expanded the scope of the erstwhile GATT beyond all confines of the past. It imposed obligations in the new areas, particularly TRIPS, without giving the member states an opportunity to exercise their right to oppose and defeat such measures. The provision also sanctioned cross-sector retaliation by integrating these separate agreements under one umbrella agreement.

With this ended the cross-border paradigm of GATT, while the confrontation between developed countries and the developing world was decided in favour of the US-EEC-Japan axis. From here begins the WTO's regime of intrusive and expanded rights in the name of trade, and the opening up of economies in developing countries under the guise of trade. This is the shift from GATT's very marginal reference to trademarks and patents, to an intellectual property rights regime that 'homogenizes' global patents in favour of Big Pharma and chemical companies. The WTO can now trump national legislation in ever-widening areas, in the name of 'harmonizing national systems'. This is the paradigm shift between GATT and the WTO: from what was a treaty on trade to a global system rigged in favour of the rich and powerful, particularly the global MNCs.

When I quit the government in 1991, Keayla invited me to join the National Working Group on Patents Law, as co-chairman. Justice Krishna Iyer was then chairman of the working group. We also built a people's campaign against the WTO; V.P. Singh was the chairperson and other former prime ministers like I.K. Gujral, H.D. Deve Gowda and Chandra Shekhar were part of it. The Left was also there, as were all the major parties, except the Congress and BJP. Even Murasoli Maran from the DMK and Murli Manohar Joshi used to come to the parliamentary forum that Keayla had organized.

I first came in contact with Amit at a meeting of the working group. When I was ambassador to GATT, I had met Dinesh Abrol, Vandana Shiva, Praful Bidwai and others. I came into contact with Amit later, when we worked intensively on the issue of the 2004 amendments to the Patents Act. Sitaram Yechury had called me in the context of a meeting between the Left and the assigned group of ministers from Manmohan Singh's UPA government. The group of ministers, constituted under the chairmanship of Pranab Mukherjee, was to negotiate with the Left on the draft amendment that the UPA was placing before Parliament.

India was forced to change its process patents regime in order to comply with the TRIPS provisions, as the ten-year 'grace' period of retaining the original Patents Act of 1970 was over. The deadline for harmonizing the Indian Patents Act with the TRIPS Agreement was December 2004. The Left wanted to use what legislative leverage they had during the first UPA government, in order to utilize the TRIPS loopholes—limited as they were—and see how much we could still salvage from India's capitulation during the GATT/WTO negotiations.

We used to meet in the Delhi Science Forum office in a basement in Saket, where Amit and D. Raghunandan used to work. Amit used to work till late in the night. He was excellent at drafting: he understood the issues in depth, and also understood the politics of it. Amit, like Prabir Purkayastha and Dinesh Abrol, understood the larger politics of intellectual property issues, which others in the National Working Group did not fully grasp. It was drafting these amendments to the Draft Patents Bill of 2004 that really brought us together. The amendments that we drafted—after a lot of discussion—became the position of the National Working Group on Patents Law, and the basis of changes that we were later able to introduce in the 2005 Patents Act, with the Left's leverage.

Frankly, after the total surrender of April 1989, and India's later acquiescence with the terms of the WTO—doing so without even a whimper of protest—I had become completely frustrated. For some time, I had withdrawn from intellectual property rights issues. The Doha meeting of the WTO had taken place in 2002, during the first NDA government led by Vajpayee. At that time our hands were tied, substantive issues were already closed, and we did not have much negotiating margin. The WTO meetings in Singapore and Doha were completely dominated by the US.

My interest was rekindled because the Left took a position of 'let us see what we can still do'. I thought we could start the process of picking up the pieces, try and see what could be salvaged. I met with Prakash Karat and Sitaram Yechury, who asked me to be a part of the Left delegation for the meeting with Pranab Mukherjee, who was the industries minister, Kapil Sibal, the law minister, and others in the group of ministers. They also said that they had full confidence in whatever stand I took, that it would be our stand. The Left took the National Working Group's draft as the basis of its negotiating position. I give credit to the CPI(M) and the Left MPs, who gave me the go-ahead to speak on their behalf.

During the discussions, Kapil Sibal started arguing in favour of Big Pharma and IT companies on issues such as pre- and post-grant opposition to patent applications, compulsory licensing, and why mailbox applications of MNCs should be granted patents. He rejected the idea that only a new molecule should be patented. He was pushing arguments in favour of big capital, using the language of intellectual-property lawyers. I spoke why these provisions in the draft amendment put forward by the NDA earlier, and now the UPA government, were dangerous for the country. These were basic issues for us. These basic issues would need to be addressed before we could support the amended patents bill. Pranab Mukherjee was chairing the group and, being the good politician he is, intervened. He urged Sibal to consider that the government needed the support of the Left. 'This is coalition politics,' he said.

'You may not agree, but we have to reach a compromise if we want the Patents Act amendments to be passed.' So he overruled Sibal and reached a compromise, including on Section 3(d).[9]

On 3(d), we had, initially, a much stronger definition of what could be patented. We wanted a rule that only new chemical molecules could be patented. The government offered a softer definition it had received from the Indian Drug Manufacturers Association (IDMA), the indigenous drug industry. We accepted this as a compromise, because we felt it would still protect us against the evergreening of patents that the MNCs wanted. This is how the language used in the current 3(d) of the Patents Act evolved. But as we know now from the Novartis judgment, this too was enough protection against predatory evergreening.

There was one year when we did some picking up the pieces after the Geneva surrender of April 1989, with Ambassador Zutshi in Geneva and I the commerce secretary in Delhi. The second round of picking up the pieces, prior to the 2004 amendment, was when the Left asked me to join their team during the discussions with UPA. My interest got rekindled because the Left was there. Unless you have political support, you can't push these things. That's how we could get 3(d) and whatever else we achieved.

Amit was quite frustrated by what had happened in Geneva in 1989 and what happened later with the WTO. He was right in saying it was the AIDS issue that once again built the campaign against patents, created a new coalition and made it into a global movement. That is why the Novartis judgment rang out across the globe. As he notes in his obituary of Keayla, it was hardly conceivable that what Keayla was doing in 1986 would become so important twenty-two years later. Very true. Things don't happen quite as you argue and expect. You argue and develop a course of action to realize your objectives. But those objectives are not

9 See the essay by Kajal Bhardwaj in this volume, as well as essays by Amit Sengupta on Section 3(d).

the main thing in the march of time, when so many situational factors are far beyond the control of simple, linear projections. You may get defeated, frustrated. But you have to pick up the pieces and bounce back. This ability to bounce back is what Kajal Bhardwaj notes here about Amit's view on resistance: *optimism as a purposeful act of political resistance*. That's a great insight. Amit's strong point was that he could relate technical and scientific issues to larger political questions.

It is absurd that I have to say these things about Amit, when he was so much the younger of us. He should have been remembering me in an obituary.

Nobody can guarantee success, and when you are trying to transform things, you are necessarily on the defeated side most of the times. If this is so, then picking up the pieces and bouncing back are important. Again today, we find that the Patent Office is compromised in its grant of patents; it is interpreting the Patents Act to suit Big Pharma and big capital's interests. The US is pushing different laws in Colombia, Argentina and other countries. At the same time, there are voices being raised from the other side. This is a continuous battle. And, without optimism, there will be no resistance or the will to fight.

3. Alma-Ata to Astana: From PHC to UHC

DAVID SANDERS

David Sanders presents an overview of the global health movement, focusing on Asia and Africa where he has worked nearly all his life. He discusses the concept of primary healthcare, its evolution, its distortion and weakening, before returning to it as globally revised in Astana at the fortieth anniversary of the 1978 Alma-Ata meeting. Sanders also looks at what is happening with universal health coverage (UHC), and concludes with some of Amit's proposals on the way forward.

Undoubtedly, health and life expectancy have improved in most parts of the world, though Southeast Asia and Africa, particularly the latter, still lag behind the rest. Many aspects of ill-health are concentrated in Africa and South Asia. Besides, there are growing inequalities between the global North and South, at least between the North and Africa. The chances of a young child dying before his/her fifth birthday are many times higher in Africa in relation to the global North—and the gap has widened over the past forty years. And, of course, within countries, there are increasing inequalities. In India, comparing the under-5 mortality among the poorest 20% and the corresponding figure for the richest 20%, we discover a three-fold difference.

The historic conference at Alma-Ata took place in 1978, and the goal of 'Health for All by the Year 2000' through primary healthcare (PHC) was proclaimed. In fact, the issue of *health equity*, a buzzword now, was central to the PHC debate at the time. There were four other notable principles that focused on comprehensive care with an emphasis on disease prevention, health promotion, community involvement, and the involvement of other sectors and appropriate technology.

A point lost in the current debate is a statement from the preface of the Alma-Ata Declaration—that economic and social development based on a new international economic order is essential to the fullest attainment of health for all. It was already recognized that past and continued exploitation of the global South demanded compensation, and that the transnational corporations—which were not as powerful then—needed to be regulated. Preferential treatment for developing countries was necessary, as was the transfer of new technologies, and an end to the wastage of natural resources.

If we look at our situation today, four decades after the Alma-Ata Declaration, we can agree that it was prescient; it predicted our plight. Comprehensive PHC, which the People's Health Movement (PHM) insists on, is a term no longer used all that often. But it covers the full span of promotive, preventive, curative and rehabilitative services. PHC had two related aspects. One was to address basic healthcare needs. Today, the first level of care, the primary level, is in shorthand called PHC. However, PHC actually means much more than just the first level of care. It also involves addressing the underlying determinants of good healthcare through inter-sectoral action and policies.

In the 1980s, there was a split in the PHC movement; what emerged came to be called selective PHC. This was less than ten years after the Alma-Ata conference and the first programmatic manifestation of that was called the 'child survival and development revolution'. The acronym GOBI stands for these child survival technologies—the growth monitoring of young children, oral rehydration therapy, promotion of breastfeeding, and immunization—all of which are very important and effective, especially breastfeeding. We did not argue against these initiatives. What we argued against was the narrowing down of the PHC agenda, with very little emphasis on addressing the social determinants of healthcare.

The rise of PHC coincided with the global debt crisis and structural adjustment policies. The fiscal stringency and user charges that were imposed (nowadays called austerity), actually limited the implementation of PHC in many countries. In the late 1980s, a subset of conservative macroeconomic policies—which we now call neoliberal—were introduced in the health sector. Neoliberal health reforms have a very strong focus on cost effectiveness; on the decentralization of management, often to district or sub-district level; increased marketization of healthcare; privatization of service delivery; imposition of user charges; under-funding of the public sector and growth in public-private partnerships. This is exactly what has happened in India, as in many other parts of the world.

This move from equity and comprehensiveness to technical and economic efficiency and selectiveness has aggravated the verticalization of healthcare—from general health services to particular programmes receiving prominence at the expense of other areas. For example, in my country, Zimbabwe, HIV and TB are given great prominence, but nutrition is a Cinderella. Nutrition, which affects all age groups, is a Cinderella in India too. Malnourishment is a complex and vexed problem; there is no magic cure. So, the neglect of social determinants, the erosion of inter-sectoral work and of community health infrastructures has characterized global health policy over the last thirty to forty years. In fact, the WHO's *World Health Report* issued in 2008, on the thirtieth anniversary of Alma-Ata, stated these findings. It listed a disproportionate focus on narrow specialized curative care; health systems in which commercialization has been allowed to flourish;

and a fragmentation of services caused by the domination of a disease-control approach focused on short-term results.

All of this was happening from the late 1980s onward; the picture I have briefly and superficially painted is that of the backdrop to the first people's health assembly (PHA). We called it a PHA to counterpose it to the world health assembly (WHA), which is held every year and to which our government delegations go. Some fifteen years ago, South Africa had the third-largest delegation in the WHO, after China and the US. I wrote a letter about it to a newspaper, which made me very unpopular. I calculated what the delegation cost our government. Such junkets are predominantly a shopping spree for the official representatives of many Southern countries, while the influence that weak countries can have there is very limited.

Since 2000, when we held our first PHA, we have had another three assemblies. I was not very much aware of Amit till I went to the second national Indian people's health assembly in Bhopal. Amit remained in the background, but often played a determining role. I learnt that Amit began his political career young, in student movements. I also learnt in Bhopal that in every meeting, he would say something which would point out the path ahead, occasionally even change the direction of our discussion. Amit was absolutely central to many of our initiatives, not least the last two people's health assemblies—one in Savar and the other in Cape Town. I know this, because he and I drew up the programmes for the most part, and that was a big job. We spent much time together, often at very unsociable hours, to flesh out the programme.

Amit was a leader and was central to many of the global activities of the PHM. Our capacity-building courses at the International People's Health University (IPHU) could last anything from a few days to twelve days. Amit taught in these courses and when he said, 'You see, it's like this . . . ', you knew that you were going to suddenly see the core of the issue with greater clarity. Amit was also central in WHO Watch—a project in which we take up to twenty youngsters to Geneva to watch the World Health Assembly or the Executive Board of the WHO. They undertake policy analysis, basically writing policy briefs and sending these, along with our analyses of all the resolutions, to delegates. There are some younger colleagues in the PHM, Susana Barria, T. Gargeya and others, who now lead in WHO Watch; they were mentored by Amit. In WHO Watch, we provide an analytical digest of what is going to be debated at the Assembly. The national delegations do not read the pile of documents, which goes up almost to the ceiling, but they read our digests. In fact, the WHO Secretariat, far from being pleased that we are doing this work for them, often gets irritated with us for providing an alternative analysis of the Resolution.

To go back to PHC: we know that the selective PHC approach has neglected inter-sectoral action on social determinants. A paper published in the *WHO Bulletin*, in one of the few robust quantitative analyses made by the organization, says that around half of the reduction in child mortality that took place since the 1990s in low-to-middle-income countries (ten countries were studied), was due to investments made outside the health sector. This confirms that the holistic PHC approach, which is about basic healthcare, but also about inter-sectoral action, was correct. And, of course, this is now illustrated by the seventeen Sustainable Development Goals (SDG),[1] which recognize that human well-

[1] 'The 2030 Agenda for Sustainable Development', adopted by all United Nations Member States in 2015, provides a shared blueprint for peace and prosperity for people and the planet, now and into the future. At its heart are the seventeen Sustainable Development Goals (SDGs), which are an urgent call for action by all countries—developed and developing—in a global partnership. They recognize that ending poverty and other deprivations must go hand-in-hand with strategies that improve health and education, reduce inequality, and spur economic growth—all while tackling climate change and working to preserve our oceans and forests. See https://sustainabledevelopment.un.org/?menu=1300.

being depends on action in at least seventeen areas. Of course, many of us in the movement are sceptical about whether the targets, a total of 169, will ever be reached. But we welcome the fact that there is a focus at last on determinants. As with everything else, we interrogate them critically. So SDG 3, adopted in 2015, is the one focused on health, and there are more than ten targets. What is now capturing the focus of the health policy community is universal health coverage (UHC).

The focus has shifted from PHC to UHC. UHC is about equitable access to health services, to quality health services, and protecting from financial risk all those who use the services. This is all very welcome and we support it. The fortieth anniversary of Alma-Ata was held in Astana,[2] the new capital of Kazakhstan. The declaration that came out of Astana has some reference to PHC, and PHC now seems to be the cornerstone of a sustainable health system for UHC. This is a bit like putting the cart before the horse. UHC should have been a component of PHC; but here UHC is the goal everything is designed to meet.

A key phrase for the big UN meeting on UHC in September 2019 is 'We will each pursue our paths to achieving UHC.'[3] For those of us with suspicious minds, this suggests that it would not be just public systems that pursue this path. It is acknowledged that there are many unaddressed health needs, and that remaining

[2] In March 2019, it was re-named Nur-Sultan.

[3] The UN High-Level Meeting (UN HLM) on Universal Health Coverage took place on September 23, 2019, during the United Nations General Assembly (UNGA) high-level week. The theme of the HLM-UHC was 'Universal Health Coverage: Moving Together to Build a Healthier World':

'This UN HLM was the last chance before 2023, the mid-point of the SDGs, to mobilize the highest political support to package the entire health agenda under the umbrella of UHC, and sustain health investments in a harmonized manner. To do this, it is critical to identify how the political declaration on UHC can add value to these efforts and set milestones towards achieving UHC by 2030.' See 'Moving together to build a healthier world' (https://www.uhc2030.org/un-hlm-2019/).

healthy is challenging for many people, particularly the poor. But there is no mention of why inequity persists, and is, indeed, increasing. There is a focus on the growing burden of non-communicable diseases and other terrible manifestations of inequality, the power inequality in our world that manifests itself in wars and violence and so on. However, there is no mention of the structural underpinnings of these threats to health.

And then there is a call on all stakeholders—health professionals, academia, patients, civil society, partners, agencies, the private sector and so on, to align with national policies, as though there were no contradictions between them; such as in envisaging the private sector as a partner to reduce the commercial determinants of health. There is also a commitment to involving more stakeholders in the achievement of health for all, while addressing and managing conflicts of interest—but we want to know how this will happen. The Astana declaration is, thus, a very muted and different version of an approach to PHC, and it does not satisfy many of us. There is no reference to any new international economic order despite the fact that wealth is more concentrated now than ever before, with eight people—eight men—controlling as much wealth as 50% of the world's population. I recall Amit pointing this out.

In theory, UHC says coverage is a *right*. It has critical implications for the choices made in terms of revenue sources and the basis for entitlement. Establishing this right is seen as a government responsibility, and it must be progressively realized. However, in many countries, there are different health systems and different financing for different groups, particularly in Latin America, but also in other regions. There is one system for the insured or the employed, quite another for the uninsured or the unemployed and the poor. It has resulted in segmented health systems, unequal almost by design. Yet this is repeated in many countries around the world. Of course, the better-off people are favoured. When countries start with these kinds of silos—different health systems and different financing for different groups—it becomes very difficult to change things. Mandating coverage boosts the privately insured.

The stance of the PHM—as also of Amit's writing—insists on a single payer, and a public payer. This is because different financing organizations, different health insurance organizations, are being enrolled. This is true for India as well. If you want universal coverage and do not want a fragmented multi-payer system, with different benefits for different groups, then there had better be a universal system with a single payer, based on public funding. Several years ago, Amit wrote a very influential paper[4] interrogating the rhetoric of UHC. There is now evidence that what he predicted might happen. We find that utilization has increased for some whose healthcare is funded under certain schemes, but not for others. There are big differences based on geography, rural-urban divides, and social groups, particularly with regard to indigenous populations.

There is over-servicing, with unnecessary obstetric operations, for example. Utilization is concentrated on a small set of services, cherry-picked by private providers. A large number of needs remain unmet. Financial protection has not been achieved in many countries. Most private facilities continue to charge extra, despite insurance coverage promising zero co-payments; and the extra billing leads to out-of-pocket expenditure and coverage without financial protection.

In other words, private providers are the biggest beneficiaries in many countries. They often benefit from public money contributed to a national fund, a fund that goes to subsidize the private sector and private insurance companies. An article by Vandana Prasad

[4] 'Universal Health Coverage: Beyond Rhetoric', Occasional Paper No. 20, Municipal Services Project, IDRC, November 2013. It has also been included in Section 3 of this volume.

and Amit Sengupta underlined the ethical dimensions of this persisting inequality.[5]

So, UHC, which everyone now supports, obscures more than it conveys. It obscures four critical policy debates. First, around healthcare financing—viz. a single-payer or health insurance market. Unfortunately, the latter is growing dominant. Then healthcare delivery: should it be integrative and comprehensive, or focus particularly on hospital-based curative care? On approaches to strengthening health systems: will these be prescribed by donors? Or will there be more democratic control of health? Oxfam wrote of this about the same time as Amit did. Both pointed out that in the name of UHC, some donors, and developing country governments, are promoting health insurance schemes that exclude the majority of people, and leave the poor behind. The big risk is aggravating the privatization of all aspects of healthcare—from financing to provision—and increasing the size of the market. Amit saw this in the final plenary of the fourth PHA—held in Savar again, in 2018.

It was also in Savar that Amit received thanks for his tremendous contribution to the PHA; for his insistence on the burning need for political organization to challenge what is happening in health, and beyond health as well, because we are *a subset of the bigger system*. Amit spoke of the pioneer Rudolph Virchow[6]—whose phrase this is. Amit, I think, is a Rudolph Virchow of our own.

[5] 'Perpetuating Health Inequalities in India: Global ethics in policy and practice', *Journal of Global Ethics*, vol. 15, no. 1 (2019).

[6] Rudolf Virchow (1821–1902) was a German physician who is known as the 'father of modern pathology' and the founder of social medicine. In addition to his scientific contributions, his ideology linked social inequality with the cause of disease; he also stressed the need for political action to address this strong link.

4. A Pioneer of People's Health and Science Movements

B. EKBAL

B. Ekbal writes of his friendship with Amit Sengupta from the late 1970s, a friendship based on their involvement in progressive movements. He also traces, over the decades, Amit's contribution to, and leadership of, health movements at the national and global level.

Amit and I became close in the late 1970s. I was an activist in the Kerala Trade Union Congress (KTUC), and got to know the Delhi Science Forum (DSF) because of our discussions on science and technology. Also, at this time, up to the early 1980s, there was a global movement against the marketing of hazardous drugs in developing countries. There was also a call to make essential drugs available to the people.

In 1985, a national conference was organized in Kerala to mark ten years of the Hathi Committee Report. Amit came to Trivandrum and made a presentation on various aspects of the Hathi report, and we also published a book the same year. In 1986, the Indian medical representatives association, FMRAI and DSF organized a conference on the 'Drug Industry and the Indian People' in Delhi. Amit, Amitava Guha, J.S. Majumdar and others played an important role in this conference, and Amit also edited a volume examining the positive and negative aspects of the Indian drug industry.[1] This volume discussed technical issues around essential drugs, hazardous drugs, etc., but it was Amit who brought in the political economy aspect.

Amit was also the first to focus attention on intellectual property rights (IPR). At the time, the Indian patents regime allowed 'process patents' which helped us develop the essential drug industry in India. Amit's contribution was phenomenal in the field of IPR and its relation to the drug industry. Very few health activists saw the nuances of the patents issues in the way Amit did, and he kept us updated on IPR in addition to providing us with information about the drug industry.

A large number of Indian groups were working on people's health and access to medicine in the 1990s. There was consensus that all these groups should come together and form a common platform—a people's health movement. This is how the idea of the Jan Swasthya Abhiyan (JSA) came about. It was difficult of course—not only were the ideological moorings of these groups different; they were also, on occasion, divergent, even contradictory. There were Gandhians, there was the extreme Left, the moderate Left, and there were religious groups. It was Amit's tenacity, wisdom and tactical approach that brought these groups together, and kept the movement going despite their differences. I recall how every time a difference of opinion surfaced at a JSA national coordinating committee meeting, Amit would appear like a magician, with a solution acceptable to all.

Again, Amit played a pivotal role in organizing the national health assembly (NHA) at Kolkata's Salt Lake Stadium in December 2000, bringing together seventeen people's health networks. He was one of the joint conveners of the JSA that was formed after the NHA held in Kolkata. After the NHA we headed to the Gonoshasthaya Kendra (GK) in Savar, Bangladesh, for the first people's health assembly (PHA). In Savar, nearly 1,500 participants

[1] See J.S. Majumdar's article in this section.

from seventy-five countries formed the People's Health Movement (PHM) and adopted the Global People's Charter for Health. We encountered a number of hurdles. Even the auditorium was not ready. Zafrullah Chowdhury, founder of the GK, asked Amit and me to come early. Amit never stopped working; he barely slept. He made sure the PHM was formed. Years later, in 2018, the fourth PHA was held in Savar with over 1,400 activists from seventy-three countries. Again, it was Amit's intervention that made the assembly a success.

Amit was the associate global coordinator of the PHM. He led the International People's Health University which was formed to train health activists under the People's Health Movement. He also edited three volumes of *Global Health Watch*, published by the PHM as an alternative to the WHO's health reports. He made an impact at the global level. PHM Global faced many problems—there are various interest groups and organizations with different approaches. Amit brought them together and became their common link.

Amit was not just an activist; he was also an academician. His writings demonstrated sound academic rigour. His study reports on IPR and the availability of essential medicines laid the theoretical foundation for the struggle for a people's medical policy in India. His interventions enabled the introduction of amendments in India's new patent law in keeping with the country's interests. He also published articles in reputed journals like the *British Medical Journal*, on topics related to primary and universal health service. At the same time, his politically insightful articles on various themes in *People's Democracy* have also been widely read.

Amit was an active member of the All India Peoples Science Network (AIPSN). He played a major role as the general secretary of the AIPSN and as a science educator. Amid all these responsibilities, he found time to participate in literacy campaigns in Delhi slums. He was a close friend of the Kerala Sasthra Sahithya

Parishad, and participated in many of our meetings in various districts.

It was not just this wide range of involvement—participation in various causes and movements—that marked Amit's life. Most admirable was his style of functioning. He believed issues should be kept open for further debate. But if a decision needed to be made at a particular point in time, say, in organizing a campaign, he would take a clear, concrete position. Equally important was the way he functioned among disparate groups: he was always a consensus builder. His approach was always democratic. And that is a very important characteristic for building movements. When building a consensus, it is easy to take a vote and go along with the majority view. But Amit always tried to take the minority along with him. He had his own politics; indeed, he was a member of a political party. Many constituents of the JSA were opposed to that political ideology. But all of them remained on friendly terms with Amit; he was acceptable to all. This was because Amit had no secret agenda. His interest was to keep the people's health movement going so that 'Health for All' could be achieved.

Above all, he was a good friend. One fine morning he would call you and enquire about your health, or call to ask about your children. He had this kind of personal relationship with several of the PHM activists, even those he disagreed with ideologically.

How do we carry on the good work Amit began and built over the years? It will be difficult, but we must do it. Amit used to say that we must change the slogan of Health for All by 2015–20, to Health for All *Now*. We have to take up this slogan, continue his fight and make it ours.

5. The Political Journey of Jan Swasthya Abhiyan

SAROJINI NADIMPALLY

As Sarojini Nadimpally traces the journey of the Jan Swasthya Abhiyan (JSA), she recalls how Amit brought his enormous political, organizational and leadership capacity to people's health and science movements. She also writes of his solidarity with related movements, such as the health component of the women's movement.

When Amit Sengupta passed away on 28 November 2018, the health and science movements in India lost a comrade. He has left behind a monumental legacy: the magic of his life, his intelligence, warmth, honesty, joy, wry humour and, above all, his steadfast commitment to a just and equitable world.

Amit was acutely intelligent, passionately committed, exceptionally strategic and focused, and hardworking. But he was also tenacious; uncompromising in the struggle for the health of the people. He could easily and simply communicate complex analytical information to grassroots health activists of the JSA through his speeches, workshops and discussions. He was remarkably clear in his politics, as well as in his analysis and articulation of issues related to public health, access to medicines, and patents laws. He was determined to ensure that the Indian Patents Act retained its flexibilities in the face of TRIPs. These—and his involvement in many other issues—provide us with inspiration and the impetus to mobilize afresh.

We in Sama, the Resource Group for Women and Health, found Amit's clarity of understanding, analytical ability, and calibre of writing exceptional. Perhaps even more important was his camaraderie—his willingness to support me and Sama. His expertise and engagement with issues of medicines, patents, public health, and science is well known. Not so visible perhaps is his significant contribution to the discourse on assisted reproductive technology. He made an important contribution with his essay, 'The Commerce in Assisted Reproductive Technologies'.[1] Amit was part of extremely critical national and international convenings, and contributed to the national and international discourse on assisted reproductive technologies (ARTs). It was inevitable, given Sama's deep engagement with reproductive technologies through research, policy advocacy and public engagement, that we benefited from Amit's constant support to our work. We could always count on him. I find that in an email dated September 11, 2008, I wrote to him: 'This Consultation (on ARTs) is a very important one for Sama as the opportunity has presented itself after almost two years of advocacy efforts to ensure an open and fair legislation. Spending time with you has helped us gain a lot of clarity as far as the structure of the Consultation goes and has also helped put some of our fears to rest. I am always touched by your concern for Sama at such times and highly appreciate your help.'

In January 2010, Sama organized an international consultation on the commercial, economic and ethical aspects of ARTs. Amit had agreed to be part of the consultation, and co-coordinate the final session, 'Challenges and Strategies: Where do we go from here?' With less than a week to go before the consultation, we received news that one of our key speakers, Professor Catherine Waldby, author of the book *Tissue Economies: Blood, Organs, and Cell Lines in Late Capitalism* (2006), had to drop out for personal

[1] Sandhya Srinivasan (ed.) *Making Babies—Birth Markets and Assisted Reproductive Technologies in India*, Zubaan, New Delhi, 2010.

reasons. We were in panic. Who would we approach at the last minute to speak competently on the political economy of this issue? It didn't take us long to find the answer. Amit Sengupta, of course! When my colleagues told him what had happened, he reassured them, then agreed without hesitation to speak at the consultation. He merely said that he would not speak on the same theme, but on 'Technology, Markets and the Commoditization of Life' in the session on 'Biogenetic Transactions: Politics and economics'. As always, his address was extremely well researched and presented with remarkable clarity.

Amit was a founding member of the People's Health Movement, and was instrumental in building it as a global people's health network, bringing together movements, organizations, academics and activists committed to the struggle for health for all. He helped organize the International People's Health University, a capacity-building programme for young health activists; and the WHO Watch in Geneva, which intervenes in, and contributes to, the body's debates through statements and policy briefs at the World Health Assembly.

Amit was the editor of the *Global Health Watch* (*GHW*), civil society's alternative report to the WHO's *World Health Report*. *GHW* covers almost every aspect of the state of global health within the prevailing social, economic and political realities. Amit brought his enormous political, organizational and leadership capacity to both the People's Health Movement and JSA.

Amit strongly believed that addressing the root causes of health inequity, and investing in society, is the only way to achieve health for all and sustainable development. This is what he wrote in his last article:

> The broader context, shaped since the late 1980s by neoliberal economic globalization, has profoundly influenced our health situation today. This can be seen in the impact of globalization on social justice, the effect of climate change on livelihoods;

> the loss of biodiversity, the detrimental effects of agribusiness on peasant farmers and small-holder farmers, who provide most of the world's food; the impact of land grabbing and the grabbing of water bodies by big business; the influence of patriarchy on society; tax evasion leading to the lack of public funds; the unbridled growth of the arms trade; and the effects of migration, to name only a few. All these issues require collaboration across sectors and policies that will address the root causes of illness and the determinants of health inequity.[2]

I still recall the heated discussions on universal health coverage (UHC) a few years ago after the release of the *Report of the High-Level Expert Group on Universal Health Coverage* (HLEG), and also the shift of global health organizations towards *coverage*. Amit never accepted the term coverage; he believed in care. According to him, 'UHC is essentially designed to universalize "coverage" rather than "care" ... [It] is built on, and lends itself to, standard neoliberal policies, steering policy makers away from universal health options based on public systems.'[3] He argued that by glossing over the importance of public provisioning of services, many proponents of UHC actually end up helping create health markets that can be exploited by capital.

Amit never wavered about articulating critiques of healthcare, whether it was the role of pharma, of international NGOs, of the corporate sector, or the WHO. Even the PHM was not spared—Amit once said:

> When you create a global movement that is issue-based, it is virtually impossible to build from the ground. Many global movements are built from the top by a few individuals.

[2] See Chapter 7 in Section 3 of this volume.

[3] Amit Sengupta, 'Universal Health Coverage: Beyond Rhetoric', Occasional Paper No. 20, Municipal Services Project, IDRC, November 2013; also see Chapter 5 in Section 3 of this volume.

They may be extremely well meaning and democratic. But structurally, they are built from the top. You can't get away from it. It does not mean that people who built the movements do not work with the community. I am not arguing against global movements. The best you can do is to try to put as many checks and balances in place to make sure that global movements understand their own limitations and that you have an extremely limited mandate to do a small number of things, which means it requires a certain level of humility not to be asserting on behalf of seven billion people.

Within the PHM, we have this debate about PHM upper case and phm lower case. PHM upper case is global leadership; phm lower case is the different organizations on the ground. The whole challenge is to build a relationship between the upper case and the lower case where the upper case is at least open to what the lower case is saying and doing and puts in place processes that are open.[4]

Amit expressed similar concerns at the fourth people's health assembly in Dhaka where more than 1,400 health activists from some seventy-three countries came together.

The untimely and unexpected demise of Amit is an irreparable loss to the community of the national and global health movement. JSA/PHM remembers him with a heavy heart; but we also have the fondest of memories of him as a long-standing friend, colleague and comrade. At a personal level, I feel he is still around. I sometimes think he has gone out of town for a meeting and will be back in a few days. He will then call and ask, as usual, '*Kya chal raha hai?* [What's up?] Let's meet.'

Adieu my dear friend, till our next meeting.

[4] Jennifer Chan, *Politics in the Corridor of Dying: AIDS Activism and Global Health Governance*, Baltimore: John Hopkins University Press, 2015, pp. 204–05.

6. Ensuring Accountability of International Organizations: The WHO Watch Programme

DAVID G. LEGGE

David Legge focuses here on the WHO Watch, an intervention in global health governance that seeks to ensure the WHO plays its role of the paramount global health authority. In the context of setting up and sustaining the WHO Watch programme, Legge describes Amit Sengupta's broad-ranging scientific knowledge and sharp analysis of policy argument, and political force; inspirational writing; generous and sensitive mentorship; and a deep commitment to a more caring world. These characteristics were all manifest in his work in the People's Health Movement's WHO Watch programme; indeed, they were critical to the successful foundation of WHO Watch.

What is the rationale of the WHO Watch programme? WHO Watch is an intervention in global health governance. This includes defending the WHO from corporate interests, and from member-state representatives who are determined to restrict the WHO's reach. As the paramount health authority at the global level, the WHO needs to be strengthened and adequately funded to play this role. WHO Watch seeks to generate support for a reformed WHO, restored to its proper place in global health governance.

WHO Watch also aims to democratize decision-making within the WHO—by supporting, in particular, delegations from smaller developing countries who need resources on issues of concern to them. WHO Watch provides a resource that covers most items on the agenda, and overstretched delegates from small developing countries can refer to the Watch for ideas and resources. Thus, WHO Watch aims to share knowledge of, and increase participation in, various engagements across the broader field of global health governance. It aims to change the balance of power in framing global decisions which impact on health. Decisions which affect global health are taken in many different fora beyond the WHO; but the WHO remains the pre-eminent global public health authority and provides a unique window on the wider field of global health action. WHO Watch is the first phase of a broader ambition, the democratizing of global health governance.

WHO Watch is also a resource for advocacy. It provides a current account of the policy arguments and political dynamics in relation to a wide range of global health issues. While the focus is on issues being considered through the WHO, the background documentation provides a more broad-based account of these issues.

WHO Watch is a strategy to promote convergence in a time of globalization; convergence across issues, borders, identities and ethnicities. It seeks to strengthen the various streams and networks across the global Health for All movement, by ensuring that activists whose concerns arise from their grassroots involvements can learn more about the global dimensions of the problems they face, and identify forms of action through which they can engage with the global dynamics.

What does WHO Watch actually do? As an intervention in global health governance, and a resource for advocacy and organizing in the era of globalization, WHO Watch involves a number of different, mutually reinforcing activities. Centrally, it brings small groups of young health activists from around the globe to follow and engage with decision-making in the WHO's governing bodies in general, and the Executive Board and World Health Assembly in Geneva in particular.

Actually, policy engagement begins well before the governing body meetings. Briefings at the national level involve PHM members and other civil society groups meeting with ministers and ministry officials about the agenda items for the forthcoming meeting of the global body. This aspect of the programme is not yet operative in all countries.

The watchers arrive in Geneva (or other cities for the regional committees) before the official meeting begins. They participate in a planning workshop focused on the policy issues to be raised before the governing body (the Board or the Assembly or the regional committee); identifying the politics of each issue; and the wider political context. The agenda items are allocated to small groups, and short statements prepared on priority items for the delegates to read. The workshops in Geneva are organized with the support of the Third World Network (TWN). The PHM's presence in Geneva (and other capitals) during governing body meetings also provides the opportunity to engage with other public interest civil society organizations, and share analyses and perspectives. At the governing body meetings, the watchers take notes of the debate into a common Skype channel to share more widely the direction of the debate. The Skype channel for the Geneva meetings has several hundred subscribers. The PHM's participation in governing body debates is supported by Medicus Mundi International.

A core resource for WHO Watch is the WHO Tracker website, which provides links to governing body meetings, official documents, reports of debate and resolutions. The Tracker provides links to the current meeting, including PHM item commentaries as well as the official documents. It also has a search function to locate previous meetings in which specific issues were discussed, or to locate the record of debate when particular resolutions were adopted.

The PHM's commentary development team prepares

commentaries on most agenda items as the official documents are published, in advance of each meeting. This includes broad consultation with various civil society experts and special interest organizations. These commentaries serve to inform the pre-watch planning workshop. They are also disseminated more broadly, including to many of the official member state delegations, through the WHO Watch newsletter (*The Updater*). After the meeting, the watchers' notes are edited and added to the PHM item commentaries; and item reports are disseminated through *The Updater* and various other social media.

What role did Amit play in WHO Watch? Without Amit, WHO Watch might never have got off the ground. When the concept was first broached in the PHM steering council, there was some scepticism about its strategic priority. Amit honoured the scepticism, but also articulated, clearly, the potential gains from such an initiative.

Amit's role as mentor in the context of the WHO Watch planning workshop was critical. His knowledge of the issues, his political insights and his generosity of spirit provided leadership, inspiration and confidence to watchers from all over the globe. Amit brought together watchers with different training and experience, and built a powerful watching team.

Amit's skills as a policy analyst played an important role in maintaining the quality of PHM comments and statements, and ensuring their alignment with the people's charter for health.[1] Again, Amit's organizing skill—behind the scenes—was a critical element in mobilizing the necessary funds to ensure the Watch was held.

[1] The 'People's Charter for Health' is a statement of the shared vision, goals, principles and calls for action that unite all the members of the PHM coalition. It is the most widely endorsed consensus document on health since the Alma-Ata Declaration. The People's Health Charter was formulated and endorsed by the participants of the First People's Health Assembly held at Dhaka, Bangladesh in December 2000.

WHO Watch is moving from its dependence on the vision and enthusiasm of a few people to being 'institutionalized' in the yearly life of the PHM. More people are involved in planning and organizing, in drafting item commentaries, and in mentoring the watchers. There is a move from individual vision to organizational responsibility. There is a lot more to be done. Still, the WHO Watch project has acquired a degree of stability and a collective sense of direction—and this is just one of the many legacies of Amit Sengupta.

7. The PHM's Alternative World Health Report

SUSANA BARRIA

Global Health Watch *(GHW) is the pre-eminent alternative world health report that brings together cutting-edge analysis, movement-based perspectives and stories of struggles on the global politics of health. This flagship publication of the People's Health Movement (PHM)—coordinated and edited by Amit Sengupta—wove together perspectives from five continents every three years.*

At *GHW*, Amit played multi-faceted roles: he was political activist, editor, alliance builder and mentor.[1] Amit was a firm believer in the need for an alternative world health report. For a broad-based network like PHM that brings together country circles in more than seventy countries, it is important to give visibility to the understanding and arguments behind its positions—to disseminate these arguments widely. The *GHW* was a response to the need for a publication that addressed the politics of health outcomes, looking into the dynamics at play, the actors involved, and the interests that motivated them; and, thereby, asking questions on the policy choices that were made, or omitted. In contrast, the *World Health Report* (*WHR*), published by the WHO every year from 1995 to 2013, stayed away from these questions.

[1] From 2009 to 2018, Amit coordinated three editions of *GHW*. *GHW*3, *GHW*4 and *GHW*5 were published in 2011, 2014 and 2017, respectively.

The UN structure constrained the *WHR* authors to remain, for the most part, within the realm of measuring policy outcomes, rather than delving into the politics behind policy choices.

The *GHW* aims at providing a political understanding of global health issues—an understanding rooted in the PHM's founding document, the People's Charter for Health. In keeping with the Charter, the prism through which the key factors influencing the health outcomes of individuals are viewed is central to the PHM's political understanding of health policies. So are the struggles required to intervene in the politics of health. The PHM believes that health outcomes are strongly defined by political, economic and social determinants. This is one of the first frameworks Amit taught me when I began working with him at the PHM secretariat. He had this slide that read: 'What good does it do to treat people's illness … then send them back to the same condition that made them sick?'

The political and economic architecture of the country in which people live has a profound influence on their health. Economic policies that prioritize equity, decent jobs and social well-being go a long way towards improving the health of a people. Political structures that promote people's participation in governance, and the design of social institutions, facilitate better health outcomes. This resonates with the 1978 Alma-Ata Declaration of the WHO and UNICEF—which highlighted the importance of the political and economic context of nations, by supporting a 'policy of independence, peace, détente and disarmament' in 'keeping with a new international economic order'. This new order was to promote a more just and equitable international economic system. Also, the social conditions in which people live and work affect individuals' health. The distribution of income, power, resources and access to social services are, in turn, shaped by public policies that reflect prevailing political ideologies. This is an important distinction. Focusing on individual risk factors, such as behavioural factors or genetics, could lead to victim-blaming.

The *GHW* structure—which Amit consolidated—reflects this

understanding of health politics. It takes the readers through (a) the global political and economic architecture; (b) issues and debates in health systems; (c) key social determinants 'beyond healthcare'; (d) watching the key actors of global health; and (e) stories of resistance and progressive change. Not only does the *GHW* help in understanding global health politics; it also contributes to the fight for a better world.

GHW plays a key role in providing a regular space to develop and share the PHM's perspective on the politics of global health. So the *GHW* is about creating new alliances, as well as consolidating existing alliances, through a joint ownership of a project that brings together more than seventy contributors in each edition. Amit brought in five new partners into the fold; the editing team was also expanded. Yet Amit liked to work on his own. The *GHW* process allowed for tracks of work to coexist and thrive.

The May Meeting, held each year on the weekend preceding the World Health Assembly in Geneva, began the process of bringing together all the partners: the PHM's networks, and members of the PHM secretariat and editing team. This was the time for collective reflection on the previous edition, brainstorming for the next edition, and formalizing responsibilities. Amit would run the meeting with great clarity, while ensuring that everyone contributed. It is another matter that not all the responsibilities undertaken were met, and much of that extra work ended up with Amit. But he was fine with it. This meeting was not aimed at decreasing his workload or bringing in efficiency, it was about getting people to share ownership. 'That way more people will read the book,' he laughed.

One of the challenges for the *GHW* was being recognized by the academic world while building on the experience of activists and practitioners, so as to make it a cutting-edge articulation of current policy debates and struggles. There are several systems built into the *GHW* that allow this to happen: case studies collected across PHM networks and knitted into more technical articles;

stories of struggle by activists; collection of inputs from several authors merged into a coherent article; and exhaustive editing, mostly by Amit, to bring both rigour and coherence to the overall narrative. This was partly due to the peculiar system of authorship in *GHW*—academic credit is not given to the authors of a specific article. Instead, all of them are listed at the end of the book.

Amit had excellent editing skills. For me, one of the things that made his editing special is that it was empowering. Amit would improve the expression, sharpen the argumentation, and often re-write pieces considerably. He would keep the core ideas, only to sharpen them. His editing made lucid what was a tentative piece by someone less experienced. At the same time, his editing process would turn into a learning exercise for the writer. The process was similar to what he would do at the WHO Watch workshop. He would listen to the presentations of the 'watchers'—the young activists following the WHO governing body discussions for the first time. He would also listen to the reactions from the other watchers in the room. Then he would identify the pieces of the puzzle, and the conceptual frameworks necessary to articulate and develop the arguments. The different documents that emerged from these discussions, say policy briefs or statements from the floor, were strongly influenced by Amit. But the watchers' feedback from this process was that they felt empowered to be part of developing and articulating these ideas and documents.

Over the years, the *GHW* has become more than an alternative world health report. First, it engages with the challenge of producing a book recognized by the academic world for its rigour—yet it is rooted in the experience of activists and practitioners. Second, it puts together the grassroots activism of a movement to give it a cutting edge. Third, it captures trends, making links across vast distances—between countries and regions. Finally, it plays a critical role in building the knowledge and understanding of a new generation of health activists.

Acknowledgements

This book began with Tanushree Sengupta, Alka Narang and Gargeya Telakapalli putting together Amit's writings. Without them there would be no book. The next step was contextualizing Amit's writings—most of which document the science and health movements. We needed to include some of the history of these movements. This is how the book became a reflection of how Amit saw his work, including his writing—as part of a larger history; a larger political story.

We were not sure how to convert a set of essays into a book. Githa Hariharan helped us conceptualize the book and its different sections, and taught us how a book is put together. Salim Yusufji edited the book, and Abhilasha Chattopadhyay painstakingly went through the entire text, including the footnotes and web-links. Rajesh Kalithody and Pratheesh Rani Prakash transcribed several pieces with patience and good humour.

Kajal Bhardwaj's essay, 'Medicines for All: A Reality Check, a Glimpse of Hope', is a revised version of the author's tribute to Amit Sengupta at a memorial meeting on May 5, 2019, India International Centre, New Delhi.

The articles and essays by Amit are edited versions of what he published over the years. We gratefully acknowledge:

'Patent to Plunder'. *Frontline*, 29: 8, April 21–May 4, 2012.

'Two Decades of Struggle: The Glivec Precedent'. *Economic and Political Weekly*, 48: 32, August 10, 2013.

'B.K. Keayla: A Personal Reminiscence'. *Economic and Political Weekly*, 45: 51, December 18, 2010, pp. 25–26.

All pieces on biological drugs were originally published by Third World Network, 2018.

'Health in the Age of Globalization'. *Social Scientist*, 31: 11–12, 2013, pp. 66–85.

'Global Governance of Health: A Minefield of Contradictions and Sectional Interests'. *Indian Journal of Medical Ethics*, 8: 2, April–June 2000.

'The Rise of Private Medicine in South Asia'. Co-authored with Indranil Mukhopadhyay, Manuj Weerasinghe and Arjun Karki, *British Medical Journal* (Clinical Research Edition), April 2017.

'Universal Health Coverage: Beyond Rhetoric'. Occasional Paper 20, Municipal Services Project, November 2013.

'Creating, Reclaiming, Defending Non-Commercialized Alternatives in the Health Sector in Asia'. D.A. McDonald and G. Ruiters, eds., *Alternatives to Privatization: Public Options for Essential Services in the Global South*, New Delhi: LeftWord, 2013.

'Forty Years of Alma-Ata Declaration: "Health for All" Still a Far Cry'. *Newsclick*, October 9, 2018.

Prabir Purkayastha
Indranil
Richa Chintan

Glossary of Terms

SECTION 1

Bioavailability: It refers to the exact amount of the active substance available in a drug for it to perform its therapeutic function in the body.

Biological Drugs: Biological drugs (commonly referred to as 'biologics' or 'biopharmaceuticals') are drugs produced through biological processes. These drugs are distinct because they are produced in living cells. Biologics are larger in size and more complex than the 'small-molecule drugs' manufactured using chemical synthesis processes. Biologics have several potential advantages as they can, theoretically, be tailored to hit specific 'targets' in the human body. They currently target diseases which, hitherto, had very limited or no available treatment options—including several types of cancer, autoimmune diseases and other non-communicable diseases.

Biosimilars: A biosimilar is a biotherapeutic product which is similar in terms of quality, safety and efficacy to an already licensed reference biotherapeutic product. It is not an exact duplicate of another biologic. There is a degree of natural variability in all biological products and it is not possible to generate a precise copy of a product that comes from living cells. A biosimilar may have a different structure from the reference product, but the active substances are essentially the same in molecular and biological terms.

Compulsory Licence: This is when a government allows someone else to produce a patented product or process without the consent of the patent owner, or plans to use the patent-protected invention itself. It is one of the flexibilities in the TRIPS Agreement.

Evergreening (of patents): Evergreening of pharmaceutical patents aims to delay the generic competition by extending the length of the exclusivity period beyond the legitimate patent term without any considerable improvement in the therapeutic benefits of an already patented pharmaceutical drug. It thus poses a serious challenge to access to medicines.

Free Trade Agreements: FTAs are treaties between two or more countries designed to reduce or eliminate certain barriers to trade and investment, and to facilitate stronger trade and commercial ties among participating countries.

Generics: A generic medicine contains the same active pharmaceutical ingredient as its bioequivalent, an originator medicine. Since generic medicines are identical in the active pharmaceutical substance, dose, strength, route of administration, safety, efficacy, and intended use, they can be substituted for the originator product.

Intellectual Property Rights: Intellectual property rights refer to the assignment of property rights through patents, copyrights and trademarks. These are legal rights that protect creations and/or inventions resulting from intellectual activity in the industrial, scientific, literary or artistic fields. These property rights allow the holder to exercise a monopoly on the use of the product for a specified period. By restricting imitation and duplication, monopoly power is conferred, but, the argument goes, the social costs of monopoly power may be offset by the social benefits of higher levels of creative activity encouraged by the monopoly earnings.

Pre-grant and Post-grant Patent Opposition: Many countries provide opposition mechanisms in their patent systems which offer third parties an opportunity to oppose the grant of a patent within a certain period of time provided by the applicable law. An opponent must allege at least one of the grounds of violation among those established by the applicable law. An opposition may be requested before the grant of a patent (pre-grant opposition) or after the grant of a patent (post-grant opposition).

TRIPS: The Agreement on Trade-Related Intellectual Property Rights is a multilateral agreement which came into effect on January 1, 1995, at the end of the Uruguay Round of GATT negotiations. The areas of intellectual property that it covers are: copyright and related rights; trademarks; geographical indications; industrial designs; patents; the layout designs of integrated circuits; and undisclosed information including trade secrets and test data. The TRIPS Agreement is a minimum standards agreement, which allows Members to provide more extensive protection of intellectual property if they so wish.

TRIPS Plus: In recent years, many developing countries have been coming under pressure to enact or implement even tougher or more restrictive conditions in their patents laws than required by the TRIPS Agreement; these are known as 'TRIPS-plus' provisions. Common examples of TRIPS-plus provisions include extending the term of a patent longer than the twenty-year minimum, or introducing provisions that limit the use of compulsory licences or that restrict generic competition. One of these provisions is known as data exclusivity. This refers to exclusive rights, granted over the pharmaceutical test data submitted by companies to drug regulatory authorities for obtaining market authorization. It means that information concerning a drug's safety and efficacy is kept confidential for a period of, say, five or ten years.

SECTION 2

Small-Molecule Drugs: Small-molecule drugs are compounds with low molecular weight that are capable of modulating biochemical processes to diagnose, treat, or prevent diseases. They can enter cells easily because they have a low molecular weight. Conventional small-molecule chemicals have a molecular weight typically between 100 and 900 Daltons.

International Non-proprietary Name: INN is the globally recognized name used to identify the active ingredient in a medicine. That is, the INNs facilitate the identification of pharmaceutical substances or active pharmaceutical ingredients. Each INN is a unique name that is globally recognized and is public property. A non-proprietary name is also known as a generic name.

Monoclonal Antibodies: A type of protein made in the laboratory that can bind itself to a substance in the body. These are antibodies produced artificially through genetic engineering and related techniques. A monoclonal antibody (mAb) is so made that it binds with only one bodily substance. Monoclonal antibodies are being used to treat some types of cancer. They can be used alone or to convey drugs, toxins, or radioactive substances directly to cancer cells.

Clinical Trials: Clinical trials are a type of research that studies new tests and treatments and evaluates their effects on human health outcomes. People volunteer to take part in clinical trials to test medical interventions including drugs, cells and other biological products, surgical procedures, radiological procedures, devices, behavioural treatments and preventive care. These trials are the primary means by which researchers find out if a new treatment, like a new drug or diet or medical device is safe and effective in people. Often a clinical trial is used to learn if a new treatment is more effective and/or has less harmful side effects than the standard treatment.

SECTION 3

Agreement on Agriculture: The AoA is an international treaty of the WTO negotiated during the Uruguay Round of the GATT negotiations, coming into force with the establishment of the WTO on January 1, 1995. The goal of the AoA was to establish a market-oriented agricultural trading system and to initiate a reform process to this end. The reform programme comprises specific commitments to reduce support and protection in the areas of domestic support, export subsidies and market access, and through the establishment of strengthened and more operationally effective GATT rules and disciplines.

Alma-Ata Declaration: In 1978 the International Conference on Primary Healthcare meeting, held in the city of Alma-Ata (now called Almaty) in Kazakhstan, expressed the need for urgent action by all governments, all health and development workers, and the world community, to protect and promote the health of all the people. This culminated in the Alma-Ata Declaration of 1978 which emerged as a major milestone in the field of public health, and identified primary healthcare as the key to the attainment of the goal of Health for All by 2000.

General Agreement on Trade in Services: The GATS was the first multilateral agreement covering trade in services. It was negotiated during the last round of multilateral trade negotiations, called the Uruguay Round, and came into force in 1995. The GATS provides a framework of rules governing services trade, establishes a mechanism for countries to make commitments to liberalize trade in services and provides a mechanism for resolving disputes between countries.

Gini Coefficient: The Gini coefficient is a summary measure of income inequality. It summarizes the dispersion of income across the entire income distribution. The Gini coefficient ranges from 0, indicating perfect equality (where everyone receives an equal share), to 1, perfect inequality (where only one recipient or group of recipients receives all the income). It is based on the difference between the Lorenz curve (the observed cumulative income distribution) and the notion of a perfectly equal income distribution.

Market Failure: Market failure is an economic situation defined by an inefficient allocation of resources in the free market. Market failure occurs when individuals acting in rational self-interest produce a less than optimal or economically inefficient outcome. Presence of externalities, where benefits of consumption do not remain limited to the consumer, is a very common form of market failure relevant to healthcare. Market failures provide one of the many rationales for government intervention.

Merit Goods: These may be defined as goods whose consumption is considered meritorious (by government), but due to imperfect knowledge, individuals would choose to consume too little of them. In such cases the government should intervene to encourage consumption, on terms that are more generous than the marketplace. Many countries and societies consider healthcare as a merit good where government investment ensures health for all.

New Public Management: 'New public management' strategies include introducing private-sector management, organization and labour market ethos and practices into the functioning of the public sector with the expectation that public services can be made to deliver with an 'efficiency' that the private sector (and its competitive environment) has supposedly realized. More specifically, there has been an aspiration to introduce 'internal markets' within the domain of public provision. Public-Private Partnerships of various kinds are seen as NPM strategies. A key element of the NPM was abolition of permanent recruitments and contractualization of human resources in the health sector.

Out-of-Pocket Expenditure: Out-of-pocket expenditure is defined as direct payments made by individuals to healthcare providers at the time of service use. This excludes any prepayment for health services, for example in the form of taxes or specific insurance premiums or contributions and, where possible, net of any reimbursements to the individual who made the payments.

Primary Healthcare: Primary healthcare is essential healthcare based on practical, scientifically sound and socially acceptable methods and technology made universally accessible to individuals and families in the community. It functions through the community's full participation and at a cost that the community and country can afford to maintain at every stage of their development, in the spirit of self-reliance and self-determination. It forms an integral part both of the country's health system, of which it is the central function and main focus, and of the overall social and economic development of the community. It is the first level of contact of individuals, the family, and community with the national health system, bringing healthcare as close as possible to where people live and work, and also constitutes the first elements of a continuing healthcare process (Alma-Ata Declaration, 1978).

Public Goods: Public goods are non-excludable, i.e. those whose consumption benefits do not remain limited to individuals. They are also non-rivalrous, in that their use by one individual does not reduce availability to others. These goods can be used simultaneously by more than one person. Many preventive public health programmes, like control of disease vectors, food and water safety are measures where individual interventions are ineffective (vector control) or too costly (water purification) or practically impossible (food safety). These are examples of public goods.

Selective Primary Level Care: The Alma-Ata Declaration was criticized by donor agencies for being too broad and idealistic, and setting an unrealistic timetable. A common criticism was that the slogan 'Health for All by

2000' was not feasible. Several donor agencies came together to propose an 'interim' strategy of entry points through which basic health services could be developed. They also emphasized attainable goals and cost-effective planning. The term 'Selective Primary Level Care' meant a package of low-cost technical interventions to tackle the main disease problems of poor countries. Four interventions were identified, which are best known as GOBI—for growth monitoring, oral rehydration techniques, breastfeeding, and immunization.

Social Determinants of Health (SDH): The social determinants of health are the conditions in which people are born, they grow, work, live, and age—as also the wider set of forces and systems shaping the conditions of daily life. These include economic policies and systems, development agendas, social norms, social policies and political systems. Health equity, human rights and distribution of power are the central values shaping the understanding of SDH.

Strategic Purchasing: Strategic purchasing has been defined by WHO as 'a continuous search for the best ways to maximize health system performance by deciding which interventions should be purchased, how, and from whom'. It is primarily meant to achieve efficiency and relies on 'new universalism' promoted by the WHO and World Bank. According to this approach, public or private ownership of facilities does not matter and the more efficient providers may be contracted to get the services delivered. Under 'new universalism' government role has been transformed from provisioning to 'stewardship'—mainly deciding priorities for funding and providing the funds.

Structural Adjustment Programmes: SAPs are sector-specific reforms intended to infuse market principles in areas where the state has a considerable presence, through measures like user charges, contracting out of services, shifting from direct provisioning to insurance-like mechanisms, and injecting market principles into the functioning of the public sector. They were introduced as per terms set by the IMF and the World Bank during the 1990s, as part of their bail-out packages for countries in the grip of economic crises.

Universal Health Coverage: In order to tide over the situation of crumbling health systems in developing countries and rising burden of household healthcare costs, by the mid-2000s international institutions espoused universal health coverage (UHC). There was a renewed call for increasing public spending on health to finance different types of demand-side financing mechanisms and ensure financial protection. The underlying belief appeared to be that if the finances were secured, provisioning of health services could be taken care of by the existing mix of private and public sectors. The use of the term 'coverage' rather than 'care' symbolizes the move away from concerns of health-systems design towards financing. UHC is conceived as a system that will progressively move towards: a) the coverage of the entire population by a package of services; b) an increasing range of services; and c) a rising share of pooled funds as the main source of funding for healthcare, and thereby a decrease in co-payments by those accessing healthcare services.

User Fees: User fees are defined as 'contributions to costs by individual users in the form of a charge per unit of service consumed, typically in the form of cash'.[1] User fees are paid at the point of service use and there is no risk-sharing. User fees can entail any combination of drug costs, supply and medical material costs, entrance fees or consultation fees. User fees were introduced by the IMF and later on advocated by the World Bank, on the grounds of low demand for poor quality services, generating revenue, discouraging unnecessary use of healthcare services, inequitable distribution of benefits, making services more responsive to the end users.

Washington Consensus: The Washington Consensus refers to a set of broadly free-market economic ideas, supported by prominent economists and international organizations, such as the IMF and the World Bank. This was a set of economic policy recommendations for crisis-ridden developing countries, particularly in Latin America, during the 1980s. The set of policy recommendations were an agreement between the IMF, World Bank, and US department of the treasury who shared the view that the operation of the free market and the reduction of state involvement were crucial to economic development in the global South.

SECTION 4

Section 301: Section 301 of the Trade Act of 1974 is the principal US statute for addressing foreign unfair practices affecting US exports of goods or services. The Act was passed at a time of large and growing trade deficits, increasing flight of manufacturing activities abroad, the rise of Japan as an industrial giant, skyrocketing foreign debt and economic crises caused by dependency on foreign oil imports. The US export industries blamed the country's economic woes on the weak enforcement regimes of the General Agreement

1 S. Reddy and J. Vandemoortele, 'User financing of basic social services: A review of theoretical arguments and empirical evidence', Staff Working Paper No. 6, Evaluation Policy and Planning Division, UNICEF, New York, 1996.

on Tariffs and Trade (GATT). Section 301 can be used to enforce US rights under international trade agreements and to respond to discriminatory foreign government practices that burden or restrict US commerce.

Single/Multi-Payer System: In many developing countries healthcare costs are mainly borne by households, with a supplementary role played by various levels of governments, employers, voluntary organizations and to some limited extent by insurance agencies. Since there are multiple payers involved in paying for healthcare, these systems are called multi-payer systems. In contrast many developed and a few developing countries have organized healthcare financing mechanisms in a way that governments or autonomous bodies (like social security agencies) mobilize resources from various sources like taxes, mandatory deductions from income, contributions from employers and pay for healthcare needs of the people through a single source. The National Health System in the UK is an example of a single payer system.

Super 301 and Special 301 Acts: 'Super 301' refers to an annual process by which the US Trade Representative identifies those practices of a foreign country the elimination of which is likely to have the most significant potential to increase US exports. Under the 'Special 301' provisions in US trade law, the USTR annually identifies those countries that deny adequate and effective protection for intellectual property rights or fair and equitable market access to persons who rely on intellectual property protection.

Abbreviations

AICAPEF	All India Chemical and Pharmaceutical Employees Federation
AIDAN	All India Drug Action Network
AIDS	Acquired Immune Deficiency Syndrome
AIIHPH	All India Institute of Hygiene and Public Health
AoA	Agreement on Agriculture
ARTs	Assisted Reproductive Technologies
ASHA	Accredited Social Health Activists
AusAID	Australian Agency for International Development
BJP	Bharatiya Janata Party
BJVJ	Bharat Jan Vigyan Jathas
BMGF	Bill and Melinda Gates Foundation
BRAC	Bangladesh Rural Advancement Committee
CBOs	Community-Based Organizations
CGHS	Central Government Health Scheme
CHW	Community Health Worker
CL	Compulsory Licence
CMH	Commission on Macroeconomics and Health
CML	Chronic Myeloid Leukaemia
CRHP	Comprehensive Rural Health Project
CSDH	Commission on Social Determinants of Health
CSIR	Council for Scientific and Industrial Research
CT	Computed Tomography (scans)
DMSC	Durbar Mahila Samanwaya Committee
DSF	Delhi Science Forum
EEC	European Economic Community
ESIS	Employees State Insurance Scheme
FARC	Fuerzas Armadas Revolucionarias de Colombia (Revolutionary Armed Forces of Colombia)
FCHV	Female Community Health Volunteers
FDC	Fixed Dose Combinations

FDI	Foreign Direct Investment
FMRAI	Federation of Medical and Sales Representatives' Associations of India
FTA	Free Trade Agreement
GATT	General Agreement on Tariffs and Trade
GHW	Global Health Watch
GIPAP	Glivec International Patient Assistance Programme
GOBI	Growth Monitoring, Oral Rehydration, Breast-Feeding, Immunization
GPPI	Global Public Private Initiatives
HBNCs	Home-Based Neonatal Care
HIV	Human Immunodeficiency Virus
HLEG	High Level Expert Group on Health
ICTSD	International Centre for Trade and Sustainable Development
IDPL	Indian Drugs & Pharmaceuticals Ltd
IFAD	International Fund for Agricultural Development
ILO	International Labour Organization
IMF	International Monetary Fund
IP	Intellectual Property
IPAB	Intellectual Property Appellate Board
IPHU	International People's Health University
IPR	Intellectual Property Rights Regime
JSA	Jan Swasthya Abhiyan
KTUC	Kerala Trade Union Congress
LGBTQI	Lesbian Gay Bisexual Transgender Queer Intersex
LMICs	Low and Middle Income Countries
MNC	Multi-National Corporations
MPP	Medicines Patent Pool
MRI	Magnetic Resonance Imaging
MSF	Médecins Sans Frontières
NACO	National Aids Control Organisation
NCMH	National Commission on Macroeconomics and Health
NDA	National Democratic Alliance
NGO	Non-Governmental Organization
NHA	National Health Assembly
NHS	National Health System
NRCMS	New Rural Cooperative Medical Scheme
NRHM	National Rural Health Mission
NWGPL	National Working Group on Patent Laws

OECD	Organization for Economic Co-operation and Development
OPPI	Organisation of Pharmaceutical Producers of India
OT	Operation Theatre
PFHI	Public-Funded Health Insurance
PHC	Primary Healthcare
PHE	Private Health Expenditure
PHM	People's Health Movement
PMBJP	Pradhan Mantri Bharatiya Jan Aushadhi Pariyojana
PPP	Public Private Partnership
R&D	Research and Development
RAS	Rajiv Aarogyasri Scheme
RCEP	Regional Comprehensive Economic Partnership
RSBY	Rashtriya Swasthya Bima Yojana
S&T	Science and Technology
SAP	Structural Adjustment Programmes
SCA	Save the Children Australia
SDG	Sustainable Development Goals
SEARCH	Society for Education Action and Research in Community Health
SHGs	Self-Help Groups
SHIP	Sonagachi HIV/AIDS International Project
SPSM	Sanitary-Phyto-Sanitary Measures
SUS	Sistema Único de Salud (the Unified Health System)
TB	Tuberculosis
TBAs	Traditional Birth Attendants
TBT	Technical Barriers to Trade
THE	Total Health Expenditure
TPP	Trans-Pacific Partnership
TRIPS	Trade-Related Intellectual Property Rights
TWN	Third World Network
UC	Universal Healthcare Coverage scheme
UHC	Universal Health Coverage
UNDP	United Nations Development Programme
UNESCO	United Nations Educational, Scientific and Cultural Organization
UNGA	United Nations General Assembly
UNHLM	United Nations High-Level Meeting
UNICEF	United Nations International Children's Emergency Fund
UPA	United Progressive Alliance
USAID	United States Agency for International Development
USFDA	United States Food and Drug Administration

VHWs	Village Health Workers
WDR	World Development Report
WHR	World Health Report
WHA	World Health Assembly
WHO	World Health Organization
WTO	World Trade Organization

Notes on Contributors

B. EKBAL is a public health activist, neurosurgeon, and academic. He is a serving member of the Kerala State Planning Board since 2016. He has also served as the Vice-chancellor of the University of Kerala. He is an activist of the Kerala Sastra Sahitya Parishad and is one of the National Convenors of Jan Swasthya Abhiyan.

DAVID LEGGE graduated in medicine in 1968. He has blended a number of streams into his career—clinician, researcher, teacher, planner, manager, policy analyst, activist. He has been active in the PHM since its formation in 2000 and was a part of the International People's Health Council. He worked closely with Amit in the PHM Steering Council, in the development of WHO Watch, in the preparation of several editions of *Global Health Watch*, and in various IPHU courses.

DAVID SANDERS was an internationally renowned paediatrician and public health researcher and activist. He worked for over fifty years with liberation movements and governments in the areas of primary healthcare, child health and nutrition, and human resources for health as part of health systems development. A legend in African health, he was the founding director of the School of Public Health, University of the Western Cape, South Africa. Sanders passed away in September 2019.

INDRANIL is a health economist and activist trained in Economics and Public Health. He is associated with the Jan Swasthya Abhiyan. He also teaches Public Health and Development Economics in OP Jindal Global University, Sonipat.

J.S. MAJUMDAR has been involved with trade unions for more than three decades. He is one of the founder members of Federation of Medical Representatives Association of India (FMRAI) and has served as its General Secretary. He was also elected as the All India Vice-President of Centre of Indian Trade Unions (CITU).

KAJAL BHARDWAJ is a lawyer based in Delhi. She has worked on trade, health and rights over the last two decades.

PRABIR PURKAYASTHA is a free software and a science activist. He has worked in the energy and information technology sectors for more than four decades. He is the Founder-Editor of the website Newsclick.in, President of Free Software Movement of India, and a founding member of the Delhi Science Forum and the All India Peoples Science Network.

RICHA CHINTAN is an activist associated with Jan Swasthya Abhiyan. She works full time with the People's Health Movement organization.

S.P. SHUKLA is a retired 1957 batch IAS officer. He served as Commerce Secretary and Finance Secretary, Government of India, during the late eighties and early nineties. He was also the Ambassador to GATT in Geneva. He was the main negotiator with GATT under the V.P. Singh government when he was also the Commerce Secretary.

SAROJINI NADIMPALLY is a public health researcher and social scientist with the SAMA Resource Group of Women and Health, and advisor to the Patient's Rights Panel of the *British Medical Journal*. She was part of the Mission Steering Group of the National Health Mission and member of the Central Ethics Committee of the ICMR. She is a National Convenor of the JSA and previous Co-chair of People's Health Movement.

SATYAJIT RATH is a trained physician and pathologist, but has worked on mechanisms involved in the functioning of the immune system. He was a faculty member of the National Institute of Immunology, and is currently working in an honorary capacity at various premier institutes. He also works with government on issues of science and society-related policy, with small companies on drug discovery, and with civil society groups working at the interface of science and society.

SUSANA BARRIA is a health and trade union activist based in India. She is a member of the Steering Council of the People's Health Movement and contributes to the WHO Watch programme. She works with the Public Services International as Trade Justice Coordinator for Asia Pacific and also contributes to PSI's campaigns for health workers' rights.